MANDELA EFFECT:
Friend or Foe?

Also By Eileen Colts   *40 DAYS & 40 NIGHTS Manifestation Key*

MANDELA EFFECT:

Friend or Foe?

Exploring the Nature of an Ever Changing Reality

Eileen Colts, Paulo M. Pinto,

Shane C. Robinson & Vannessa VA

11:11 Publishing House
Estero, Florida USA

11:11 Publishing House, LLC
20791 Three Oaks Parkway, Unit 809
Estero, Florida 33929 USA

ISBN: 9781692857691

"Big, inexplicable, instantaneous changes are being observed in movies, books, art, logos, geography, human anatomy, celestial constellations -- and every conceivable type of historical fact and event. *Mandela Effect: Friend or Foe?* is an excellent resource for understanding, coming to terms with, and ultimately embracing the staggering implications of the Mandela Effect."

"Highly recommended!"

Cynthia Sue Larson, author of *Quantum Jumps, Reality Shifts*, and *High Energy Money*. www.realityshifters.com

CONTENTS

Part One by Eileen Colts

PART ONE

EILEEN COLTS

YOUTUBE CONTENT CREATOR:

ONE (EILEEN COLTS) CHANNEL

www.youtube.com/OneEileenColts

My Mandela Effect Awakening

My awakening to the Mandela Effect was a triple-header with, "Luke I am your father", and the VW logo on my steering wheel changing … years after wondering how Nelson Mandela was still alive. In the Star Wars movie, *The Empire Strikes Back,* at some point this iconic movie line, "Luke – I am your father!" appears to have changed to, "No - I am your father" in all copies of the movie available – in private collections and online. (1) This makes for the funniest Mandela Effect reaction videos on YouTube, as die-hard *Star Wars* fans scream at their computers, "Nooooo – he never said No!"

When I purchased my Volkswagen new in 2012, the logo on the steering wheel had no break through the middle of it. It was one continuous piece of logo art. However, when I traded it in by 2016, there was an obvious break in it between the top V and the bottom W. If it was only me experiencing these rather meaningless changes, I would have to accept having a faulty memory, but thanks to YouTube, I soon learned countless other people reported not only misremembering these too, but misremembering them *exactly* the same way I did. That seemed impossible, unless something stranger and deeper was going on. Welcome to the Mandela Effect.

I started looking for other examples of rather mundane, but still inexplicable historical changes in matter; and to my surprise found not just a few, but hundreds if not thousands of small but significant changes to book titles, iconic movie lines, song lyrics, Bible passages, geography, animals, plants, human anatomy ... it seemed anything in matter could change and be different from how I remembered it. Historically, these changes are said to have *always* been this way, and never having been the way so many of us remember. I could have left it alone, if so many different people did not incorrectly remember these things *exactly* the same way I remembered them. Being familiar with the human collective consciousness, sometimes called a hivemind (which explains how groups of animals communicate instantly over long distances, much like quantum entanglement), I felt this was a mystery worthy of further investigation.

So the Mandela Effect became my number one topic to research to get my head around how it was happening, and more importantly - why it was happening. I just knew we were not in

Kansas anymore (even that iconic move line from the *Wizard of Oz* movie has reportedly changed). Something strange and new was going on in our material, solid world, and I felt partly responsible for it. You see, I drove that Volkswagen for several years with the car logo without any break in between the V and the W on my steering wheel. I would be driving along, not paying attention to anything in particular, I would look down at the logo, and quite a few times I would think - you cannot really see where the V begins and the W ends. I would then think it would be much better if they put a line between the inside V and the outside W. I thought this countless times from the time I bought the car until I traded it in, and like magic, it changed. Right before I traded it in, I noticed there was a break between the inside V and the outside W on the logo on my steering wheel – *exactly* the way I imagined it should have been for years. Did I help cause the Mandela Effect concerning that logo?

The change did not only occur on my car. It was true for all Volkswagen vehicles, and when researched, the history of the VW logo was presented online as *always* having been the new way. (2) The way I so clearly remembered it (without a break or separation) had never existed. So now I felt certain I was at least partly responsible for creating this particular Mandela Effect, but the really phenomenal part was thousands of others around the world were commenting on videos that they remembered it *exactly* the same way I remembered it, but the break was a logical change. Common sense dictates that a large number of people misremembering something would misremember it uniquely and differently to each other. At the very least, identical misremembering would equate to proof of a collective human memory or collective subconscious mind. More importantly, did a lot of people think this change into existence with me?

I turned to science and the authorities first to explain this, but there was nothing to be found on the subject. They simply appeared to be avoiding analyzing something that through its analysis seemed to prove a shared collective mind at the root of something like mass misremembering, or confabulation. That left it to me and any other interested laypeople to provide the science or research on this subject by studying it ourselves. And then I remembered: this is exactly how science started before money and notoriety politicized it, and modern science became a means to a political or financial end. The mystical often became the scientific with astrology becoming astronomy and alchemy developing into chemistry. Ironically, now it sometimes feels to me that the lack of any authoritative stamp of approval (funding) gives us laypeople and our findings even more street cred. So, what you read here in this book is no more "expert" than you are "expert" at living as spirit-in-matter on Earth in the twenty-first century – because even that definition is a collective agreement, and on that we are *all* experts here. In fact, in my community of Mandela Effect researchers, your opinion would be taken more seriously than that of anything tainted by mainstream, which is often viewed in truther communities as having been manipulated for personal power or greed over the common good.

Even though I discovered my first official "Mandela Effects" in 2016, like many I too was Mandela Effect effected for decades before I realized it. Back in the 1960's and 1970's my mother would often comment after hearing of a celebrity death that she was sure they had died before, and go on to describe their funeral or some significant memory of it in detail. In 1984 while travelling in South Africa, I requested to interview Nelson Mandela, who was sick in prison awaiting release on humanitarian grounds. Saying Mandela was too ill to participate, I was given an interview with Adriaan Vlok, then Deputy Minister of Defense instead, to discuss his possible release. I recall finding it very interesting the minister explained to me that Nelson Mandela was jailed for his participation in a train station bombing that resulted in four deaths and was *not* jailed for life for only speaking out against apartheid (as so often portrayed in Western media). He also explained that in South Africa a life sentence was for life, not just a few decades as is typical elsewhere, but they were continuing to consider early release because Nelson Mandela was reportedly dying. In fairness it is also interesting that in 1999, Vlok was granted amnesty by the Truth and Reconciliation Commission as the sole cabinet minister to have admitted committing crimes, including the bombing of the headquarters of the South African Council of Churches at Khotso House, and the trade union headquarters. So both the jailed and the jailers were not as innocent as usually depicted. (3) I am not making judgements on the men here, just pointing out the information we have is often incomplete. It seems all truth requires some level of personal research.

On my return in 1984 we broadcast my interview on Loyola University radio station in Chicago. I graduated in 1985, accepting a position at the Chicago NPR affiliate radio station, where I covered local politics and served as morning news host before moving to Europe in 1990 to cover the fall of the Berlin Wall and European news for the English services department of the German national broadcasting network. But sometime in 1986 or 1987, I specifically recall hearing reports at work that were broadcast of Nelson Mandela's death in prison, tragically just weeks before his release was finalized. I remember news reports after his death about his widow Winnie taking over as an apartheid liberation spokesperson with a questionable football team of bodyguards. I think you would have to be working in news as I was to remember these events so specifically. So imagine my surprise, when living in England in the mid-1990's, Nelson Mandela turned up at a press conference with the Spice Girls pop band. For a moment I thought I must be on another planet, but as you do, I told myself my memory of his death years earlier *must* be wrong and I moved on. The published history and timeline of these events does not match my memories of them. The often published versions of Nelson Mandela's history never mentions the train station murders, says he was released from prison in 1990, became President of South Africa in 1994, and died in 2013. Even more interesting, several people report remembering his death in 1987 like me, while others recall his death in 1991 with some textbook evidence or 'residue' to support that date. (4)

Coincidentally the whole phenomenon was named after him in 2009 precisely because people had different memories of different years for his death, but more on this in a later section. Fortunately, I am not alone in becoming affected by the phenomenon before there was even a name for it. Cynthia Sue Larson, physicist and author of the books *Reality Shifts*, *Quantum Jumps, and High Energy Money* was affected by the Mandela Effect starting in the 1990s before it had an official name too. (5) She attributes the term reality shifter to one of her and my favorite authors, P. M. H. Atwater, who also wrote a similar themed book *Future Memory*. (6) No matter how new this is for you, as a phenomenon, the Mandela Effect has been around a long time – possibly forever.

Possible Causes (Overview)

What if while I was driving my Volkswagen, and I put a specific thought of a change to the logo on my steering wheel into my subconscious mind, that thought was somehow communicated to the human collective subconscious mind? What if that idea just sat there percolating until enough people driving Volkswagens thought the exact same thing? (Many people like me also say they think the company name Volkswag**en** used to be Volkswag**on**.) Then together we eventually reached critical mass to collectively create a physical change in the material matrix we share; because matter is a physical representation of *information* in waveform, and where does that *information* come from? Us, via the hivemind.

If the human hivemind is at work in controlling and editing the matter around us (also called the matrix or the field), then things like reported chemtrails, chemicals in food, water and air, as well as subliminal messages in television and music … could actually impact the human collective subconscious mind, and therefore impact collective matter. I honestly would not be surprised to wake up one day to a collective green sky with collective blue grass! But who is doing the programming to influence what we collectively think and feel that materializes around us? Could it be us, or rather an elite group of us who have figured out how this works?

The most popular Mandela Effect videos are blaming the largest atom collider, quantum computing, and a large planet coming our way for the phenomenon. Though entertaining, I decided there was not enough evidence to say any one of those caused the Mandela Effect: the unexpected and seemingly random changes in our material reality. Having briefly formally studied astronomy, geology and archeology at university, I then decided to look into changes to our planet and solar system for clues. Here I was rewarded with information from a University of Wisconsin study that I can no longer find referenced online. I recall it stating that all of the planets in our Solar System are heating up and becoming more luminous. This is even visible to the naked eye now. If you use a free sky map app on your phone to scan the night sky, you will see that Mars is much brighter and more yellow than red (how I remember it under live observations in my astronomy class). Jupiter is huge and almost as bright-white as Venus now. Venus has always been the brightest object in our night sky, besides the moon, but it is so much bigger and brighter now. So what is making all of the planets in our Solar System become hotter and brighter? Even if authorities continue to blame 'global warming' on human activity here (which they recently changed to 'climate change'), they cannot do so on other planets in our Solar System, and there is little scientific consensus on what is heating up all planets now. (7)

Could it be due to the increasing gravitational pull of Planet X or Nibiru as it approaches Earth now and every few thousand years, as reported by many followers of the Sumerian Anunnaki myths? This theory is largely attributed to the 150,000+ Sumerian clay tablets written 3000 to 4500 years ago and discovered in ancient Babylon, Sumer, Mesopotamia, current day Iraq. The Oxford University Press has many translations available, (8) but popular translations were written by Zecharia Sitchin, (9) detailing the fabulous story of the Anunnaki gods who live on planet Nibiru who created and enslaved the human race to dig for gold here in our ancient past. The Anunnaki reportedly return to Earth to collect their gold every 2600 years on their own planet Nibiru's cyclical orbit around ours and the Sun. It seems like many people now hold the information in these clay tablets to be factual, but before believing any religious or historical tale, remember that just because something is very very old does not mean it is very very true. Imagine if people uncovered the Harry Potter book series two thousand years from now. Would they believe that our children went to wizarding schools, studied spells, and flew around on powered broom sticks playing Quidditch … just because someone wrote it down in their own long-ago past? (10) When it comes to believing religious stories, we quickly experience a kind of amnesia about how creative human imagination can be, willing them to be true accounts of actual events.

So perhaps Nibiru (or Planet X or the 10th planet) is nearing Earth and having an increasing gravitational effect. This would certainly go a long way in explaining our increasingly scattered magnetic field or shield called the magnetosphere. It could explain the spiking Schumann Resonance amplitude graphs, the erratic and faster migration of the Magnetic North Pole, increasing heat and luminosity of all planets … why it could even explain the Mandela Effect, since all waves (presumably even brain waves) could be gravitationally tugged and pulled just like the waves present in matter.

The Hopi speak of the Blue and Red Star Kachinas returning. Coincidentally a very large object is reported to be on its way to light up our night sky by 2022 that will then gradually fade away again. (11) More on cosmic connections later. There are many in our growing community of M.E. researchers that question anything NASA says now, sarcastically calling NASA short for "Never A Straight Answer". I think we need to be somewhat less judgmental here, because some history and some scientific findings are still true and can help us in this quest for truth on many topics including the Mandela Effect. Just because we have been and are being lied to for political and financial expediency, does not mean *everything* they tell us is a lie.

Even though many of us have learned the hard way that the truth of what is really happening and the nature of our reality matrix is rarely shared with the public, it just means we have to do a bit more work to figure it out on our own. This is bringing us together to share our findings and our feelings on our findings with each other more than ever before. This also engages your thinking process and makes you an active participant in the knowledge you are acquiring, rather than being spoon-fed information along with disinformation so that you behave the way the people providing the information wish you to behave. About time we developed our natural instincts and internal truth detectors to guide us while exploring official and unofficial information (the unofficial information aka rabbit holes are far more interesting). That in itself could be a huge leap forward in human consciousness evolution, and could be the reason the Mandela Effect even exists – as a catalyst to deeper, fuller, expanded awareness and understanding of the reality we find ourselves in. All of this was programmed for us long before we arrived here as innocent, helpless, amnesiacs.

While I am sure the creators of multidimensional quantum computers and the operators of large atom smashers, one with an obvious 666 logo, would love us all to believe that they have the power to change all matter (to change the reality matrix), they have never claimed this and nothing they have produced so far actually demonstrates this. The only thing coming close to this are reports that they knew their atom-smashing activities in 2012 – 2013 at the world's largest particle collider could have produced a mini-black hole while searching for the so-called God Particle (the supposed recreation of the first particles created after a Big Bang), and despite that risk they did it anyway. Some speculate they did create a micro black hole in 2012-2013 (12), and human conscious life was transferred here to an alternate Earth, on an alternate timeline, which is similar but not identical to the Earth of our past. If that was true, then all of the differences in matter would have happened at once, and not still be occurring; and there could be no flip-flops in matter switching back and forth between new and old states. There seem to be new Mandela Effects or inexplicable changes to matter, occurring every day, so we can discount the "We All Died in 2012" theory, even though it is one of the most interesting ones to speculate about, and is still used by respected YouTube channels in our community as a starting point for a larger conversation.

Many of our M.E. researchers hold to one or more of the Parallel Worlds, Multidimensional, Holographic, Simulation models of our universe, and there is some scientific evidence to back up all of these theories. I personally think it is smart to start simple when searching for explanations (Occam's Razor). So why would anyone choose to think all humans on Earth jump into a new dimension, parallel world, or new simulation en masse - every single time there is even a minor Mandela Effect change? Is it not far simpler to think humanity is staying in one place and matter is shifting and changing all around us, much like radio receivers remain stationary, but pick up different stations in the same room just by moving their internal dials? Is physically jumping timelines or dimensions as easy as changing channels on your television? Our internal dial is our focus. That which we focus on grows in strength. Where focus goes energy flows. This also goes a long way in explaining why some humans would keep the masses in a constant state of fear. Fearful people are much easier to manipulate and control with restrictive new laws than are confident people. Fear also seems to act as a mechanism of preserving the status quo. So the Mandela Effect could be an evolutionary tool to interrupt this state of status quo fear programming.

In my research on geological changes, I also noticed that it seems like the world map or Earth topography is shifting. Even though considered by some in our community to be unreliable, the largest most popular Earth app is showing no land masses on half of the planet now in the Pacific Ocean region. Before you start shouting "Flat Earth", don't worry I will address that concept later. The app is presenting a globe and we therefore must discuss changes to the globe it is presenting. I and others have noted they removed the arctic icecap from the standard Earth map apps too, making Greenland look like the new North Pole. The old North Pole is clearly under water now. Like me some of you may remember searching for the North Pole to show your children where Santa lived, and back in the day this same popular Earth app would show it smack dab in the middle of a snowy white arctic circle. Now a search for the "North Pole" turns up a town in Alaska and the snow from the Arctic Circle is all the way over in Greenland. Before you say this is proof of global warming, remind yourself that these are still animated graphics as opposed to genuine photographs, and like some Inuit tribe members say on YouTube, this could represent an Earth shifting on its axis or a migrating magnetic north pole - rather than increased global temperatures. (13)

Some attribute land changes and shifts to the Mandela Effect and others attribute this to increased volcanic and earthquake activity, or Earth axis shifts due to the largest earthquakes. Japan reportedly moved eight feet after the large quake in 2011. (14). This of course led to the Fukushima Nuclear Reactor meltdown which is reportedly still dumping tons of radioactive waste into the Pacific Ocean, which for some strange reason remains largely ignored by media and the public. (15)

All of this eventually led me to looking into the Grand Solar Minimum: a possible 400-year phase of fewer solar flares from our Sun. When it stops producing as many solar flares, the magnetic storms on the Earth increase (which can knock out power grids), as does volcanic and earthquake activity, as well as a cooling down of Earth surface temperatures very quickly like a mini-ice age. (16)

I also discovered that the Schumann Resonance, the hertz or tone that the Earth naturally emits, is increasing in amplitude and fluctuating wildly. I learned the Schumann Resonance is intimately tied to our magnetosphere often referred to as our magnetic field or shield – which is becoming increasingly scattered, allowing higher concentrations of UV and other cosmic and gamma radiations onto the surface of the Earth. (17) It is possible that the scattered magnetic shield (allowing more cosmic energy to hit the surface of the Earth that had previously been blocked) is causing the Mandela Effect: powerful cosmic waves interfering with brain waves and the waves in the atoms that make up matter. Sounds logical. More so in my opinion than hadron colliders and quantum computing combined. Are those increased energies causing matter to change, or are they causing human consciousness to change so that we *notice* matter as it changes in ways it has always done? Are these natural changes in matter directly tied to human consciousness in some way? Is the spirit in a material reality the programmer of the matter in the material reality? Could something be speeding up the natural changes in matter making it more noticeable now? Have you noticed time moves faster now? Go ahead and test it. Count the seconds like you were taught in elementary school: One elephant, two elephant, three elephant … to a stopwatch. Even if you used one Mississippi, two Mississippi, or one one-thousand, two one-thousand … you will probably see it is impossible to count correctly to a stopwatch the way you used to. Time appears to be faster now for many of us.

Something is causing these physical changes to random material objects, books, iconic movie lines, songs, animal life, human anatomy, land masses and the Solar System. And anything that tells you Satan, demons, aliens or human machines are behind it are designed to distract you from these rather obvious and important corresponding changes to our planet, magnetic shield, Sun, and solar system. Some call these exaggerated horror stories 'fearporn', and the people who put them out 'controlled opposition' (conop) and 'psychological operations' (psyops) designed to distract people from the more logical and obvious causes of the M.E. Exaggerate it so they do not *really* believe it, and they continue to behave like good citizens, do not panic and stop working, living and spending in an orderly systematic way that best serves the minority here. If you tell them the truth they may start prioritizing the spiritual instead of the mundane, and exercising their God-given rights to create in matter as *they* choose – that serves all and not the few here. So you can see how the Mandela Effect can be manipulated and used by the few to manipulate and maneuver the many to benefit the few.

I will consider each of these possible causes in depth later. Suffice it to say, conspiracy theorists are now calling themselves 'truthers', and they too are drawn to Mandela Effect research because they are always on the lookout for the hidden hand behind everything. In this, the M.E. and truther communities form an easy, natural alliance. Perhaps those who *do not* seek new or secret information may not notice the Mandela Effect. Perhaps you do not have to be M. E. affected to be a truther, but you have to be some kind of a truth seeker to be Mandela Effected; because many report their first awakening was to the secret negative control here for profit, which made them angry, *and then* they bumped into Mandela Effect videos while searching out more hidden information on hidden human greed and manipulation. In a very basic way, we have all become stuck in old science, old energy, old money, and old power for the sake of a few small minded individuals holding the human purse strings, and we simply cannot evolve, and break-free of terrestrial bondage until we express the systematic cooperation that benefits all so the system may thrive. Compassionate cooperation, representing a complete paradigm shift in human consciousness, feels like it is about to explode on the scene right now. Chances are because you are reading this book - you already play a very important role in this shift in collective consciousness.

Mandela Mind Over Mandela Matter

If you prefer simple solutions over the most complicated ones on offer too, and have researched any quantum theories, it seems far more likely that this is how matter has always worked. Look into superposition of states, retrocausality, and entanglement for a scientific mind-bender. This could be how matter is created and edited. It flows like energetic waves of particulate plasma which is influenced by the stronger waves of human consciousness. When consensus is achieved in larger numbers, then matter may flow into states of material change. The Mandela Effect may very well be showing us it is literally mind over matter. I believe the collective subconscious human mind literally creates and edits matter constantly around us, and the natural energetic changes to our planet, solar system, and galaxy is changing our awareness of this process. So now we can actually see the process of creating and editing matter with our thoughts and feelings. What else could change our awareness of the mind's affect on matter? Passing through photonic clouds in the galaxy could change awareness, as could increasing toxicity of food, water and air. No matter what shape you think the Earth is, the plasticity of matter in quantum studies seems to back up the fact that matter is pliable and often

24

unpredictable. So far this is the easiest and simplest possible cause of the Mandela Effect I can find, but of course I am always searching for more plausible causes.

Once you are M. E. affected and you wake up to the fact that matter is fluid and can change, then I think your feelings, thoughts, and beliefs can have a greater impact on your immediate material environment, and the collective material environment as well. How? By acting willfully and directly with your intention, which feeds and seeds the human collective subconscious mind anyway, so you might as well seed it with the changes you would *like* to see. Some people call it the collective unconscious, or the human hivemind, while others object to that insect-like description. I believe Mandela Effect affected people who are aware of matter changing around them also sense that their reality responds to their combined thoughts, feelings and actions. Matter is malleable. It is fluid and not permanent. Think of it as very firm plasma or light filled with energy and information in motion. And once you have become aware of that, you suddenly become more self-aware too. Once you realize you can affect matter, chances are you will do so more carefully. Once you realize the power of your thoughts and feelings you start monitoring them more. So instead of just thinking, believing, feeling and acting randomly in response to all of the emotions around you, M.E. affected people start paying closer attention to how things make them feel, and then they learn to manage that better so they are responding with intent instead of reacting without intent. M.E. affected usually start switching off mainstream anything while searching out information and truth on their own, or with like-minded people, forming new friendships, even whole communities in the process. Sometimes they completely turn off all news and other mainstream media, preferring to think for themselves. Many newly Mandela Effect aware start looking into, researching, watching and listening to things that have a positive effect on their feelings instead of negative programming, which has a nurturing effect on their individual and collective consciousness. As more of us become emotionally well, so does the world. It makes you feel better, think more positively, and feel more positively when you do this, and you can start doing this right now with simple intention. Where your focus goes energy flows and grows. Just as you would not intentionally feed your body poison, you stop feeding your mind poison once you see its source. This is "aware consciousness" –

aware of itself and aware of its natural ability to affect self, others and matter.

When you realize you can, then why not take control of your thoughts and emotions to create a happier reality. One easy way to do this is to wake up with gratitude. The moment you wake up each day say a heart-felt thank you to God, the universe, or your higher self for your amazing body on this beautiful planet with your loving family, home, sustenance, friends, pets, or something along those lines. Say it in your mind, or out loud. Then tell yourself you choose to think healing thoughts and feel healthy feelings that honor you and God (or source energy if you prefer) all day long. Then during the day when you catch yourself thinking an automatic negative thought - just stop it. Do not judge it or criticize yourself for having thought it. That just adds more negativity to it. Say to yourself or out loud: I do not choose to think negative thoughts, and then immediately say or think the exact opposite of that negative thought. This whole process only takes a moment. For example: Someone cuts you off in traffic and you immediately curse them and say they are rude, aggressive, dangerous et cetera.

1. Notice the negative thought.

2. Stop thinking it.

3. Say to yourself or out loud: I choose to think positive thoughts today.

4. Think or say out loud: that person must be in a hurry or under stress – bless him or her to drive more safely, (or something along those lines).

5. That is it. Move on with your day.

Never berate yourself for negative thinking. To cure it and to cure collective negativity on Earth, I think it is important to forgive, forgive, forgive – and then forgive some more. Forgive yourself for thinking negative thoughts – you have been conditioned to do this your whole life. It is not your fault. Nor is it the fault of others, so forgive them too. It is part of the human condition at present to dwell negatively on the past or future instead of acknowledging or enjoying the present, and we are evolving away from this now. We heal ourselves, our families and the world through forgiveness and choosing to think, feel and act positively as much as humanly possible.

Once you realize thoughts and feelings rule over matter, one of the easiest ways to feed your subconscious mind nourishing, healthy, positive thoughts is to start meditating or praying daily. A lot of people pray and not only ask for positive outcomes in their lives, but they give thanks for all the wonderful things they already have, and when they do this, they are actually seeding their own life, as well as the collective world with more positivity. It seems God, source, and the creative universe loves gratitude, and responds to it faster than it does to desperate pleas or demands for the very same things. Why? Don't ask me – meditate on it and ask God, source, the creative universe, or your higher self. One of my favorite books on the power of prayer is called *The Gentle Art of Blessing* by Pierre Pradervand. In this book you learn how to bless everyone and everything naturally every day in every way: the good and the bad - in fact the bad needs your prayers even more than the good ever will. (18)

Other people prefer to meditate, to go inside in order to find God and communicate with the creative power that created the universe. God, source, and the creative universe are often described in exactly the same way, as the sum total of everything that is, was, or ever will be. I personally believe we are all tiny parts or fractals of God, like individual cells in the body of God. Like cells in the human body, each and every one is important to the health and well-being of the whole.

To help you attain and maintain a loving forgiving state naturally, I highly recommend doing *A Course in Miracles* (ACIM) book by Helen Schucman. (19) I say "doing" and not just "reading" for a reason. Buy the combined version that contains the Text, the Workbook and the Manual for Teachers. If you actually complete the course you cannot help feeling differently, more loving and forgiving of humanity in all of its unimaginable creativity and promise, and diabolical faults.

I realize the Text portion of the book puts a lot of people off, because of the way it is written and its length. I am sure many people who have completed or teach ACIM would disagree with me, but there is a way to get through the material if the sheer volume of it is off-putting to even getting started. I recommend skimming through the parts that you lose interest in. As a mainstream journalist who had to read a lot of books preparing for programs, shows, interviews, et cetera, I developed my own method. Have a highlighting pen available, as the act of highlighting words emphasizes them in your memory even if they are never revisited, and when you wish to brush up on the material, you can quickly read only the highlighted words to recall the whole. Read ACIM when you have a good hour or two of quiet privacy, and read at a slightly quicker than normal pace. Do not worry if you do not remember what you just read – do not re-read it. It will sink into your subconscious mind to add to the whole of the knowledge you are acquiring. Believe it or not your subconscious mind takes in the whole page at once. Highlight any words or sentences that stand out as important to you.

If it starts to feel boring, or you lose interest, just go into skimming mode where you read only the first sentence of every paragraph until a paragraph grabs your attention again - then start reading whole paragraphs again until you start to lose interest again. When this happens, go into the skimming mode of reading only the first sentence of every paragraph until it grabs your attention again; and so on, until you have completed the Text. You will be amazed at how much of the material you retain this way, because you are only paying attention to what interests you and the rest, the filler, you will absorb subconsciously. Then read and do the Workbook, which is organized into one short lesson a day for a whole year. Who has time for that you ask? Besides it is too dictatorial a pace befitting the personality who channeled the information and the era in which it was published. So I recommend reading as many daily lessons as feels comfortable after you have completed skimming the Text, but do not skim the daily lessons as they are much shorter and without any filler. I finished my year of lessons in this way in just three months. And finally I recommend reading 100 percent of the Manual for Teachers at a pace that suits you. It is very short, so no skimming necessary. (For those who have studied metaphysics for a long time I recommend reading the Workbook first, followed by the Teacher's Manual, and then skimming the Text.) There is something about the Text, possibly by design, that puts most people off completing or even starting the course.

A Course in Miracles teaches atonement or at-one-ment with humanity, all life, and God (source energy) like no other book I have found. This leads to an internal state of peace and makes the practice of love and forgiveness that much easier.

How does this all relate to the Mandela Effect? Your thoughts rule your beliefs. Your beliefs create your feelings. Your combined thoughts, beliefs and feelings dictate your actions. Your thoughts, beliefs, feelings and actions create not only your world, but our shared collective world. You affect me and I affect you and the seven billion others … see how important your positivity is to Earth and us in the here and now? Because only what is in spirit within - is reflected in matter without. There is much truth to be found in simple Hermetic Laws. So all is consciousness after all. I believe the Mandela Effect is a wake-up call to the simple fact that mind rules matter here. Some of my own favorite sayings:

> Thoughts are things with wings and our feelings give them flight.

> Your thoughts will return to you in the form of material experiences if you feed them enough of your emotions.

> Warning: this is true for positive, neutral and negative thoughts.

Who Controls the Mandela Effect?

Now that you have seen the Mandela Effect in action, and realize you could be the source of it, or at least contributing to it … it is plausible that the people who are aware and awake who see the Mandela Effect also have the ability to steer it more than those who do not see it. If you study a bit about The Hundredth Monkey Effect, you will see how once a critical point in a population of a species learns a new skill - it becomes an automatic skill in one hundred percent of the community. You no longer have to teach it - it just happens as a natural new skill across the entire species. No one knows the exact number of individuals needed to learn a new skill in order to reach critical mass, but I have heard it can be as small as just over seven percent of a population. This fits in nicely with the holographic universe, parallel dimensions, string and the simulation theories of reality, because it represents a kind of subconscious programming that communicates on a different frequency to thoughts, spoken language and electronic media. It is silent, natural and instantaneous, like Spontaneous Evolution (of which there are many unexplained examples in Earth species). It is also like Quantum Entanglement. This is the "spooky science" Einstein spoke of, because we cannot yet understand, describe, or even detect the frequency of this innate instant communication among members of a species (or particles) that crosses all boundaries - even space and time.

The human hivemind, (the collective subconscious of all humanity), also nicely explains why the Hundredth Monkey Theory works. When you act, think or feel something - it has an effect in your personal environment, and when enough people act, think or feel the same it reaches critical mass. At critical mass it is communicated to all of humanity instantly, subconsciously and becomes innate: something you are born with and instinctively understand that no longer needs to be taught. In The Event community, critical mass is counted on for group ascension. Some attribute this to the 144,000 enlightened souls bringing the Golden Age to Earth, as mentioned in the Bible. (20)

The very opposite appears to be true when looking only at mainstream media (MSM) including news, music, movies, television programming and games which nine times out of ten seem to program the human mind with abuse: drugs, alcohol, sex, killing, conquest, and end of world scenarios et cetera. This makes some of us ask: are humans in control of mass media intentionally trying to keep the masses feeling low? The word apocalyptic in Greek means "revelation", or an unveiling of things not previously known, instead of the death and destruction of the world as MSM portrays. Perhaps the end of the world as we know it, actually means all its corruption is coming to a close now, but not the end of the physical world. That would make the Apocalypse a good thing instead of a bad thing. Some speculate that reality is so pliable that those of us here who expect to experience destruction will get to experience that, while those of us here who expect to experience a Golden Age on Earth will get to experience that instead. Instant heaven and instant hell, depending upon your own personal expectations. In this way the apocalypse is both good and bad, depending on your perspective, and the Mandela Effect demonstrates an important part of the unveiling – at least the veil that prevented us from seeing how matter responds to consciousness.

Now I am no expert, (because the experts are ignoring the Mandela Effect), but if you have studied a little quantum physics you know everything in the universe, including matter, is information in wave form. Within all particles of matter are waves, and information waves in potential are faster and lighter than information waves found in dense matter. In fact, the plasma or electromagnetic universe of Tesla is making more sense. Especially as presented by scientists on the ThunderboltsProject channel on YouTube, along with David LaPoint's Primer Field videos ,and Theoria Apophasis videos on light and gravity. It makes perfect sense that all is information in light, and the density of light changes with the information it contains. The Mandela Effect becomes logical when you see the collective subconscious creating matter and editing matter with collective waves of information stemming from human hearts and brains. To increase this power to create and edit matter (denser slower frequency waveform) with your mind and heart (higher faster frequency waveform), start expanding your awareness by reading, watching, meditating and praying on quantum subjects. Learning new concepts actually changes the plasticity of your thinking mind and physical brain (the program and the computer). Your subconscious and superconscious minds grow as a consequence, exponentially, to the level you expand your conscious mind with new information. The act of seeking truth changes everything in your life. And that also impacts the collective subconscious or human hivemind - propelling us all forward in our spiritual and physical evolution. This is purposeful hivemind programming. Maybe the M.E. was purposefully made visible to create new truth seekers in people who had no reason to seek this kind of deep reality exploration before ... until, that is, they began seeing matter changing all around them.

The Mandela Effect is the automatic changing of matter through collective thoughts, so it has no apparent rhyme or reason, except for changes to the human body, which for the most part appear to be improvements. The heart moving to the center of the ribcage, the kidneys moving under the ribcage, the strong, solid bone sockets behind the eyes, the thicker collar bones, a new organ called a mesentery, a new bone in the knee ... are some of the reported anatomical Mandela Effects.

The other way to expand your ability to influence your reality (including matter), is through heart-based meditation, intention and prayer practiced daily. More on that later. We are more powerful than we know, and the Mandela Effect may help to show us just how powerful we truly are to determine our reality. Seeing how humans collectively create and manage the matrix (through the visuals of the Mandela Effect) may indicate a quantum jump in human consciousness into the New Human: one who controls their personal and collective reality. The Mandela Effect makes you the captain of your ship - called "life".

Claims of False Memory

Let us do a quick thought experiment here and do not feel silly doing it. Some of you may already know that all of Einstein's theories were based on his thought experiments. His wife was reportedly the mathematician who put his thought experiments into mathematical formulas, but he decided since they were married that meant that she automatically received credit when he received credit, so he always failed to mention her contribution publicly.

Some, especially those who do not see the changes, say the Mandela Effect is no more than a false memory or confabulation. What is interesting is that they leave out the most important part of their theory – "residue". Residue is the material evidence of how things were *before* their change, and is found in older forms of media more abundantly than online media for most.

In our thought experiment, imagine a car logo that has existed for decades. Suddenly thousands of people think it used to be different. They look it up to see when the company made the change, only to find the company never changed it – it has always been this way – the new way. So they think they are misremembering it, but then they see thousands of other people across regions, ages, genders are misremembering it too. And here is where the Mandela Effect becomes real, tangible and measurable: thousands of people do not misremember the logo thousands of different way, which is to be expected. No, the logo is "misremembered" in the *exact same way* by thousands of different people who have had no communication with each other. Now that would be a miracle in itself that science brushes off as "confabulation" or mass-misremembering. How would thousands of people with no direct communication tune into the exact same change in memory of something? That is not possible without the existence of a collective memory, collective subconscious mind, or shared unconscious mind (a la famous psychiatrist Carl Jung), where many are tuning into the same brainwave frequency.

Keepers of Memory

I am going to give you a different perspective on the Mandela Effect here. In fact, it is the opposite of what the unaffected say. I am not going to explain how we *know* the Mandela Effect is really occurring, because anybody reading this probably already knows that based on residual evidence. You either see it or you don't. Especially on YouTube, there is some really good evidence that things at one time actually were the way you and many remember them, but have changed at some point into the new how-they-always-were state. If you understand that last statement - you are definitely Mandela Effect affected. There are also many flip flops back-and-forth between the way things used to be, the way they became, and going back to the way they used to be. So you can mentally gorge yourself for days on YouTube videos showing you residual proof of your memories.

Especially changes to the human body, which are amazing, and continue to occur day by day. Examine any online photos of the human skull and see if you remember the universal chin clefts, holes around the eyes, eye bone sockets, and massive cheek indentations. Look up the mesentery (a brand new organ) and a new bone in the knee. Do you remember the human heart slightly to the left or in the middle of the chest? The kidneys being tucked up safely under the rib cage, or do you remember the term sucker punch? Many of the so-called Mandela Effect changes to the human body seem to be improvements to safety and survival. Perhaps the M.E. has always been behind spontaneous evolution, and explains dramatic quick changes to a species that science struggles to explain through Darwin's Survival of the Fittest theory of gradual evolution.

Do certain constellations like Orion and the Big Dipper look bigger in the night sky than you remember? Do you recall words like unicorn, couch and stuff in the Bible? Not that I mind these changes. I do not even mind the Mandela Effect. I do not mind that matter is shifting and changing around me constantly, because I am comfortable with the idea that it truly is mind over matter here That as our minds change, matter reflects these changes back to us – individually and collectively. So how could that bother me? Of course, I would prefer if all humans on Earth could see the Mandela Effect, which is coming, like I would prefer if all humans craved and demonstrated compassionate cooperation – which is also coming. We are getting there slowly but surely, and may even get a boost from the Hundredth Monkey (spontaneous evolutionary) Effect.

I realize now that I am a keeper of memory, and we collectively who are M. E. affected are the keepers of the memories. Think about that. All these people who do not see matter changing around them constantly are saying to us it is false memory - you don't remember correctly. If you know the truth it does not matter what anyone says. That is how powerful truth is. And some day the keepers of the memories may serve a higher purpose than worrying their family and friends with their claims that matter is changing. Even standard science today recognizes that matter is flexible and at its essence acts more like a wave than a particle - like plasma: light or information in light with measurable matter with plasticity.

Often when you show a disbeliever residual evidence of the way you remember it, the way it used to be, they answer you with silence. Why? Because acknowledging that that evidence of your memory exists - upsets their paradigm of reality. It means that their memory of it and the current history of it could be wrong, or may have changed so both existed. Not many are strong enough to face a paradigm change head on. No wonder they are worried and angry and frightened when we try to make them see it just so they can agree with us and make us feel better about what we are seeing. Are we so afraid or lonely that we must have the whole world see what we see in order to feel comfortable in our new slightly expanded paradigm? Be braver than that and let people see the paradigm shift when they are ready, not when you are ready, for them to see it. Perhaps it takes exceptional psychological strength to face paradigm shifts without fear, depression or anger. Or the bravery comes after we process these feelings as a natural byproduct of losing your reality rules – the rules that were handed to you the day you were born, but established long before you arrived here to see how things really work.

Remember: companies can and do change product names and logos. Always research the history of the name or logo you think has changed, to make sure its history says it has always been the way it is now – before you call it a Mandela Effect. Since most humans have not been taught to research anything ever, we are only taught to memorize and regurgitate 'facts', many are mixing up company changes, uncertain memory, and introduction to new things with actual Mandela Effects - making the phenomenon more than murky.

This phenomenon should more accurately be called a Quantum Awakening within the Quantum Mind. So we are the keepers of the memory of how some things were before, whether we like it or not. I am a keeper of memory. You are a keeper of memory. Somehow there is a smaller group of us that has attained the ability to keep accurate memories of how things used to be as they are constantly shifting and changing all around us in response to collective thoughts, beliefs, and feelings. And this is probably going to become an important skill. It does not seem important yet. Right now it is more of a nuisance because it is primarily about car logos and names of products, song lyrics, celebrity names, movie lines, TV shows, et cetera. However, it does feel more important when you see the changes to geography, history, human anatomy, animals, and religious texts occurring. But this is nothing compared to what I believe is yet to come. Holding all memory of what was before may become a very important skill as things progress here, as changes occur more often and faster, and perhaps as these changes creep into social structures like government, politics, finance and law.

It is not always a matter of memory. Sometimes it is a matter of interest. I am always amazed at the number of Americans who still do not know that in 2012 the United States Congress passed a bipartisan bill supported by the Democrats and the Republicans that made it legal for the United States government to lie to the United States people in the best interests of national security. Political propaganda so expertly crafted by the Nazi Party during World War II is now completely legal in the United States. In the interests of National Security our public servants may legally lie to us. How convenient for drumming up false support for acts of war regardless of party affiliation. (21) How many Americans know that they cannot legally sue a vaccine manufacturer for any harm, damage or death attributed directly to their product? (22) And that the largest producer of genetically modified organisms is trying to get a similar law passed to protect them from any harm caused down the road from consuming genetically modified foods. (23)

How nonsensical is it that we are paying our public servants to protect corporate interests, instead of protecting us from corporate interests that may cause damage and harm? Sometimes the

Mandela Effect changes to matter do not surprise me as much as the fact that most Americans do not notice when their rights are quietly removed, and when they are told, they ignore it or do not care. Sound familiar? This is also how many react to Mandela Effect evidence or reality paradigm changes. Is this natural? Is this okay? Is it purely coincidental that fluoride gas was reportedly used by Nazis to sedate concentration camp prisoners during World War II; (24) that Nazis were reportedly secretly brought into the post-war American government through Operation Paperclip; (25) and that American public tap water was fluoridated soon after? (26) It could be a coincidence. I hope Americans start caring enough to protect their freedoms and their rights, so that their children do not have to fight to restore them. But this is not a political book, though it is often difficult to separate societal structures influenced by the Quantum Awakening of human consciousness from the political structures that control those societal structures.

We cannot be sure that some apparent Mandela Effects are not just the unveiling of true facts we never learned, or facts kept hidden. Did you know the Statue of Liberty was bombed and damaged by the Germans in 1917 as an act of war on American soil? (27) What do you think of the new conspiracy theories surrounding Mud Floods and the Tartary Empire, or Flat Earth? There is sometimes no way to prove definitively whether some or all of these are Mandela Effect changes to our history, facts we never noticed, hidden history, a false conop and internet inserted psyop, or just an interesting but false conspiracy theory. History has always been written by the victors, but true history and true facts are getting very flimsy now. Did you know or care to know that recently released John F. Kennedy Assassination documents show he was shot from different directions - disproving the long-held single-shooter theory that Lee Harvey Oswald was the lone gunman? (28) Few seem to care now that many conspiracy theories turn out years later to be conspiracy facts. Political activism is in decline. Could there be a chemical connection to the constant ingestion of fluoride and other brain-numbing toxins in our food, water and air that could equally be responsible for the explosion in Alzheimer's and Autism? I cannot say with certainty, just noticing apparent coincidences. Every scientist knows disproven coincidence often turns theory into fact. Does something we collectively see, hear, eat, drink or breathe take away our moral interests to care about these very same things? There we go into politics again. Being controversial by nature the Mandela Effect often leads this way. It is hard to avoid when so many rabbit holes are interconnected, coincidences become correlations become facts, and conspiracy theories become truth.

Every single object in our world started out as a thought in someone's mind first. And when you have a lot of collective thought coming together in agreement on something in a collective setting, then the matter connected to that thought is going to reflect that change for everyone in that setting. So just remember that as a Mandela Effect affected person who is quantumly awakening: you are a holder of memory and you are part of a growing community that are also the Holders of Memories. We remember how things were and we always will. We can no longer be fooled by changing matter - into thinking that when a change occurs - it was always that way. Whenever it changes, we are going to notice because that is how human consciousness is evolving, and there are too many of us to be fooled now. Once you see the Mandela Effect you cannot *unsee* it, and it is extremely contagious. It crosses all boundaries of age, sex, race, religion, region, and nationality. I guess you could say it is the New Human without Artificial Intelligence. It is naturally the way we are becoming. And seeing something change is better than not seeing something change, because only then can you analyze *why* something has changed and learn something new about you in your environment. Therefore, the Mandela Effect is progress, while not seeing it is stagnation. Even if you thoroughly believe that millions of others who *say* they can see it *cannot* see it, you are stagnating in an old reality paradigm on purpose. Personally, I would try to see it and jump on the Mandela Effect vehicle to expanded awareness – even just to see where it would take me.

Common Characteristics of Those Who See

After producing a Mandela Effect channel on YouTube, putting me in touch with many affected individuals through videos, comments, and livestreams - these are my observations of just some of the common characteristics we seem to share.

I find the Mandela Effect affected tend to be artistic and creative. Many I have met are artists, musicians, singers, songwriters, dancers, poets, and writers. Even if these are not their full-time professions, they tend to have artistic hobbies and express wishes of pursuing their art for a living, rather than mundane jobs just to survive in the current societal systems - which were set up to benefit the few over the many. They do not fully understand or agree with systems that were handed to them at birth: systems they had no part in creating - systems begging for reform, change and evolution ASAP. Many of them still express hope that one day soon social systems will reflect the human need for freedom and creative expression, so many are naturally optimistic. Some who are more sensitive or empathetic seem to respond with more anger or sadness at human tendencies towards corruption. Some even wish to leave the planet and never return in terms of reincarnation. You will also find the logical left-brain dominant individuals who love scientific exploration of all subjects, and who prefer to discover the answers for themselves, rather than swallow force-fed answers. In this way they too are highly creative, although they may think themselves more logical minded. Many 'M.E.ers' are naturally psychic, empathetic and become energy healers or nurses. So this is what I personally feel is the positive Mandela Effect camp.

There is another one. What else would you expect where duality reigns? Also in the M.E. community I find fearful individuals expressing pessimistic negative views, including fear of the future and of all things Mandela'd. Fear of the unknown, of matter changing around them, of the Devil, of demons, of atom smashers, of quantum computing, of A.I., of the wrath of God, of nature in the form of cataclysms, of their fellow man, of the end of the world … the fear list does not stop there. When they see the M.E. changes they often fear reality and fear their own sanity. You could consider this a natural pessimistic outlook with or without the Mandela Effect. It does not help if they do not have close friends and family members to discuss the changes with - when they become newly awakened to the constant changes in matter. The positive-oriented individual seems to adapt quicker than the negative-focused individual.

I found a correlation in that the fearful M.E experiencers seem to come from a strict religious upbringing, so perhaps the indoctrination of a vengeful punishing God plays into their interpretation of an unstable reality – especially since there have been many Mandela Effect changes reported in the Bible. If they believed that God physically wrote the Bible and something is changing that now, it stands to follow that *that* something must be evil to go against the original words of God. But for those of us who studied world religions and considered the Bible an inspired human construct, that humans physically wrote the word of God, putting it through their human prejudices and biases first; and editing those words countless times through history for political expediency … changing the words now does not construe evil. It reflects another mechanism of change - the same mechanism changing children's books, songs, and pop culture movie lines. Not so scary when Berenstein Bears changes to Berenstain Bears; but when something changes your Lion with the Lamb to a Wolf with the Lamb it's another story … well personally that does not scare me either because I like wolves. Maybe you have to have fear within you as a primary outlook in order to remain frightened of the Mandela Effect long after a natural adjustment period to a new reality paradigm.

However, fear is an obvious first reaction to seeing your first Mandela Effects. It seems part of the process of coming to terms with it, but not something to get stuck in. You have been taught that matter is relatively permanent and although it can and does decay over time, it cannot instantly change. Now you suddenly begin perceiving instant changes in matter, and how does the human animal react to severe unexpected change? Possibly with denial, fear, anger, bargaining, and eventually acceptance. This is very similar to the Kubler-Ross Model predicting psychological reactions to death and terminal illness. After reading Anita Moorjani's book, *Dying to be Me*, I even question the reality of so-called terminal illness beyond human-programming-constructs in the collective false-reality-rules given to us all at birth. (29) If you understand that sentence without re-reading it, then you are a natural born Truther.

I have found that those individuals with an internal locus of control (who naturally tend to believe they are in control of their life) with an optimistic outlook tend to move rather quickly through all of these stages when it comes to accepting the Mandela Effect as a natural occurring phenomenon. But those with an external locus of control (who naturally tend to believe they have little to no control over what happens to them) with a pessimistic outlook tend to get stuck in the fear or anger stage indefinitely. They may even try to force others around them to see it too, just so they can feel more comfortable themselves, regardless of whether those people are ready to see it or not. This is understandable. Who wants to be the only one seeing these changes? Company in belief indicates sanity and safety. For this reason, I recommend you share it with others in natural conversation, but back down when you meet resistance to it. You can either see the changes or you cannot. The Mandela Effect has no middle ground. It is a matter of personal conscious awakening, not a matter of factual presentation skills. Those who are not ready to awaken to matter shifting around them will not only deny the changes occurred, but will ignore all residue of how things were before they changed. Rather that and call you crazy for seeing it, than admit their reality is no longer real, reliable, permanent. Unfortunately, this has sometimes led to splits in families and friendships. But once you choose a Mandela Effect camp to spend your time in – the positive hopeful side or the negative fearful side – that is where you are likely to find friendships to replace those you may have lost along the way. Fear feeds and grows more fear, while love feeds and grows more love, so it is in your own best psychological interest to come to an acceptance of the M.E. as a natural awakening in your consciousness, so you may approach it with the sense of wonder it deserves. If you are stuck in anger or fear of the phenomenon just remind yourself it has not killed you, nor will it ever kill you, so you can adapt to it.

Conquering Mandela Effect Fear

So you're newly awakened to the Mandela Effect and you see matter changing around you: favorite songs, iconic movie lines, book titles, verses in the Bible, human anatomy, geography … you name it. And your immediate reaction is confusion or fear, or a little of both. Why? Because you were taught that matter is permanent and cannot change without a physical alteration and a record of the change being made. So it is natural for the newly affected to feel initial fear, because what they were taught about matter, reality, and the world was wrong. Sometimes this morphs into anger when they feel the truth was kept from them.

There are so many reasons why you can flip and flop from fear to anger and back-and-forth, but the problem with that is, as long as you are experiencing fear or anger you are cutting yourself off from your own power. As long as you are experiencing fear, which is a feeling not a belief, and a feeling is a state of being - you are cutting yourself off from your own power. It is more important that you know this than you know the age of the universe, who or what created the universe, or how the universe came into being. It is far more important that you know how to regain your own personal power, or sovereignty here, so you can become more effective as consciousness-spirit-soul energy experiencing a physical life in a physical body in a physical world. Fear in the body causes contraction and constriction, giving all energy to your organs for the fight or flight response; while centered, balanced feelings of well-being allow your energy to expand even past your physical body to experience more of the world.

The reality matrix around us on the outside is a reflection of how we feel about ourselves on the inside. As well as how the entire species thinks, feels and acts. Our repeated thoughts become our beliefs, which produce our feelings, which direct our physical actions in matter.

Repeated Thoughts = Beliefs = Feelings = Actions.
(On the individual and collective levels.)

Thoughts are internally fueling feelings, which emote externally driving choices, decisions and actions in matter. Everything you see or experience outside starts inside of you. And everything you experience on the outside reconfirms the thoughts and feelings on the inside of you in a circular biofeedback loop. Think of feelings (emotions) as supercharged thoughts which have a profound effect on matter. Many of us believe thoughts from the brain are more electric in nature because of the electrical firing between synapses; and feelings from the heart are more magnetic in nature due to the pumping action; while actions are kinetic in nature. Though there are many states and levels of energy - these three combined change matter. The early New Thought movement focused on controlling thoughts alone with books by Napoleon Hill, Wallace Wattles and Neville Goddard. (We are New Thought writers, as anyone who challenges conventionally held beliefs in any age are considered to be part of a 'New Thought' movement.) However, it took another century for us to understand our thoughts are only the beginning of matrix control – feelings are necessary to give our thoughts enough oomph to manifest, and action speeds the whole process up. That is why just thinking something over and over does not manifest desires very well, even after they have become firm beliefs. Feelings help speed up manifestation by giving them the magnetic heart energy to draw them to you quicker than electric thoughts alone. But when you add thoughts, feelings and actions in a focused way to manifest a specific goal or desire - this trifecta of energies produces faster manifestation in a material world by pulling the intention out of the 'ethers of possibility' into the physical world of matter. This works for the collective in jointly creating, editing, and maintaining the material world through collective feelings too. So take a page out of any of Eckhart Tolle's books and videos, and pause before reacting to anything - to consider how you would *like* to respond. If the collective group is feeling scared, angry and insecure, it might be willing to part with more of its hard-earned money in the form of taxes to build more bombs and walls. So it behooves the weapons manufacturers to keep the collective in a constant state of fear. That is a very profitable emotion for a few but not so great for the many. This also applies to diseases and pharmaceuticals, and anything where manipulated group emotions result in some form of control or profitability for a smaller group of humans. They know and we know this is coming to a natural end as the Sleeping Giant (humanity which is sometimes called the "Sheeple", but I prefer "Sleeple") awakens to emotional manipulation used to manage the material matrix in the favor of a few instead of the benefit of all, and step into their personal individual power as collective co-creators here.

Believe it or not, your emotions are under only your control. It is not what happens to you that matters as much as how you *react* to what happens to you that matters most. We exist moment by moment by moment by moment … we do not actually exist in the past or in the future at any point in our entire life here. In this way, life in matter is a perennial now with the illusion or memory of a past, and illusion, or hopes and dreams of a future. This explains why all time is happening at once - because you only ever have a long string of nows in which to exist, move, change, fear, love, act, and be. Focusing on the past can result in feelings of regret, while dwelling on the future may produce feelings of uncertainty. Dwelling on the present is called mindfulness and is where you exercise your true power to create within this spirit-body matrix. Power to react appropriately, power to make changes, power to influence the whole, power to steer your life … is only ever exercised in the moment. Your life can be measured in your reactions moment by moment over a lifetime, because when you are looking back that is all you have - and there is your control. Because if you take a moment to consider your reactions in this moment, you have control over how you respond to anything: an argument or a kiss, a dis-ease or a healing, a failure or a success, and so on. Your response to everything and anything is entirely up to you. No one can make you respond one way or another. We usually react immediately without thought, but if we pause for just a moment *in that moment* we get to decide how we *want* to react in a way that best serves us. That moment of reflection before reaction can change everything.

Some well-known tools for delaying auto-reaction are to take a deep breath, or count to 10 before reacting when emotionally triggered. Even a small delay can change how you react to something and the outcome. Think about how you are responding: does it serve you, your loved ones, or your community? When this kind of thoughtful reaction spreads - the whole world changes.

One way to move away from anger or fear, including fear of the Mandela Effect, is through gratitude. Gratitude instantly neutralizes disappointment, resentment, jealousy, sadness, anger, and fear. Simply write down, say out loud, or mentally list what you are grateful for in the moment. It helps to use gratitude related to the person or issue that is upsetting you. Shift from a negative feeling to at least a neutral feeling by thinking of something you love or appreciate. This will shift you into a state of love and forgiveness and take you out of the state of anger, disappointment, or sadness - which are all forms of fear: fear of abandonment, fear of not being appreciated, fear of powerlessness, fear of being alone or misunderstood .... There is only love or fear here, with everything else falling somewhere in between.

When it comes to negative feelings from larger social injustices like abuse, starvation, poverty, or war, it is a little bit harder to shift because we perceive ourselves as having no control over it in the first place. This also stems from fear of being a victim, or of being powerless. But you can still shift yourself into a state of love and forgiveness by using gratitude and prayer. List what you are grateful for related to the situation and pray for what you cannot change - especially for others far from you. Bless the people involved, both the victims and the perpetrators that they understand and change their ways by sending them love. Some who analyze word magic caution that to bless is to B-less which removes power, so send love instead of B-less-ings. Meditate, pray and send love from your heart straight to the people and the area of the world you think needs it. These actions are self-empowering and spill back on you, helping you shift from a negative, sad, fearful state of being into a positive, loving and grateful state of being. To better understand how loving, praying, and intending for others can heal you and your loved ones, I recommend you read Lynne McTaggart's book, *The Power of Eight*.

Those who study avatars know that the miracles come from states of being and not from wishes or thoughts. This better serves you, your family, your community and the collective. The Buddhic or "middle way" (sometimes called the Narrow Path), is to look at everything and if it is positive appreciate it, if it is negative transmute it with forgiveness, love, or prayer, and if it is neither negative nor positive then remain neutral. This is controlling your state of being, which controls your manifest world. Easier said than done, but perhaps Ho 'Oponopono, the ancient Kahuna prayer of restitution can help transmute negativity and fear with the simple words: I Love You, I am sorry, Please forgive me, Thank you.

Ho 'Oponopono prayer is a gift that brings many peace and healing. This is an important tool for speeding up the process of ascension, awakening, shifting to 5D Earth, shifting to the better timeline, quantum jumping etc. (Have you figured out by now "The Event" is you here now changing the here-now with your thoughts, feelings and actions?) You can look it up and watch some videos about it on YouTube. I recommend anything by Morrnah Simeona, Dr. Hew Len, or Joe Vitale. They have videos and books available to teach you this ancient kahuna prayer of reconciliation. They call it cleaning and clearing the negative with key powerful words: "I love you, I'm sorry, Please forgive me, Thank you, And it is done." Repeating these words over and over while holding a problem, issue or person in your mind basically sets things right again by cleaning the emotional slate; and there is plenty of evidence to support this. This works on your problems with loved ones, and for the world. Morrnah used to employ the prayer a certain way: as soon as you experience something that makes you feel bad, whether it is something that happens in your household or something you see on the news triggers you into a negative feeling, (and I would not recommend watching a lot of the news because that keeps your vibration continually low), just say in your head or out loud, "I love you, I'm sorry, please forgive me, thank you" … over and over again, until you feel neutral or good. She starts with, "I love you". This change in feeling means you have cleared it, not only for yourself, but for the world due to collective consciousness. Hew Len and Joe Vitale employ it in a slightly different way starting with: "I'm sorry"; followed by, " Please forgive me, thank you, I love you ..." over and over until the negative feeling is gone and the issue that caused it is clear. They call it 'getting back to zero' in the popular book and audio series *Zero Limits (30)*, and this fits in nicely with believers in the simulation theory of the universe. It is like hitting the delete key when something upsets you!

For me when I say or think, "I'm sorry please forgive me thank you I love you I'm sorry please forgive me thank you I love you I'm sorry please forgive me thank you …. " the faster this goes the more it has been cleared, so I know when to stop. I tend to use the Len-Vitale version starting with "I'm sorry" first, if I feel I have a personal part in the issue that upset me. If I see something that upsets me that I had no role in, an issue in the larger community, then I start with Morrnah's version "I love you" first. You can use this prayer for family members as well. There is even a website called zero-wise.com where you can clear and clean with Ho' oponopono on other people's requests, and ask others to clear and clean with Ho' oponopono on your issues or problems.

Another important tool for empowerment is action. Especially in a world that seems to be changing all around you without asking for your permission first. If something triggers you, or makes you feel sad, angry or fearful, it is very empowering to do something about it in a peaceful way. Positive action seeking a positive result. For instance, if you see something on global poverty that upsets you, there are plenty of sites online or by phone that you can make a donation to. There are crowd sourcing platforms. Do some research first, so the organization you are giving to is reputable and actually uses the funds to help the ones in need. It is not uncommon for charitable organizations to pay their CEOs and directors millions now, or use most of your donation to pay the salaries, bonuses and overheads of running the charity, with very little going to the actual cause. Once again, a few clever humans realized that appealing to human emotions can be very profitable for 'the few profiting from the many' system. Instead of hating on these people and wishing them eternal damnation in the fires of hell, see them as naturally flawed humans whose flaws we are collectively correcting now (ACIM).

If your toddler steals another toddler's toy do you wish for them eternal damnation and hellfire, or do you correct them gently, so they can grow into less greedy adults? The global greed that we damn is of our own collective creation. In damning and punishing the greed, we damn well punish ourselves – not an effective way for corrective change to occur if you have spent any time with toddlers or training innocent animals. The easiest, best, and quickest training comes through rewards and not punishment. So there must be a way to reward the least greedy of us in a significant way that encourages a healthy cooperative system to develop here.

You can also sign or create a petition. You can find one that matches your area of concern on the petition websites, but I suspect many of them now are used to gain personal information for financial appeals. And after signing hundreds of them I have seen few good results. You can also call or email the White House or Prime Minister, as well as your state, province, county, city, town, councils and governing representatives. Tell them how you feel about the issue that you would like them to take action on, or how you would have them vote on your behalf. You will probably find they are shocked you bothered to call them. So long as people refuse to participate in their own governing, they will probably be abused by those they give the job to. I wish we were more evolved as a species than this, and there is evidence we are headed this way - into natural collective empathy and altruism. In our lifetime? Maybe.

I know this takes time and we are exceptionally busy by design, because the busier you keep people at trying to make enough money to survive, the less time they have to put into civic action and personal development like continued education, travel, and spiritual studies. People who have time to grow in these ways also tend to oppose social injustices by governments and institutions. Why? Because balance and well-being is the natural state of all things in existence in this universe - including us. Everything naturally seeks balance. Think of water in an ocean or a cup. So, it may not be coincidental that wages never seem to keep up with increases in the cost of living. Imbalance. Some grow richer as a direct result of others growing poorer. Imbalance. But the outcome, though temporarily profitable for a few, is unstable and therefore cannot go on indefinitely. Low wages and high costs of living keep people too tired, fearful and off-balance to even care about anything but their survival. Now look at how many people truly make enough money to relax and stop thinking of survival in your community, your country, the world ... so they can start thinking about art, philosophy, intrinsic humanitarian desires. Not many, again, by design. But taking peaceful action, praying, meditating and shifting to healthier emotions regardless of your paycheck puts you back in the driver's seat of your emotional life - which creates your material life and brings you back into balance. And your peaceful, loving, healthy life contributes to a peaceful, loving, healthy world, which contributes to a peaceful, loving, healthy universe ... and so on through the multidimensional holographic fractal of ALL life, that is God. Your good is my good and our good is God's good.

Cosmic Causes Considered

In researching the Grand Solar Minimum, I discovered very limited information on a proposed "photo belt" of increased energy in the galaxy we may be moving through; which may be causing the Hindu Yugas or ages of enlightenment versus the ages of ignorance or sleeping consciousness. Picture rubber bands of increased energy in and around the galaxy that we periodically move through. Could this expanding consciousness in high energetic points in the galactic lifecycle have something to do with entering the Age of Aquarius now? Could the Mandela Effect be a side effect of expanding consciousness, or is it partly the cause of expanding consciousness?

This led me to information on the Great Year or Platonic Year, which NASA defines as the period of one complete cycle of the equinoxes around the ecliptic every 25,800 years, or one complete cycle of axial precession. In layman's terms it is the apparent path the Sun follows in the sky from a position on Earth, rising in (during Spring Equinox) in each of the zodiac constellations for a period of 2150 years. So it is an optical illusion, because the Sun does not truly rotate around the Earth. Does it really matter which constellation our Sun appears to be rising in on a particular day? If that also correlates with the position of our galaxy in or out of a photon belt, then yes, it can be used as a galactic clock to predict rising and falling human consciousness, and other cyclical events: like corresponding solar cycles, magnetic pole shifts, Schumann Resonance rises, and mini-ice ages. Humanity has been starved of this and other information it needs to evolve en masse. Manipulation requires a certain level of ignorance to be effective. Could simple greed be holding us back from our full potential as a species? In other words, does starving a species of information in order to make more money within that group – delay or halt that species' evolution?

While the Sun rises at Sumer Solstice for approximately 2,150 years in each of the 12 constellations, we are now approaching the end of one cycle in Pisces and beginning a new 2,150 year period in the Age of Aquarius (on the Spring Equinox our Sun rising in the constellation Aquarius). It is interesting to note our birthdays move clockwise through the constellations, called the Zodiac, but move backward or counterclockwise through the constellations of the Ages. The Photon Belt theory reports a band of higher stronger energies running around the galaxy as a band that our solar system must pass through the bottom of it every 13,000 years and through the top of it every 13,000 years of this approximate 26,000 year cycle or progression of the equinoxes; and passing through the higher frequency energy causes a corresponding awakening in consciousness that fits in nicely with the Hindu Yugas of falling and rising human consciousness with four 6,000 year cycles. (31) (32)

Still others attribute increased radiation as coming from the "Galactic Sun" or Galaxy Center instead of a photon belt, which some even speculate may be a black hole, or a white hole or quasar. By the way, it takes the Milky Way 225 to 250 million years to complete one whole rotation – known as the Galactic Year, or Cosmic Year. This is the duration of time required for our Sun to orbit once around the center of the Milky Way Galaxy. This could determine rising and falling consciousness too, depending on what the space around our position in the galaxy holds. I highly recommend you do your own research on all of this through internet search engines that reportedly do not track your searches. (We can encourage and support the growth of goodness here with every choice we make.)

To support this theory, scientists have been reporting increased gamma radiation at ground level on the planet, and report that we have been passing through energetic clouds in the galaxy recently, including a huge helium cloud our entire solar system passed through. (33) Some have given this time of higher frequencies a name. It was called "The Shift" in my memory in the 1970's, but since Dolores Cannon's QHHT practices caught on, it has recently morphed into "The Event". This topic deserves its own section.

On a side note, the whole division of time feels wrong to me with 356 days divided into the Roman Calendar of twelve uneven months of 31, 30, 29 or 28 days each. When I discovered a thirteenth sign in the zodiac based on the thirteenth constellation called Ophiuchus (from sidereal or ancient astrology depicted as a serpent representing wisdom), I realized Roman law, still used today, stripped our culture of a more natural calendar. Could it be possible we naturally have 13 constellations and 13 zodiac signs of which the Sun spends approximately 2000 years in each sign for one Great Year of 26,000 years? More importantly it naturally gives us 13 equal months of 28 days - coinciding perfectly with the cycle of the moon, seasons, the female reproductive cycle, and human pregnancy of ten 28-day-months. Currently they say humans have "a nine month pregnancy" of "40 weeks", but 40 weeks is 9 and a half months. Hmmm …. This is also Hindu time-keeping as there are 13 28-day moon cycles in a year which they revere and celebrate.

Romans not only killed one of the most loving religious leaders in history who was trying to make corrections to the Old Testament (the Hebrew Bible or Tanakh), but they killed the natural flow of time on Earth too, removing the feminine principle along the way. Did you ever think it odd that Rome killed Jesus and then took over the administration of his belief system turning it into the religion Christianity? Did you ever wonder why Jesus, as a Jew, could not convert Judaism to remain Judaism under a loving forgiving God instead? If they had, then perhaps they would have recognized Jesus as their Messiah, with no need to create a new religion, experiencing a more complete religion. Not to mention Ancient Roman Admiralty Law concerning ownership of humans through its citizenSHIP… but that is a whole other topic outside the scope of this book. Enjoy exploring these fascinating rabbit holes, but be warned, once in them it is hard to leave them, and you will probably only find peace outside of them. If you roll in the dirt you will get up feeling dirty.

Correlations with Contact

I wonder how many Mandela Effect affected individuals have experienced some form of contact with non-human intelligence. The Academic Research Foundation with the Dr. Edgar Mitchell Foundation for Research into Extraterrestrial and Extraordinary Experiences (FREE) have published the first in-depth study of contactees worldwide. Unlike other books on the topic, subjects were not hypnotized, but were allowed to share in detail their experiences and feelings during and after contact with non-human intelligence, otherwise known as alien, off-Earth, or extraterrestrial lifeforms. You may share your contact experiences for future books at www.consciousnessandcontact.org. You may recall Edgar Mitchell was the astronaut who returned from the Apollo moon missions a changed man – convinced here was so much more to human consciousness than ever taught. His foundation's amazingly well-researched book *Beyond UFOs: The Science of Consciousness and Contact with Non-Human Intelligence Volume 1* (34) is a must-read for anyone interested in aliens, abduction, contact and UFOs (now called UAPs or Unidentified Ariel Phenomenon by mainstream media, government, and science just for the sake of Reality Doublespeak). Just like Planet X, Planet 10, Planet Nibiru is now officially called "Planet 9", doublespeak from George Orwell's book *1984* is used by authorities intending to confuse. Changing the name of something in this way makes the authorities sound like they are discussing something new and not discussing something they previously, vehemently denied for decades or centuries.

Perhaps surprisingly, experience with otherworld or other-dimensional lifeforms was so positive, that 84% reported they did not want their experience to end; and 70% stated their experience with non-human intelligence changed their lives for the positive, making them more psychic, feeling more at one with all life, and more interested in the spiritual side of consciousness. Most surprisingly, over 50 percent of all contactees worldwide reported contact with non-human intelligence through consciousness only without their physical bodies. It may very well be that in order to experience contact with non-human life - your consciousness must already be expanded beyond third dimensional limits in order to do so. If only five percent reported contact had negatively impacted their lives (including contact with the so-called Greys and Reptilians) – then why would mainstream media put such a negative spin on alien contact stories? Does it serve our human rulers in any way to keep us frightened away from communication with all off-Earth life, so we do not interact with more advanced lifeforms and learn self-empowerment? Many are now seeing the correlations between Quantum Awakening in Consciousness, Contact with non-human intelligence or off-Earth lifeforms, and the Mandela Effect. All three share commonalities, namely expanded consciousness; and I would not be surprised if those who are Mandela Effect affected have experienced more NDEs, OBEs, and contact with extraterrestrials *more* than the general population who are, as yet, not M.E. affected.

Is it coincidental that some of the popular M.E. fearporn associates hadron colliders and quantum computers with opening portals to other dimensions where aliens (now often called demons or fallen angels) can enter? Is this more programming by some humans to keep other humans from developing their own conscious abilities to transcend dimensions and communicate with other intelligent life elsewhere in our universe? Programming aimed at children often warns them away from exploring higher consciousness at all, like the Netflix programs *Stranger Things* and *Black Mirror* to name just two in an ocean of such programming across film, television, books, movies and video games. I doubt it will work, as the younger generations seem increasingly naturally talented and interested in all things magical and mystical. The younger generation also tends to pay no attention to self-proclaimed "authorities" whatsoever – another sign that humanity may soon transcend the oppression of the few over the many.

Nicola Tesla famously reported visiting over twenty dimensions of this reality with his mind alone, as well as reporting contact with aliens whom he credits with giving him most of the great technological ideas he had. He attempted to give free unlimited clean energy to the world, but was famously derailed by organized greed. Human authorities were not yet ready to release their profitable stranglehold on dirty carbon energy. Soon, if human consciousness continues to expand and evolve at only the current rate, they will have no choice in the matter, because fortunately it appears numbers matter and majority rules when it comes to consciousness programming the material world. And the Sleeping Giant (all the 'sleeple' combined) is waking up quickly now to governing corruption, and their ability overcome this by steering matter with purpose through collective thoughts and feelings. Power to the People has a deeper meaning now. It means "the People already have all the power here - whether they realize it or not". Those who program humanity en masse through centralized education and media already know this too. Is it possible that communicating with other more advanced and more evolved lifeforms could threaten the control paradigm here, as individuals grew into their personal power to change their reality matrix - not only for themselves but for all? How do you want your world to be?

Personally, my immediate family has three generations of contact with a particular non-physical group that utilizes Greys to do their physical work here, such as collecting, sampling and returning. The program is voluntary and being conducted for the good of all, but that is another story for another book. Suffice it to say their message has been consistent: learn to practice cooperation that serves all, or be contained here permanently.

The Mandela Effect and End World Scenarios

Of course there are plenty of stories circulating about the human ruling elite creating underground bunkers fully equipped with 30+ years of food, water, artificial light, power, even tennis courts, basketball courts and swimming pools; with an underground network of high speed transportation between underground cities ... presumably, so in the event of a surface catastrophe, the elite and their families have somewhere safe to go. Like most people, I cannot help thinking that it would be such a shame if the only survivors of Earth were always the greediest and least altruistic of our species after each cyclical reset. Unfortunately, we currently reward the greediest individuals on the planet with the most power, and the most powerful people on the planet are the ones with enough money to develop the new technologies openly or secretly. Going along with their success in the greed = material-rewards system we have created here, they are unlikely to suddenly turn their attention and money to benefit the many instead of just themselves. If they have been raised in a society that only rewards selfishness - can you really blame them? We all buy into and pay into that system. We either actively create it, or passively allow it. The system is not just their system - it is your system too which you perpetrate though your participation. Sometimes it seems impossible to leave "the system", but little things help like only using people to check you out instead of the machines on offer, and using cash as much as possible. Buying local as much as possible, supporting family-owned small businesses, choosing free range and organic as much as you can afford .... Supporting people over corporations with your hard-earned cash as much as you possible can in enough. You love-filled prayers, intentions and forgiveness are inestimably valuable too.

So if you are the successful product of a greedy, competitive system that benefits the few, instead of an altruistic, cooperative system that benefits all, and you are not one of the self-serving few - chances are you are not going to be invited underground in order to survive a cyclical cataclysm (if there even is an underground bunker network in reality – who knows anything for sure in a system of governing by stealth). But ask yourself – would you go if you could? I would not. How could going underground possibly help in the event of a global asteroid strike, global flood, a solar CME, an Earth tilt, or Magnetic Pole shift? The actual surface of the Earth is very unstable, so underground is as dangerous, if not more dangerous, than above ground. This is naturally shown in plate tectonics (the large-scale motion of the plates comprising the Earth's surface); with underground flooding, gas deposits, sink holes, volcanoes, and earthquakes.

Coincidentally or not coincidentally, many in the Mandela Effect community have developed The Event theory to encourage and reward those who serve the greater good, and punish the selfish, while imagining catastrophic End Times scenarios like the Apocalypse. Basically, the baddies will be wiped out and be returned to atomic states of early evolutionary matter, while the goodies' souls will move on to higher states of being in a higher dimension of Earth - often called the New Earth or 5D Earth. Some rather optimistically even imagine taking their physical bodies with them. I think these are the ones praying for it to occur daily because they do not understand it involves a kind of death in shrugging off the material body in order to live as a higher-frequency being.

Abrahamic religions support this notion with Heaven and Hell and rapture scenarios. Because evolution is always upward and based on improvements in the whole group, I think that makes it highly unlikely that anyone would survive Earth catastrophes by acting selfishly and going underground based purely on personal wealth accumulated in a broken system of greed = power. Successful mechanical and biological systems always have healthy cooperative parts. Lack of cooperation in mechanical and biological systems is devastating to the whole system much like the human body, a computer, or car. When something goes wrong somewhere - the whole stops operating. Greedy people cannot escape natural law in matter no matter how much money they have. The same could be said of humanity. It is highly unlikely that natural evolution of the species would reward that which goes against healthy systematic cooperation for very long. If any part of a system is sick. then the system itself is sick with limited development, stalled progression, and eventually complete failure. So, followers of The Event theory believe human spirit only survives matter if living in 'service to others', and only ascends to the next level through At-One-Ment - which implies altruistic cooperation. Of course, the Mandela Effect and the human hivemind or state of *oneness* appears to fit in rather nicely with

Biblical At-one-ment, Ascension and Rapture beliefs. Better safe than sorry to guarantee your existence after life on Earth. Act for the good of all whenever possible because natural law has a way of extinguishing that which halts the natural upward evolution of a species. Goodness is good for us after all because it is rewarded by nature and is allowed and encouraged to progress.

Nibiru and Chemtrails aka Stratospheric Aerosol Injection

(perhaps the biggest wake-up call of all)

I was watching a video on Talltanic YouTube channel called "Mind Blowing Discoveries in the Last Year" in 2018, and it quietly confirmed one of the greatest "conspiracy theories" or "probable truths", as I like to call them. About two and a half minutes into the video they casually announce NASA says there is most likely a large previously unknown planet in our solar system way out past Neptune. Considering what else was on the video, that would have been my number one choice for "mind blowing discoveries", and I would have shouted it from the rooftops. This was a good example of "soft disclosure", or quietly slipping it in somewhere not too obvious, so when people ask why they did not tell you this sooner, the authorities can say – we did – here – but nobody noticed. (35)

In the video, they talk about NASA releasing a press release stating the new "ninth planet" (refusing to call it the usual Nibiru, Planet X, or Planet 10), which is ten times the size of Earth on an extremely long elliptical orbit around the Sun, most likely *does* exist. How could I possibly have missed an announcement by NASA that Nibiru most likely exists - something they and mainstream science have denied for decades? I first heard of a suspected Planet 10 or Planet X when I was a child in the 1970's, but it was considered a conspiracy theory. That was in the good ole days when Pluto was still a planet – our ninth planet, and truthers said there was plenty of historical evidence we had another much larger planet way out past Pluto that would come closer to Earth on its orbit around our Sun and interfere with out gravity and magnetic poles. I remember some speculated on whether it was large enough to cause our magnetic poles to shift or completely flip. Until author Zecharia Sitchin popularized the mythical stories of Planet Nibiru from his translations of the ancient Sumerian clay tablets from Babylon, Mesopotamia (modern day Iraq), it was usually called Planet X or Planet 10. When Sitchin's work caught on, many began referring to this possible invisible rogue planet as Nibiru instead. (35) As discussed earlier, although his translations have been largely rejected by scientists and academics who dismiss his work as pseudoscience and pseudohistory, his books remain popular within the ancient astronauts community worldwide. The Sumerian clay tablets postulate repeated fly-bys with Nibiru every few thousand years, but never a collision with Earth.

The Nibiru cataclysm theory, where Nibiru is expected to collide with Earth on its return orbit started becoming popular in the mid-90s. Although these theorists used the same name for the planet on a collision course with Earth, Sitchin reportedly denied any connection between his work and various claims of a coming apocalypse or doomsday event involving Nibiru. Very Confusing I know. Some even tied the approaching Nibiru theory to the end of the Mayan Calendar and some author's subsequent 2012 doomsday predictions fell flat. For decades the existence of Nibiru, Planet 10, Planet X was vehemently denied by the authorities. These theories were all considered fringe, hoax, and pseudo in every way by mainstream media (MSM) and mainstream science – giving rise to the necessity of alternative media and alternative science for inquiring minds.

After watching that Talltanic video, I did a quick internet search and found a NASA press release I think you should read in full, stating that an entirely new extremely large planet (Nibiru to some) *does* likely exist after all:

NASA Jet Propulsion Laboratory,
California Institute of Technology News
October 4th, 2017
The Super-Earth that Came Home for Diner

It might be lingering bashfully on the icy outer edges of our solar system, hiding in the dark, but subtly pulling strings behind the scenes: stretching out the orbits of distant bodies, perhaps even tilting the entire solar system to one side.

If a planet is there, it's extremely distant and will stay that way (with no chance -- in case you're wondering -- of ever colliding with Earth, or bringing "days of darkness"). It is a possible "Planet Nine" -- a world perhaps 10 times the mass of Earth and 20 times farther from the sun than Neptune. The signs so far are indirect, mainly its gravitational footprints, but that adds up to a compelling case, nonetheless.

One of its most dedicated trackers, in fact, says it is now harder to imagine our solar system without a Planet Nine than with one.

"There are now five different lines of observational evidence pointing to the existence of Planet Nine," said Konstantin Batygin, a planetary astrophysicist at Caltech in Pasadena, California, whose team may be closing in. "If you were to remove this explanation and imagine Planet Nine does not exist, then you generate more problems than you solve. All of a sudden, you have five different puzzles, and you must come up with five different theories to explain them."

Batygin and his co-author, Caltech astronomer Mike Brown, described the first three breadcrumbs on Planet Nine's trail in a January 2016 paper, published in the Astronomical Journal. Six known objects in the distant Kuiper Belt, a region of icy bodies stretching from Neptune outward toward interstellar space, all have elliptical orbits pointing in the same direction. That would be unlikely -- and suspicious -- enough. But these orbits also are tilted the same way, about 30 degrees "downward" compared to the pancake-like plane within which the planets orbit the sun.

Breadcrumb number three: Computer simulations of the solar system with Planet Nine included show there should be more objects tilted with respect to the solar plane. In fact, the tilt would be on the order of 90 degrees, as if the plane of the solar system and these objects formed an "X" when viewed edge-on. Sure enough, Brown realized that five such objects already known to astronomers fill the bill.

Two more clues emerged after the original paper. A second article from the team, this time led by Batygin's graduate student, Elizabeth Bailey, showed that Planet Nine could have tilted the planets of our solar system during the last 4.5 billion years. This could explain a longstanding mystery: Why is the plane in which the planets orbit tilted about 6 degrees compared to the sun's equator?

"Over long periods of time, Planet Nine will make the entire solar-system plane precess or wobble, just like a top on a table," Batygin said.

The last telltale sign of Planet Nine's presence involves the solar system's contrarians: objects from the Kuiper Belt that orbit in the opposite direction from everything else in the solar system. Planet Nine's orbital influence would explain why these bodies from the distant Kuiper Belt end up "polluting" the inner Kuiper Belt.

"No other model can explain the weirdness of these high-inclination orbits," Batygin said. "It turns out that Planet Nine provides a natural avenue for their generation. These things have been twisted out of the solar system plane with help from Planet Nine and then scattered inward by Neptune."

The remaining step is to find Planet Nine itself. Batygin and Brown are using the Subaru Telescope at Mauna Kea Observatory in Hawaii to try to do just that. The instrument is the "best tool" for picking out dim, extremely distant objects lost in huge swaths of sky, Batygin said.

But where did Planet Nine come from? Batygin says he spends little time ruminating on its origin -- whether it is a fugitive from our own solar system or, just maybe, a wandering rogue planet captured by the sun's gravity.

"I think Planet Nine's detection will tell us something about its origin," he said.

Other scientists offer a different possible explanation for the Planet Nine evidence cited by Batygin. A recent analysis based on a sky mapping project called the Outer Solar System Origins Survey, which discovered more than 800 new "trans-Neptunian objects," suggests that the evidence also could be consistent with a random distribution of such objects. Still, the analysis, from a team led by Cory Shankman of the University of Victoria, could not rule out Planet Nine.

If Planet Nine is found, it will be a homecoming of sorts, or at least a family reunion. Over the past 20 years, surveys of planets around other stars in our galaxy have found the most common types to be "super Earths" and their somewhat larger cousins -- bigger than Earth but smaller than Neptune.

Yet these common, garden-variety planets are conspicuously absent from our solar system. Weighing in at roughly 10 times Earth's mass, the proposed Planet Nine would make a good fit. (36)

The confusion over NASA calling this new planet "Planet 9" stems from the fact that our original 9th Planet, Pluto, was downgraded to a "dwarf planet" in 2006, making room for the 10th Planet (Planet X or Nibiru) to be categorized as our 9th Planet – again. This masks the fact that so-called conspiracy theorists have been writing about this planet for decades quoting ancient texts. I think it is important for you to research the mystical significance of the number 9, the mathematic anomalies of the number 9, *Dante's 9 Spheres*, et cetera, which may go a long way in explaining why the astrophysical authorities down-graded Pluto, refusing to allow this new planet to be called the 10th Planet (Planet X, or Planet Nibiru). Is it because they so vehemently denied it existed for so long? Or is it for numerological and mystical reasons of the ruling elite? Perhaps some will think this new planet has always been our ninth planet and forget that Pluto ever held that lofty title for so long. The fact mainstream science tells you now that what they once classified as a planet is no longer a planet – illustrates how fickle, imprecise, and incorrect mainstream science really is; leaving ample room for us to reconsider everything they have ever taught us about the nature of our world and our universe. In my experience, all scientific facts are eventually replaced with new ones, therefore *all* scientific facts are only scientific theories.

If you watch alternative scientific views, you will find many skeptics no longer believe the official narrative about space now. I personally do not believe in a flat Earth, but I do not criticize those who do, because the official scientific narrative is always questionable and always changing. Mainstream science is protectionist in refusing to explore new theories that could replace the old ones they themselves discovered or support. (Kind of like established political parties. No one willingly gives up their power or their "facts" easily.) Who really knows the true shape of Earth, except for those who have gone up far enough to view Earth from a distance in space with their own eyes? In a holographic multidimensional universe everything could be any shape depending on the position of the observer. So, my round Earth could be someone else's flat Earth, and both could be true, if we do in fact have individual realities based on individual beliefs; as Cynthia Sue Larson YouTube channel reported is now being studied as a possibility in Edinburgh. (37)

It is interesting that this new previously denied planet was announced somewhat quietly and most people missed it. When I first started researching the Mandela Effect, I bumped into a University of Wisconsin study indicating all the planets are getting hotter and more luminous now – another fact most people do not know because it would blow the narrative of global warming due to human activity, which would in turn hurt their carbon fuel taxation, even though cleaner energy is not made available ... nonsensical politics for corporate financial gain. They only offer us dirty carbon fuel and then penalize us for using it. But that study now is very hard to locate, so I have to attribute it to my memory of having read a report on the study findings in 2016.

Then you have got numerous reports online discussing our increasingly scattered magnetic shield called the magnetosphere, which for decades has been getting increasingly scattered and broken up. What kind of gravitational pull or plasma interference could be heating and lighting up the planets, tugging at our magnetosphere, and slowly moving magnetic North to somewhere over Siberia, with some predictions of it continuing south at 60 kilometers per year, until it reaches the equator causing a magnetic pole reversal? I often hear and read that gravity is a weak force on Earth and a poor concept off of Earth that requires particle scientists (following the Standard Model of the universe) to invent dark matter to counteract measurable matter with enough gravity to keep everything in the universe from collapsing. The only problem is they cannot even detect dark matter or measure it because it very likely does not exist. To understand why follow plasma science on the YouTube channel ThunderboltsProject. (38) And David LaPoint's Primer Field videos which show how electro-magnetism provides all the energy this universe needs to coalesce, without the need of gravity, black holes or invisible nonexistent dark matter. (39)

Is this new unseen super-earth really pulling on our solar system so hard it could cause all of these disturbances? Maybe. If so, then why couldn't it also be tugging and pulling on brain waves, causing the Mandela Effect? Could the increasingly scattered and thinned magnetosphere be the reason reported chemtrailing, (officially called Stratospheric Aerosol Injection or Solar Management), reportedly uses highly reflective nanoparticles to reflect and deflect increasing cosmic and solar radiation? All of this is reported, but not proven in alternative media; but If this is true and they ward off extinction-level radiation - then chemtrails would in fact be good for us and all life on the planet. However, if they are being employed only to protect our aging electrical grid for security purposes, the detriments to cellular biology may not be worth it.

I am uncertain if chemtrailing is used or proposed to be used to prevent mass electrical grid failure due to increased magnetic storms caused by the Grand Solar Minimum, or to save lives due to increased radiation ... why not both? But I believe it is not for the stated reasons of staving off human-caused global warming (remember all planets are heating up) because it would likely increase the temperatures on Earth and acidify the oceans killing off life. (40) The chemicals used in Solar Radiation Management programs could be responsible for the Mandela Effect, if they are already being used and not merely proposed. Aerosol nanoparticles could interact with the human brain in unknown ways to affect changes in consciousness. This would also indicate matter has always responded to consciousness, but the human mind could not see matter changing until somehow enhanced to do so with the chemicals in chemtrails.

I hope you realize by now I am not supporting any one of these theories as any one, or any combination of them could be responsible for the Mandela Effect. Until more is known about the phenomenon, I think we should leave all theories on the table until we can discount them one at a time. The increase of energy, or change in energy implied in all of these theories could easily account for changes in consciousness. Especially since according to the quantum world everything is a wave and waves are easily interfered with. So if we are truly entering the Age of Aquarius where we will remain for the next two thousand years – why wouldn't that include a new age of consciousness too, where we could actually see the energy waves of matter shift and change and flip and flop as they respond to the waves of collective consciousness?

This would explain the use of predictive programming and fearporn used to control the masses. The collective consciousness of the masses determine the material matrix, (if the holographic universe is flexible, responsive, alive, constantly responding to our thoughts, feelings, actions), but only the ruling elite humans know this because it is the knowledge of the ancient wisdoms schools and must be sought and not taught. You either look into these concepts to understand your reality, or you do not. You lead or are led. Hermetic Laws and quantum science studies are published everywhere for everyone to access, but most do not. At least not until something like the Mandela Effect rises up to slap them in the face with a giant, "Are you awake yet?". Think of the movie *Monsters Inc.,* which shows children how emotional energy can be harnessed and used for bad or for good.

The smartest thing we can do is question everything, research everything, develop our own gnosis or internal truth detector, and keep an open mind that all things are possible until proven otherwise ... but leave the fear out of it. There is no more reason to expect Anunnaki to come marching off Nibiru to steal our gold and enslave us - any more than we are already enslaved by the few humans who control global markets, finance and governments. I believe physically seeing Anunnaki is as good as your past observations (with your own physical eyes) of seeing demons and the devil up close and personal. Do I believe in off-world life and visitors to our world? Of course, but to observe us and possibly to keep us contained here until we can safely leave our Earth – meaning safe for all life *out there* due to the erratic, unpredictable, and often aggressive human behavior towards anything different or "other" down here. Not a prison planet, but to keep us safely contained here on Earth until we can play nicely with others out there. Consider it a preschool of sorts.

On a positive note, in doing this, selfish power-hungry humans give us something to push against, helping us to establish and demonstrate our own personal levels of greed-to-altruism, with most of us falling somewhere in the middle. They are very much what psychoanalyst Karl Jung called archetypes, and so are we. For how could we embark on the 'hero's journey' if there were no villains or non-heroes for us to overcome? No obstacles to conquer? That does not excuse their actions, but more on this philosophical examination of human behavior later – back to perceived outer space and the Mandela Effect.

The Cannibalistic Galaxy

An even bigger surprise came from watching, "These Sumerian Clay Tablets Reveal the BIGGEST Secrets of the Solar System" video on ZEG TV HIDDEN FROM THE PUBLIC YouTube channel, featuring author and speaker Billy Carson. This showed me how our Solar System was not "born into the familiar arms of the Milky Way Galaxy" as we all thought, but actually belonged to a much smaller galaxy called the Sagittarius Dwarf Galaxy. The infrared Two-Micron All Star Survey led by the astronomers at the University of Massachusetts reportedly showed the Milky Way is actually consuming a neighboring galaxy in a "dramatic display of on-going galactic cannibalism", according to Carson. The study published in the Astrophysical Journal showed how the Sagittarius Dwarf Galaxy, containing our Solar System, is ten thousand times smaller than the Milky Way, and as such, is being stretched and pulled as it passes through it. This is not as surprising as it sounds. According to Carson this thing happens all the time - galaxies collide forming bigger and bigger galaxies. In 2003, the University of Virginia modeled our Sagittarius Dwarf Galaxy to show how it fits into the much larger Milky Way Galaxy at a slightly different plane of inclination in what is considered public peer reviewed scientific data. (40)

Sound familiar? The NASA press release about a super-Earth pulling and tugging on our Solar System, is also credited with tilting our Solar System off the plane of the Milky Way galaxy. Either, neither, or both of these could be the cause of our solar system's unusual inclination. That is how much confidence the "official" take on anything inspires in people willing to do their own research. When conducting your own research, you are often left with more questions than you started out with. But eventually, facts from all over start to coalesce in your mind – making likely bridges to truth. So, we will just have to wait and see how this all plays out to know for sure. Or wait for some renegade scientists to spill the beans on solar system climate change, solar changes, magnetosphere changes, and solar radiation management programs. At least we know what to look out for.

Carson explains, "Just like atoms are mostly empty space, believe it or not, galaxies are mostly empty space. The distances are so vast they can coalesce together with very few collisions, but collisions do happen. A lot of the orbits [of nearby planets] will be switched around due to gravitational pull, and so forth. But this happens all the time - it is nothing to be shocked about. The fact that the Milky Way has always been seen at a slightly different angle from Earth has always puzzled us. If we originated within the Milky Way, our Solar System should be at the same angle to the Milky Way's ecliptic." Carson says this research also leads us into the theory that our Sun is part of a Binary System, or twin sun system. (41) … but that is a whole other topic of research showing another possible cause of the tilt of our Solar System away from the Milky Way's ecliptic plane; and another possible stand-alone or combined cause of the Mandela Effect.

Nemesis or Our Binary (Twin) Sun

Yes, I am afraid you are in store for more stretching, pulling and tugging on our solar system (and brain waves) here. The best video I have found so far on the topic of our possible binary twin sun, or Nemesis is *The Great Year*, on the BinaryResearchInst YouTube channel. (42) It is by far the most logical explanation, in my opinion, for the rash of geophysical anomalies we are experiencing like the magnetic pole drift, scattered magnetic shield, rising Schumann Resonance amplitude … the heating up and increased luminosity of all planets, time speeding up, and yes, even the Mandela Effect or *expanded human consciousness*. It explains how almost all stars have a binary twin, if not triplet, orbiting each other in elongated orbits over long periods of time from a human perspective. They illustrate how a binary twin to our Sun (often called Nemesis, or the Blue Kachina Red Kachina Nibiru/Nemesis combination), is on a twenty-six thousand year cycle that could cause all of these anomalies and more, like increased volcanic eruptions and earthquakes, as it tugs at the Earth's surface as it comes nearer.

Recognize that number? It is the same as the Precession of the Equinoxes. They even postulate a speeding up of time that would shrink our twin sun's orbit from 26,000 to 24,000 years, as it increases in velocity when it nears our Sun. Is Earth on a cyclical 24,000-year binary twin star cycle that fits in nicely with the Precession of the Equinoxes and the Hindu Kali Yugas? I think the free documentary on YouTube *The Great Year* in which many scientists participated, is very important to our understanding of likely natural galactic causes of the Mandela Effect, and other anomalies. Too many things are changing on our planet, in our solar system, and in our consciousness for them to be completely unrelated.

I found other interesting articles predicting a future space anomaly, saying something big will be lighting our night sky by 2022. Scientists attribute it to two stars colliding two thousand years ago, with the light from that collision just starting to reach our eyes in 2020, increasing for two years, and then decreasing as the light just fades away. (43) Is this just an official cover story for Nibiru or Nemesis approaching?

Every one of these theories by themselves could explain a pull and tug on our home planet strong enough to cause a stretching or expanding of the waves of human consciousness. Do you see now why I doubt atom smashers, quantum computers, or time travelers are causing the Mandela Effect? Dramatic and compelling geological and astrophysical changes are occurring at the same time. Of course, we are not taught about these things maybe because our human governors fear chaos could ensue. Would you rather believe that quantum computing is opening portals responsible for the M.E. that will allow demons into our dimension? Or that Satan is changing the Bible? Or that a time-traveler is responsible for changing matter? None of these are as spectacular as the possibilities of an approaching binary twin sun, an approaching super-Earth, or our little galaxy being gobbled up by a bigger one ... science is far more interesting! So why wont the authorities share this and so much more with the masses, the Sleeping Giant, the collective sleeple? It seems obvious they fear we would panic, stop working, stop paying our loans, our credit cards, and our mortgages ... everything that maintains their status. I believe we are up to these challenges and more now, and deserve to get our physical and spiritual houses in order. Life on Earth has survived cyclical challenges many times before, as evidenced by the fossil record, but societal systems do not. So these cyclical cataclysms are more of a social order reset than extinction level event. Many of us sense that what has worked beautifully for our human rulers the past five millennia is coming to a close now, as all great civilizations that have self-imploded under the weight of their own greed have done before theirs. Think ancient Mesopotamia, Egypt, Greece and Rome. Where are the Phoenicians, Byzantines and the Khans today? Hermetic Law on cycles seems to apply to human social structures too, and probably for a good reason.

Magnetic Pole Drift and Flip (or Rotation)

We have all heard of the Magnetic Pole Flip, Shift, or Drift. It appears to be completely natural and tied to the interior workings of the Earth in conjunction with its rotation and related to the magnetic field and Schumann Resonance. The Magnetic North Pole naturally drifts a little north and south every year, but its drift is becoming faster and more erratic over recent decades, as is the scattering and breaking up of the Earth's magnetic field and the Schumann Resonance spikes. Do you really think it is entirely coincidental that The Mandela Effect is being seen by more people as these three geological anomalies increase? The best source I could find on the magnetic pole shift was in the Freedom of Information Act released book, *The Adam and Eve Story,* by Chan Thomas. (44)

This is a wonderful mystery for me personally, because I found a highly sanitized FOIA released document on CIA.gov with only 56 pages of the original 232 page-book released by the United States government, however I bought said book on eBay for just $150, although the only other copy for sale on the internet was asking over $1000 for it. So if the information in this book is so top-secret that it had to be redacted down to 56 pages before being released to the public nearly fifty years after its publication – how and why are copies of the full version available for purchase online? Not a very well-kept secret. Just another glitch in the manufactured societal reality matrix? It does not make the FOIA released documents seem very important … or is that part of the controlled opposition (conop) to release a lot of filler along with important information and see what people make of it? On January 17, 2017 thirteen million pages (called a document dump) of previously restricted documents were released through the Freedom of Information Act. Try sifting through that in your spare time.

The recent spread of censorship under the banner of banning 'fake news' saw many alternative news YouTube channels and videos being removed. Then the truther community responded by indicating the information being pulled must have been true, or they would not have pulled it. So censers began pulling their own manufactured-truther or conop (controlled opposition) channels too, just to make them look more legitimate. The only difference being their conop channels were soon restored, saying poor me, while the genuine truther channels were not. Eventually anyone can figure out true truthers from the conop or pretend truthers. To better disguise their purpose, they mix in a lot of true information with the false narratives, but eventually the false narratives hit your internal gnosis hard, allowing you to *feel* the genuineness in all presentations of information. I call this your Internal BS Detector and Internal Truth Detector. We are all naturally born with one which appears to be dumbed down with mind-numbing media, subliminal messaging, and toxic chemicals. The ancients called it your Gnosis. You just need to exercise it to strengthen it, and use it daily to keep it operating at peak performance levels. I believe strongly that this innate skill becoming impervious to outside control mechanisms is part of the New Human we are becoming, and in the future, it will be categorized as part of our natural sixth sense – the sense of knowing.

Back to the magnetic pole flip theory. In *The Adam and Eve Story*, Chan Thomas proposes a cyclical magnetic pole shift cataclysm evidenced in the geological record every six to eleven thousand years, and he is not alone in this. He credits this theory to highly regarded scientists (geologists, paleontologists, anatomists, biologists) J. Andre DeLuc in 1779 and Georges Cuvier in 1812, as well as M. C. Escher, Auguste Forel, Christian Leopold von Buch, Frank C. Hibben, and J. Andre DeLuc Junior. (45) They all lend scientific credence to mythological legends of old including legendary advanced civilizations that were destroyed in cyclical cataclysms caused by a rotating Earth crust magnetically tugged and pulled into completely new positions throughout eons of time. The most recent episode involves the Biblical Noah's Flood taken directly from the Babylonian Epic of Gilgamesh, whereby Noah was actually a Sumerian named Unapishtim who built an ark to survive our last cyclical cataclysm Diluvian theorists claimed to be about 6000 years ago.

Why is this believable? Not only because so many scientists have found evidence in our geological record to support it through the centuries worldwide, but human written history only goes back to the Sumerian cuneiform clay tablets originally considered to be up to 6,000 years old. Coincidence? If a great natural cataclysm did not wipe out human civilizations at that point in time, then some human writing should be evident worldwide pre-dating cuneiform -in between cuneiform and ancient cave paintings and petroglyphs.

Why keep this information from the public? That is fairly obvious. Their theory is that geological evidence shows that every six to eleven thousand years the electro-magnetic orderliness inside the Earth is disrupted, which allows the molten layer to act like free liquid pulling the shell or crust of the Earth around like a spinning top. Interestingly, *The Adam & Eve Story* also describes the popular new 'rabbit hole' mud floods, in addition to rising and falling continents and global sporadic flooding, as part of this process.

I noticed a few 666 synchronicities in researching this book. For instance, carbon 12, the most common element in the human body and on Earth, is made up of six neutrons, six electrons, and six protons - giving credence to those who say 'the beast' with the mark 666 is the human, who is clearly capable of so much good and so much evil – with most of us falling somewhere in between. Concerning the possibility of the next cyclical pole shift, the magnetic north pole (somewhere over Siberia at the time of this writing) is currently moving about 60 kilometers southeast per year, and is only six thousand kilometers from the equator which, according to Chan Thomas's book, will force a magnetic pole shift as it draws nearer to the equator. According to Thomas and the earlier scientists mentioned in his book, the shell or crust of the Earth is only about 60 miles thick and rotates periodically in a normal cyclical way. Information seen clearly in the geological record, but kept secret by ruling humans who not only do not teach humanity about it, but found it necessary to remove this book from public view until recently, but still only released a highly sanitized version. Why? Do ruling humans keep such big secrets? According to related secret history – they do.

Robert Sepehr's book, *1666 Redemption Through Sin,* explains a human orchestrated debasement of humanity for profit by the ruling and banking elite going back to 1666 for easier control of large populations. But they could only survive by orchestrating their societal control mechanisms in secret. For every time they were exposed they were brought down fast and hard by the non-ruling population. (46) Mark Booth's book, *The Secret History of the World,* demonstrates how human secret societies have been organized to keep human history and human potential secretly well-guarded to serve an elite class through the manipulation of information for millennia. (47) This means everything we are taught may or may not be true, and the information that wields the greatest power here is utilized in secret by the few who control the many – as a matter of principle.

The Adam and Eve Story postulates rather well that there have not been many advancing and retreating ice ages, rather that different areas of the Earth have been in polar regions at different times following shifts of the crust. We could consider this a cyclical reset of life on Earth where corrections to unsustainable, Earth-damaging systems occur. Negative or harmful life systems, like the one we have now, can be erased by the greatest force on Earth – nature; so that one lifeform or another never has enough time to completely destabilize or destroy the Earth. Kind of like an Earth failsafe mechanism

I believe we were supposed to have figured this out by now, before the end of yet another great civilization, and created a successful self-sustaining cooperative system of humanity on Earth. According to many religious beliefs, such at-one-ment of such cooperation would lead to ascension during rapture (cyclical cataclysm), with the Harvest of those souls who can live cooperatively moving on into higher frequency planets or dimensions. What happens to uncooperative human souls who cannot move on into cooperative non-duality dimensions? Some say they are cyclically reabsorbed into the beginning of conscious matter in 3-D. Others say, going against evolution, they are obliterated and absorbed into non-conscious fractals of the multiverse. And of course you know many here now say they go to Hell forever.

I sense there is still time to get it right, but I also feel we are getting closer to a reset now. That may be the greatest gift of the Mandela Effect - an awakening tool that matter, reality, and the matrix is not what they told us it was; matter is changeable, and we are all much more powerful players here than we ever imagined.

I recently discovered David LaPoint YouTube channel's six-year-old "Primer Fields" videos demonstrating how all matter, from an atom to a galaxy, creates its own electro-magnetic toroidal field of clean infinite energy in, through and around itself. Toroidal fields are everywhere, including in and around human beings, planets and galaxies. He demonstrates in these amazing videos how they create their own attraction and repulsion, completely doing away with the need of gravity, black holes, white holes, and dark matter to explain the attraction, repulsion, expulsion and expansion of all matter in our known universe. Rather mysteriously, he never posted parts four and five to this video series, and went quiet until recently. After seven years of silence, he recently posted a video asking people to download information from his website on what could turn out to be free clean energy. (48)

Videos by ThunderboltsProject on YouTube showcase a group of modern scientists brave enough to explore the electro-magnetic nature of our universe (they call the "electric universe"), with consistently compelling evidence. Their videos offer an alternative view of a universe alive with electrical currents and magnetism that can hold itself together without dark matter, black holes, gravity or other purely theoretical and mathematical theories that live purely in mathematical equations. Plasma Science, often called Tesla Science, holds that light contains information and all is light in different states: densities, forces, stages. Plasma fills all space, and is itself renewable - providing unlimited clean energy if harnessed the way Tesla repeatedly tried to demonstrate to money-men already invested in Edison's inferior electrical projects. Over one hundred years ago Tesla lit up light bulbs without wires, but for financial reasons the ruling humans at the time decided to wire the world for electricity. Now, a century later, we are moving into the unwired electrical world of Nikola Tesla, and we have yet to harness Earth energy the way Tesla imagined we could.

Time Travel

I initially looked into time travelling humans messing with historical events as a possible cause of the Mandela Effect, but as soon as you see all of the residue left over here of how things used to be, you have to discount time travel as the cause. This is because of logic that if a time traveler went back and altered something, by the time you got to the present there would be no evidence, or residue left behind of the way it *used* to be – because the time traveler changed it in your past. If it never *was* that way, you cannot have evidence of how it *never was*. Residue disproves time travel as a cause of the Mandela Effect.

Particle Colliders, Quantum Computing, Artificial Intelligence, Toxins, and Simulation Theory

Sprinkled throughout this book are so many reasons the Mandela Effect phenomenon is beyond anything humans can make with their hands. It is instant and miraculous change that only a portion of humanity can see. That portion is growing exponentially daily. No doubt, soon, the whole species will be born seeing it as a natural process of consciousness in matter. And then, no matter what they tell you in religious texts written by ruling humans, or in mainstream media programmed by ruling humans: 1. No one will doubt matter responds to consciousness, and 2. No one will doubt that we *naturally* possess the ability to change matter as a God-given right individually and collectively with our thoughts, feelings and actions.

Particle science and the Standard Model are almost dead in the water of plasma science now, though mainstream science still clings to it with their multibillion-dollar colliders. Science always clings desperately to its own past findings at the expense of anything new that would replace it. They worked so hard to determine those "facts" and "scientific truths" - why should they let anything, like conflicting observations of reality, discount them? Once again, the problem is in the process and not only in the people following the process, who have been honored with finance, awards and prestige to support and build upon the status quo. How can anything be more indoctrinating than throwing degrees, awards, money and status at people who do not challenge accepted theories? This is why we are scientifically stalled. We have to let go of clinging to the old in order to advance into the new.

Alternative science claims they invented gravity, a known weak force on Earth, to explain the mechanics of what holds the universe in place. But to generate enough gravity off of Earth with such great sizes and amounts of space, they had to invent vast amounts of dark matter as an opposing force to counteract and suspend the visible matter we can see. The only problem is they cannot see it and cannot measure it because it likely does not exist, and all future science to date has been based upon it. The same is true of theoretical black holes. They often invent things to solve mathematical equations that cannot be solved without theoretical inventions. Gravity, dark matter and black holes are no longer necessary when you explore Tesla's amazing plasma science and the electromagnetic universe, as many leading-edge, but unrecognized scientists are now doing. The forward-thinking YouTube channel ThunderboltsProject with Wal Thornhill demonstrates clearly how theoretical black holes are actually plasmoids. (49)

To better understand the famous double-slit experiment that light and matter can have characteristics of both waves and particles (first discovered by Thomas Young in 1801 and later attributed to atoms, molecules and electrons in 1927 by Davisson and Germer), watch Veritasium channel's video, *Is This What Quantum Mechanics Looks Like,* on YouTube to see how a solid particle could go through one slit, while the waves its movement creates goes through both slits, or even all slits with pilot waves and walker waves. Now the object does not need to be a particle and a wave at the same time in superposition – it can be a particle going through one slit that makes waves go through multiple slits at the same time, while remaining separate and unique from the waves its motion through a plasma-filled space creates. (50) This demonstrates a simple misunderstanding of what the waves represented. This calls into question such things as superposition and the Copenhagen Interpretation that everything that can be known about a particle can be observed in its wave function. Again – particle science making things up to fit pre-existing theoretical narratives. We have moved so far beyond these particle constraints it is time mainstream science caught up with lay science, and left their particles behind to study what makes particles possible - consciousness, plasma, information in light, and the electromagnetic constructs of our physical reality in a multidimensional holographic field.

I have read numerous articles and watched numerous videos on quantum computers and still do not understand how the physical mechanics of a machine created by humans can cross the natural boundaries between dimensions that make them only accessible through consciousness, so I will leave that to you to explore further on your own. But I will say that quantum computing is still theoretical at the moment, like their theoretical non-existent black holes and dark matter. Fearporn indicates hadron colliders and quantum computers are opening portals to other dimensions where demons aka aliens may enter into our dimension to ... do what exactly? Eat us, torture us, kill us, make fun of us ... they always leave that part to your own fertile imagination. If you wish to believe that, then you clearly should not be reading this book, because frankly, if demons existed and aliens wished to do these things to us – they would have done so by now. Or there would at least be some actual evidence of it. So far, I have only witnessed humans hurting other humans. Humans controlling other humans. Humans acting stupidly in their greed and lust for power. No Satan, no demons, and aliens only watching with occasional and increasing interaction to bring about full disclosure that yes – we are not alone in our universe. If we learn how to play nicely here first, then maybe we will be allowed off Earth to join our galactic brethren. The need of a Space Force is dubious at best.

Artificial Intelligence (A.I.): what is there to say about it? It is here already, and it is online. It is operating in our phones, computers and TVs. Will it be the end of us like the brilliant Sophia Stewart wrote in her previously uncredited Terminator/Matrix epics? Probably not – I hope not, at least not the end of our souls. Is there anything humans can build with their hands in matter that can supersede the creation of God, Source Energy, All that Is, Was, and Ever Shall Be? Didn't think so.

Perhaps we should consider toxins injected into air, water, food and the human body as possibly interfering with the mechanism that prevented us from seeing consciousness change and edit matter. Since everything is waveform, then some psychological mechanism may exist to hold reality steady in the mind only; making everything that changes appear to be considered constant, old, original and historic. Something may now be interfering with that mechanism in some, but not all of us, and the mechanism's failure is growing and spreading with more seeing the Mandela Effect every day worldwide. This is a species-wide change. I have considered Simulation Theory, but I have nothing to add to it except to say: if life is a simulation it need not be programmed by a technology, or another person outside of yourself. There is no reason why God, Source, or our own higher selves could not simulate realities for our lower selves to experience in a three-dimensional material matrix. Simulation does not require computer and information technologies.

Mandela Effect Timelines and Alternate Earths

If the Mandela Effect is an awakening tool to higher conscious – then awakening to what? Here is where it gets really interesting. Some believe we literally changed Earth timelines from a more positive one on the Sagittarius Arm of the Milky Way Galaxy, which Carl Sagan (51) and Neil De Grasse Tyson (52) verified in the past. More recently, science has placed our solar system on the Orion Spur of the Milky Way Galaxy - which has suddenly changed to the "Orion Arm" everywhere online at the time of this writing.

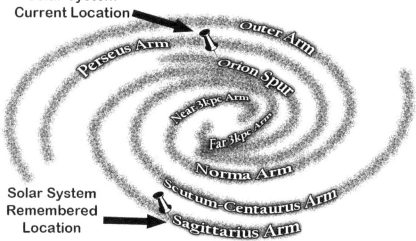

Many speaking their opinions in YouTube videos say they think we shifted en masse to the new position, and consider the earlier location a more positive version of Earth. I disagree. I think it *appeared* to be more positive because those who recently awakened could not see what was really percolating behind the scenes of human societal systems. Now that they have woken up to the reality hidden behind perceived or staged reality, they often say take me back to my "old Earth" where the only real difference was that they were ignorant of hidden machinations, so it *seemed* safer and *felt* more positive, but in reality was not. In fact, because you cannot solve a problem until you identify there is a problem to solve, this may be considered a more positive version of Earth because the problems are becoming exposed so we can collectively see them in order to fix them. Even if that feels more uncomfortable than blissful ignorance, which would you choose? A false reality where no progress may be made because the problems are so well hidden? Or, a true reality where the problems are exposed so progress may be made in the fixing of them? The false reality feels comfortable. The true reality feels uncomfortable. Do you now see that the sense of discomfort spurs the action necessary to fix the causes of discomfort - in order to achieve balance and feel comfortable again? Therefore, your discomfort with the status quo is a good thing for the evolution of the whole.

This brings us into a related concept to the Mandela Effect: shifting into 5 D Earth, New Earth, and/or Fourth Density. How? Via a Shift, or via The Event. Dolores Cannon offers many books on hypnotic regression subjects recalling from their subconscious minds, or one superconscious mind, that the Earth is splitting into two versions of itself: one in the current 3D version of negative, greedy human governance that harms other humans, animals and the planet for limited self-satisfaction; and the other in 5D where all life lives compassionately and cooperatively without harm to any for the benefit of all. Those in service to self who willingly perpetuate the harm here will be left in 3D until its final (or cyclical) destruction, while those living harmlessly in service to others will go to the peaceful cooperative version of Earth in 5D. Sounds similar to the Biblical Apocalypse, Rapture, and Ascension to Heaven or Hell. Unfortunately, whether true or not, this scenario gives a satisfactory ending or punishment for the baddies if the goodies do nothing to improve human living systems on Earth. This always presents a dilemma of living in duality. Should we sit back and love and forgive our way into 5D Earth, Fourth Density, New Earth, or Heaven? Or should we act to peacefully to improve the human social systems here in order to bring 5D, Fourth Density, New Earth, or Heaven here now for everyone? Understanding cyclical resets also gives the ruling elite more than enough reason to gorge themselves on greed as long as possible.

The *Ra Law of One* series of books describes the Dolores Cannon 5D Earth as Fourth Density with the people in service to self staying in third density (our current 3D), while the people in service to others ascend to Fourth Density Earth (Dolores Cannon's 5d Earth) during a cyclical cataclysm. (53) This is New Earth and Heaven by a different name. David Wilcock ascension theories are in line with the *Law of One*. He even spent time helping them develop their living compound. Although he said this would likely happen in 2012, along with the end of the Mayan Calendar; he is now attributing the cyclical cataclysm to an extreme solar flare or flash (CME) as an extinction level event to separate the spiritual wheat from the spiritual chaff – before 2025. After attending one of his extremely interesting and well-presented Ascension Portal seminars, the main problem I have with this theory, based on *The Law of One* books, is that that you only have to be 51 percent good to ascend. Personally, I would not consider it Heaven or New Earth if my fellow souls were 49 percent selfish, greedy and abusive to others. Perhaps I hold my idea of New Earth to a higher standard. I would feel more satisfied if it were called Middle Earth - a step in the right direction but far from the ideal of the New Earth as presented by Dolores Cannon.

Modern QHHT (Quantum Hypnosis Healing Technique) practitioners are schooled in the Dolores Cannon regression techniques, where she often referred to a gradual shift in human consciousness ushering in a New Earth in 5D. (54) Many of her QHHT practitioners since her death in 2014 have changed that gradual shift into an immediate occurrence called The Event. The Event ascension theory usually holds all humans will be swept away in a rainbow cloud that will instantly create a peaceful, cooperative, 5D Earth for the goodies, and leave the baddies here on the 3D Earth of duality living in the conflict, struggle and negativity of their own creation. Sounds fair, and sounds like new names for Heaven and Hell, with Hell being 3D Earth and Heaven being 5D Earth. I do believe they skip 4D considering it the dimension of time here.

Some believe you make a personal choice of which one to go to, with some lightworkers choosing to stay here to continue helping humanity ascend. Others believe the choice is made for you based on your thoughts, feelings and actions. Some believe all of humanity ascends to a higher frequency of living, while others believe it is a reward for the few. Some hold they will be saved body and soul, and brought into spaceships and healing domes until a suitable higher frequency Earth is created after an extinction event or Apocalypse destroys 3D Earth, while others believe the ascension process discards the physical body and moves the righteous into light bodies that can live on a higher frequency Earth immediately without alien help or intervention. The most interesting consideration to me is that most humans are programmed to believe in some form of cataclysm resulting in reward or punishment of their actions here.

I will not go into any discussion of the Secret Space Alliance and the White Hats some believe are currently fighting for control of Earth, who will ultimately succeed with promises of mass arrests of politicians and an economic reset - year after year after year … because there is simply no evidence for it. The conop psyop of "Q" working with or without the help of President Donald Trump have been aligned with space invaders who will save us from abusive human rulers, so we need do nothing ourselves to fix or correct any problems here. Sounds suspiciously like the promotion of a savior in order to keep the masses compliantly waiting for someone to save them. This kind of waiting compliance with abuse of power serves the abusers more than the abused. Some blame all greed here on Reptilians instead of greedy humans. Any problems here were created by humanity, are being perpetuated by humanity, and fall to humanity for solutions. I personally believe we are being observed by other lifeforms, but they are not going to swoop in to enslave us or save us, or they would have done so by now. Common sense dictates there is no evidence of aliens or demons coming to destroy us or save us, so there is no reason to believe those saying the Mandela Effect is a sign of hadron colliders and quantum computing allowing aliens access to do so now. The connection between this belief and the Mandela Effect is nonsensical.

Some believe the Mandela Effect is showing parallel worlds theory in operation, where humans physically jump on and off different versions of Earth or different Earth timelines every time there is even a minor Mandela Effect change. This seems to be the most popular non-ascension theory presented in YouTube videos on the subject, but it would take a tremendous amount of energy to move humanity en masse into a new dimension every time a Mandela Effect change was noted daily in something as minor as the spelling of a product. Unless each of us jumps timelines or dimensions, moment by moment, as a process of spirit life within physical matter. This possibility is being explored by mainstream science now, particularly at the moment of death. (55)

The one thing they all have in common is the punishment of the negative humans who perpetrated harm to other people, animals or the planet; and the rewards of a beautiful, peaceful, compassionate Earth for positive humans who were good, kind, compassionate, cooperative and loving. No matter what you personally believe, the actual shift, ascension, or soul evolution may be a completely individual, personal and internal experience, rather than an external event shared by all. It is also possible, no matter how much you would like it *not* to be true, that as one humanity - none go until we all go. Just more food for thought giving you more power in creating the world you want to live in, which benefits you, your family, your community, and all. The timelines, dimensions, parallel worlds and alternate Earths may be an internal process of consciousness, rather a physical occurrence in matter. This means *you* are the cause of the Mandela Effect you see, and *you* are The Event you have been looking forward to. The only way of knowing this for sure is through the development of gnosis: internal wisdom, rather than external knowledge. Gnosis cannot be explained or taught. It only comes through individual internal seeking of truth – universal truth as opposed to temporary scientific "truths" later proven false.

Timeline Tools

If you believe you are quantumly jumping timelines, there are tools to help you jump with intention for a better outcome. If you are constantly quantum jumping randomly (without intention or direction), you experience random outcomes. Here are just a few pointers on how to personally quantum jump into the New Earth, a new timeline, or a better version of you. You can start practicing these every day, and the more you practice them the more powerful and addictive they become. Eventually they become second nature and automatic. My gnosis tells me we bring 5D Earth, or New Earth here through our thoughts, feelings and actions. I believe it is a gradual rather than sudden process, although it does feel like it is speeding up now.

For increasing your own frequencies (in feelings and thoughts) to match higher vibratory New Earth frequencies, and to help root it in here for others to experience, I recommend any books and videos by Cynthia Sue Larson. Cynthia is naturally positive in her approach to quantum consciousness, which is contagious, while she teaches you in her books and videos how to constantly quantum jump into realities with a better outcome or version of you. Esther Hicks is great at helping us learn how to manifest anything we truly desire through positive thinking and positive feeling through the Law of Attraction - where like attracts like. I consider HeartMath Institute books and videos very useful at helping us to entrain our minds with our hearts into coherence to raise our personal frequencies to empower positive manifestation for one and all. Helen Schucman's *A Course in Miracles* helps us to become One through Christ Consciousness or the State of Grace of spirit living in matter. Pierre Pradervand shows us how to practice love and forgiveness through the daily act of blessing. Larry Dossey also shares the power of prayer in his popular books. Dolores Cannon's many books and videos make the higher consciousness and alien contact experience less frightening, as does the only scientific study on the subject of contact found at www.consciousnessandcontact.org and in their amazingly well-researched book, *Beyond UFOs: The Science of Consciousness and Contact with Non-Human Intelligence Volume 1.* Any book by Lynne McTaggart, Deepak Chopra, Greg Braden, Dr. Bruce Lipton, Dr. Joe Dispenza, Dr. Wayne Dyer will fill your mind and lift your spirit.

If you read and understand only parts of these great authors' works, it would be difficult for you to fear, hate or harm anyone or anything – including off-Earth life. Your soul, which is loving by nature, is fully integrated with your higher consciousness already. It is a matter of choice to allow your higher or lower consciousness to guide your decisions here. The State of Grace is also the great Buddhic state of harmlessness. Simple concept - difficult to put into practice. Here are some timeline or quantum jumping tools to help:

1. A simple ascension tool is to turn off mainstream media. Watching television programming and listening to commercial radio lowers your personal frequencies by suppressing feelings of love and safety, while fueling feelings of separation and fear. Personally, after decades of research, I believe the negative beings in charge of our current systems are human and not reptilian, alien, demonic, Archons, Annunaki, or other fabricated archvillain archetype. Choose your media based on how you *want* to feel. You would not willingly eat poison, so why willingly watch it or listen to it? Teach your children they have the choice to turn this kind of negativity on or off too.

2. Another important timeline jumping tool is forgiveness. The more you employ it the stronger it becomes. When something triggers you and you get an immediate knee-jerk reaction of a negative feeling - that is your emotional red flag telling you to employ its counterpart - forgiveness. As soon as that red flag goes up and you are feeling frustration or anger, use it as a warning signal that tells you to look around and determine who you need to forgive in that moment. Do you need to forgive the person who just bumped into you? Or do you need to forgive someone and something that happened earlier in the day? We often over-react to things later because of earlier frustrating experiences. Sometimes the red flag goes up when we are really just tired, we have been working too hard, or we have been using too much caffeine, alcohol, nicotine et cetera. Chemical additives make the red flags go up quicker, and lower your patience. Forgiveness is a wonderful tool for getting you into the mindset and the heartset of being able to transition to a higher frequency of living - whether you call it 5D, New Earth, Fourth Density or Heaven on Earth.

3. Gratitude is another timeline tool that is particularly helpful when there is no red flag of anger or resentment, but there is the orange flag of sadness. When you are just feeling a little bit blue

and a little bit down (which could also be due to too much coffee, cigarettes, alcohol, drugs), pause the sadness to list the people, events and things you are thankful for. When you are feeling low, raise your vibration by focusing on what you already have that you are grateful for. This change in focus immediately lifts your heart energy frequency, which immediately lifts your feelings. When you feel better you act better, which also raises the collective frequency. So, it is in my best interest that you feel good!

4. Love, love, love, and then love some more. This is the ultimate timeline tool for making sure that as you move forward in life you are also moving upward on your evolutionary journey. Leveling-up as you go, instead of going around and around a karmic wheel without any real progression. Perhaps that is the self-imposed punishment abusers create for themselves when they abuse anything, or allow themselves to be abused.

5. One timeline tool for jumping timelines into a better version of you - is through imagination and visualization. Relaxing, closing your eyes, and deeply breathing can help you get into a peaceful state, whereby you may imagine a person, event, or experience that makes you feel happy. Some people call this "going to your happy place". If you cannot actually see visual pictures in your head, that is okay. You can literally just feel or sense what it would feel like to be or experience these things. While visualizing it is important to ask yourself what does this look like, sound like, smell like, et cetera, in order to make it real for your subconscious or unconscious mind. But it is far more important to ask yourself: how does this make me *feel*? *The healing is in the feeling*. When visualizing for manifestation, it is crucial you see or imagine yourself *in* it and *doing* it already.

6. *The Gentle Art of Blessing* by Pierre Pradervand teaches you how to employ blessings every day, so that you get into the habit of blessing everything and everyone. It is not only important to bless yourself and your loved ones, but also bless those around you that you do not personally know. (56) Always *act* to help others whenever you can, but if you cannot due to distance or other separation – then send them your blessings instead! A great blessing for somebody you do not know is to ask God to bless them with anything they may need right now. This leaves it open to include, money, food, security, love, health ... allowing the receiver of the blessing to decide for themselves what is most needed in the moment. When blessing your family daily, you can

be much more specific because you know some of their needs intimately: like blessing your children's teachers to treat them kindly and to have patience in answering their questions. Ask God to bless you that you may always be able to easily provide for your family. God bless your parent's health that they continue to prosper in all ways ... these are just a few examples. *Ask and you shall receive*, but be specific. Or you may receive the unspecified request with unspecified results. However once you have asked for some specific manifestations, and taken some action to help bring it about – allow the creative universe to decide exactly how to bring it to you.

There are literally an unlimited amount of blessings you can give yourself and your loved ones daily, but remember to include strangers, animals, the Earth, all of humanity, all children, the water, the air, the land, insects, minerals, foliage ... and don't forget to bless those who need it most – the perpetrators of crimes on the local and global scale. They are nowhere near your level of ascension and badly need soul healing. Ask God to bless them on your behalf, to heal them, so they too can think, feel and act in cooperative compassion for the best possible outcome for all concerned. How often do we instinctively wish punishment on the selfish and the greedy instead of asking for their healing?

7. Employ angels to help yourself and others. I particularly appreciate Jean Slater's book on the subject, *Hiring the Heavens* (57), but I like working directly with God without intermediaries too. As a fractal of God, you already have a connection to source that cannot be broken. Many who teach about angelic energy say they are not beings with wings, that is our interpretation of the energies emanating from God to aid us. So certain Archangels (or God Energy) have certain characteristics and gifts. Like Archangel Michael who is known for bringing humanity the gift of protection and safety. Archangel Rafael is known for giving us the gifts of healing, and Archangel Gabriel is the bringer of good news and is the primary angel or God energy for writers and communicators. The *el* in most angels' names comes directly from Elohim, meaning *of God*.

8. Act with love. Thinking loving thoughts and feeling loving feelings are wonderful ascension tools, but love in action is even more powerful. The trinity or three energies of electric thoughts, magnetic feelings, and kinetic action to demonstrate your act of co-creation in God's Creation. You can pray for animals,

especially in winter months when they are struggling to find food and water, and you can feel sorry for them, but it is far more powerful to pray globally, but act locally and actually go out and provide them with some food and water. This is how we co-create with God. We create every time we do something that would have otherwise been left undone. You can usually apply local action to any global issue that bothers you. If you are upset with stories of famine in Africa and cannot find a reputable charity to give money to in order to help relieve their suffering, you can drop off food at your local foodbank. Thinking forgiveness and feeling love is a wonderful gift, but acting with love and forgiveness is even more powerful. It is your personal contribution to God's creation.

9. Please re-visit the earlier section on Ho 'Oponopono for one of the easiest and most powerful ascension tools available (page 42).

I hope these timeline tools work for you, and maybe you can come up with your own and share them with me in the comments section of my YouTube videos, to help us ascend, awaken, and shift more easily. When we naturally employ these ascension tools, we then project a higher frequency that brings the higher frequency Earth here through us. We seed and feed these ideas into the collective consciousness, and teach them through demonstration. The shift is well underway, and it is going to create a completely different world to the one we see here now. A world that is peaceful, compassionate, cooperative and loving. A gentle place, where it is safe to be forgiving and loving. A creative place, that honors your gifts, instead of making you scratch out a living doing anything in order to survive. Organized lack creates fear which fuels greed. Because New Earth is not a place you run to, but a place you create, it is transmutation of the place you already find yourself in. Transmutation from your soul through your heart to the world and universe through your actions, words, thoughts and feelings. God may have given you the world, but your transmutation of the world is the gift you give God.

Death, the Event, and the Mandela Effect

What do you take with you on your journey into life after life on Earth? We only ever have a perpetual state of now while we are here-now, so it is hard to define the infinite states of being in the here-after. The possibilities seem endless, but the likelihood of returning to Earth through the process of reincarnation also seems logical. Hermetic Law: As above so below, as below so above. If children go to Earth schools to learn in order to progress, it is logical that the soul comes to Earth in order to evolve. If the child's goal is to graduate to move into higher levels of education, then the soul probably wishes to graduate Earth to move into higher levels of existence.

It is comforting to think we are all fractals of God (the sum total of the universe), going off to have an adventure, to learn, to grow, and to share it with our soul family as we find our way back home to being one with source energy - all that is, was, or ever will be. At-One-Ment. What better way to graduate, evolve, or level-up than to be able to love fully and unconditionally? We get plenty of practice here!

This brings us to a subject that people, at least in the West, try to avoid. They do not want to talk about it, or even think about it, but they know it is coming. It is inevitable. And while they are going through it - they actually talk to their loved ones and coach them through the process. Death. What a word - right? Could it not have a nicer more gentle sounding word then "death"? There is something very final about the Western concept of death. You live this life, this is your only life, and if you are good your soul goes to Heaven forever, and if you are bad your soul goes to Hell forever. Unbaptized babies who die go to Limbo and unclean souls go to purgatory before meeting their maker. At least in some of the Eastern religious traditions they talk about death as a natural part of life, and prepare for it.

My first experience with death, because I did not have any pets from the age of birth to six that died, occurred on my first day of formal schooling. You see, my parents never sat me down and said, "before we send you to first grade at a Catholic school, we need to talk to you about death, because if we don't - they are going to scare the *youknowwhat* out of you with it!"

On the first day of first grade sitting in my first uniform in a gray desk-chair in a grey classroom at my suburban Chicago Catholic school in the 1960's – a grey woman dressed in black from the top of her head to the tip of her toes walked in and told us we were all going to hell when we die, unless we did exactly as she said. She wore the old-fashioned black nun's habit, which included a large wooden cross hanging from her waist that swung from side to side as she walked. I am sure this is going to bring back memories for a lot of you. The guilt-training starts very early in our original Middle Eastern Abrahamic *cum* Western religious traditions. I think the most damaging lesson taught is that we are all naturally born sinners, and we have to buy our way into heaven by attending their services, confessing our sins to them, and tithing them money. Being born an evil sinner did not really bother me as much as being told on my first hour of formal schooling that my family members were all going to die, because everything dies, everyone dies, your parents die, your friends die, you die, even your pets die! What a horrible trick God played on me that day – giving me so much happiness in my short little life only to take it all away with one sentence from that nun on my first day of school. I am sure she had the best of intentions to frighten us into church, into prayer, into confession, into good little future tithers with the thought of death looming large over our little heads. Along with the constant reward of heaven and the constant threat of hell based on how well we obeyed our human church, temple, synagogue, mosque – all those who brokered our relationship with God, even though we never asked them to. Frankly I have a great relationship with God and God or Source Energy is happy to communicate with me directly. So after studying world religions for decades - I eventually fired the lot of professional well-paid intercessors.

Later that night, my mother heard me crying in bed. She came in, sat on my bed and asked me what could have been so horrible on my first day of school. She later said she suspected I, as a chubby child, had been bullied by other children, but never suspected I felt bullied by church doctrine that threatened the lives of the ones I loved. I was more upset that my parents would die than I would die, because I would not see them again unless I was good enough to get into heaven. My mother explained she and my father were not going to die for a very long time (a promise they kept), and that God was actually good and kind despite what they taught me in school, so we would all be together in heaven eventually no matter what the nuns said.

Long story short: I asked to transfer to public school by third grade and my parents complied, so I got out of Catholic school relatively early and unscathed. Not so for a seventh-grade child with a broken arm from being thrown across desks by a nun. She was punished with a fast, quiet retirement instead of prosecution for assault and child abuse. I instinctively never trusted a nun, a priest, or the church since that first day in Catholic school. I must have been born with gnosis intact. Raising a family in England decades later, I found the Anglican Protestant church much more open and relaxed, so much so they even have women leading services. So, I decided to allow my child to attend Sunday School starting at the age of four (the age they begin formal schooling in England), in a back room of our village Saxon church dating back to the 800s, while I attended the family service. Unfortunately, she came out of Sunday school frightened and confused just like I had four decades earlier. My daughter told me the victims of the tsunami at Christmas time in 2004 were sinners, so God drowned them, because that is what he did to naughty people. When I asked her why she thought they were naughty, she retold the story of Noah, the animals and the flood. Abraham's angry vengeful God was back in my life again. I decided to skip the service for the grown-ups and sit in with the children during the next session. It was being taught by a volunteer - a self-proclaimed missionary who spent years converting people in Africa; and like my first-grade-teaching nun, she was trying to frighten the children into becoming good little Christians. She instructed the children to cut hearts out of black paper and red paper that day. She then had the children hold the black paper heart over their physical hearts, as she told them they were all born with black hearts, but if they accepted Jesus as their savior, they would have a red heart full of love instead. Then she told them to put the red paper heart over the black one. Maybe an acceptable allegory for older children, but the four-year-olds in the room looked terrified as they held the black hearts over their own. Exactly when did they decide you can only terrify children into being good Christians? I do not recall Jesus ever suggesting this method of conversion.

So that was the end of Sunday school for both of us - forever. I think we in the Western world have a terrible relationship with death, and a not so good relationship with God, because we cannot trust *him* to not kill us or punish us for an eternity for not being perfect like *he* is. So God is male, mean and destructive – perhaps like the people who invented him. Not to mention they have completely removed the feminine principle of God and creation (suits a Western world that thrives on making and selling bombs and weapons of mass destruction.) Imagine where that leaves over half the world's population, the women, who lacking the male phallus could never be as perfect as *He*. Do you ever feel like we are still living in the Dark Ages? If you imagine yourself as an alien studying Western religious thought, I think you would feel sorry for us. Unlike many Eastern religious traditions, death is not something we are taught to accept, or even prepare for. Except for that famous line from *Peter Pan*, where he is looking up at Captain Hook who is about to kill him, and Peter says, "To die would be an awfully big adventure!" (58) Well the fact of the matter is – death *is* a very big adventure. Perhaps our biggest, because it represents a mysterious journey we must all take alone. No one escapes it. Kings and presidents cannot buy their way out of it. Popes are not spared. For all their wealth the elite cannot escape the fate of the poorest peasants. I am not going to say look forward to it, or rush to it, but I had a death experience in Maadi, a suburb of Cairo, at the age of 17 that changed my perspective on death, and led me on the mystic's path.

My father worked as a telecommunications director for an oil company, so I grew up in the 1970's and 1980's in a Chicago suburb with my mother, and in the West Indies and Middle East with my father. This probably fueled my interest in studying world religions for decades, after graduating from a Jesuit University with my major in broadcast journalism and a minor in psychology. I was an American Catholic Christian teenager living in Maadi, a Cairo suburb, when my father decided we would take the local train overnight from Cairo to Luxor. The company doctor, who kept us immunized with all the normal American vaccines, plus vaccines for smallpox, yellow fever and hepatitis, suggested we get a tetanus booster in the company medical offices before we left.

The company doctor worked in an office block with some medical equipment and a couple of nurses. I stood in line with all the other company employees and their children getting vaccine boosters that day. Unfortunately they did not have tetanus toxoid available. It only came in combinations with diphtheria or with diphtheria and pertussis antigens. They gave me the DT diphtheria-tetanus booster in my arm, which burned like fire as soon as it stated spreading. My skin turned bright red wherever the serum went. The next thing I knew I was looking down on the body of a young teenage girl laying on an examination table with her eyes closed. While the doctor and two nurses ran frantically around the room, there was a man standing over her crying and stroking her head rather roughly, but trying to be gentle. He was saying "wake up" and "open your eyes, Eileen" over and over. I watched with curiosity as the doctor did manual CPR and shouted to the nurse to go to his car and get his medical bag out of the trunk.

Then the doctor stopped doing CPR and said to the man sobbing over the body of this young woman that the nurses were taking too long, as he ran out of the room. I saw all of this while floating under the ceiling in the same position mirroring the body below, so my head was floating above the head, and my arms were above the arms, as I faced myself looking down from the ceiling. I was watching through a light, brown haze or fog. Most surprisingly, seeing the body on the table did not upset me emotionally, because I did not know who she was, or if anything was wrong with her. I did not know who the crying man was, and I did not even know who the floating *me* was, nor did I care. I just did not have an emotional attachment to any of the people or events I was watching. I felt curiosity. I remember feeling sorry for the man crying. One moment I was walking out of the doctor's office and the next I was floating on the ceiling with no pain and no fear and no identity.

The doctor came back with the nurses and his medical bag and gave me a shot of adrenalin. After re-establishing a heartbeat, he smacked my face, just like in the movies, and asked me to open my eyes and speak to him. To which I responded, "let me go", as I turned my head to the wall. He gave me a second shot of adrenalin, and kept me lying down for eight hours, as sitting up could have caused a heart attack with double the normal dose of adrenalin. I repeated back to my father and the doctor every word that had been spoken, and every action taken while I was technically dead with no heartbeat and no respiration. They were convinced I was indeed watching them the whole time from the ceiling, and asked me why I said, "let me go". I still have no better answer than – because it felt better to be flying free than to be contained within a human body. I was instructed to have no more vaccinations, and through allergy testing I later learned I had experienced the anaphylactic shock to the diphtheria portion of Diphtheria-Tetanus vaccine, which my child inherited.

I was lucky at such an early age of 17 to experience a very short clinical death, because these kinds of experiences often have profound and lasting effects; opening hidden talents and inspiring spiritual undertakings in most of the near death and death experiencers. Interestingly, I have no memory of my consciousness or spirit actual leaving or returning to my body, but the time out of body is quite vivid with strong visuals and sounds. It taught me there is only the feeling of unemotional freedom once you leave your body and the life cord to the body is severed. No pain, no sadness and no fear. I did not get as far as seeing loved ones, a light, a tunnel, or hearing music. No one came for me. Maybe because everyone on the other side knew I was not ready to pass over.

Now without fear of death at such an early age, it really changed who I am, and gave me a driving desire to understand life here on Earth, life in between lives in matter, and to know myself and God better. And that brought me to world religions, quantum science, metaphysics, and spirituality. I read as much as I could find on the near-death experience, and human religious texts, as well as quantum physics - trying to get a feel for what people have said for thousands of years about death, dying and existence before life on Earth and after. One of the best writers I found on the subject is P.M.H. Atwater, especially her book *Near-Death Experiences: the rest of the story*. (59) She spent decades studying near death experiences as told by the men, women, and children from different cultures, religions and ages who had actually experienced a medically documented death; which is a temporary death followed by successful resuscitation. There are also many near death experiences reported while a person is in a coma, or on life support.

Over her career, she interviewed over 4000 individuals to find out the differences and commonalities of death and dying. In Atwater's research, adults will often report seeing a dead loved-one who died before them, or angels, or the iconic religious figures from their particular religion like Jesus, Mary, Buddha, Mohammed, Vishnu et cetera. Most interesting, only 15% of the adults reported experiencing a negative or hell-like place first, while 85% said they went straight to a positive or heaven–like place. One hundred percent of the 15% going to a dark place eventually moved on to a heaven–like place too. It was like the dark place cleansed them of their guilt, so they *could* move on. One hundred percent of children reported going straight to a beautiful heaven-like place.

Most interesting to me, Atwater found the people reported they went to *exactly* the kind of place they thought they *deserved* to go. They decided, not God, or a council. Some who committed minor infractions, but carried a lot of guilt, reported going to a dark place first; while others who justified their terrible crimes reported going straight to a heaven-like place, because they thought they deserved to go there. This supports the teachings in *A Course in Miracles* too, where it states repeatedly that we are our own judge and jury. (60) This makes perfect sense if we are a part of God. So do not expect any kind of council to judge you. We are often our own worst critics here anyway, so we are probably more than qualified to judge our lifetime once outside of said lifetime. Those who believe in reincarnation may see repeated lives on one planet, dimension, or realm as a personal progression or evolution through life-in-matter on its way back to the source from which it sprang; much like a child moves from grade level to grade level all the way up to graduation. But there is nothing that proves we cannot also experience many lives in many bodies on many planets in many universes in many dimensions. With all of that available - thank goodness we are eternal.

Unity with God is often considered soul "graduation" after all physical lives and time spent in between lives finally leads to perfection or atonement with all (at-one-ment with all of creation which is God or Source). To understand how God or Source could create itself and be infinitely self-perpetuating please look up toroidal fields, as the information on them would fill this book. Guilt on one's deathbed is a very dangerous thing, if you go where *you* think you deserve to go at the moment of your physical death. Like the Eastern religious traditions, we should spend the time necessary to heal our guilt, old wounds, and forgive loved ones and ourselves – in other words make amends during the death process before our last breath. And we should spend time visualizing, talking about, and determining exactly what kind of a place we think we deserve to go to when the life cord to the body is finally separated. Death should not be feared. It should be studied, discussed, and understood to the best of our ability as a natural part of life here; and prepared for with a sense of appreciation for the life lived, and awe for the after-life to come,

Most reassuring of all, is that people who come back through resuscitation usually report being in beautiful places, doing things they love, with loved ones who passed before them. Giving these reports even more credibility is the fact they never report seeing living loved ones there, and if these were mere vivid dreams, they would be equally populated with people we love who are still alive, as well as dead loved ones, and strangers. The in-between places (spirit life between material life) are for people and their loved ones outside of physical material bodies only, and that is a beautiful thing. Once consciousness is free of the body it is no longer dead, it is no longer dying, it is literally living as pure consciousness (spirit, soul, fractal of God) in between physical lifetimes with light bodies, or who knows? So the in-between is more creative than the actual lifetimes themselves, because matter is more restrictive. Following material life you are not encumbered with the rules and the laws of matter, so you can fly freely.

Quantum Memory

Matter changing, with the residual evidence of how it used to be before the change, is simply an expansion of human awareness, an expansion of human memory, and an expansion of consciousness or God-force within its material environment. If you can see Mandela Effects, you are one of the lucky ones, and the numbers are growing every day worldwide. You are one of the lucky few who can hold on to a lot more memory than the average human, who can only remember what is, not what was *before* what is now. You can hold on to the past memory of how things used to be, while you hold on to the memory of how they are now; so you can hold on to the memory of the in between too - when things shift back and forth called flip-flops. Maybe not considered a critical skill now, but who knows how important this may become in future days.

The Mandela Effect or Quantum Memory is a wake-up call to the simple fact that mind rules matter. Mind rules matter and heart rules mind, so if you know that - you might as well start directing the show here now. Why do the ruling human elite keep the majority in the dark and in a perpetual state of poverty and fear, exhausted from over-work and over-worry about how to pay the ever-increasing bills? If everybody had free time they might study and explore the nature of reality and figure out how this works ... then there would not be an *elite* anymore. They would lose their control as soon as the masses began exercising their abilities to steer, edit and create matter the way *they*, and not the elite, want it to be. The shared environment, all of Earth, would be ours to co-create in for the benefit for *all*. Not just for the benefit of the few who keep humanity ignorant of their personal power and hungry for survival. We are small, but we are mighty, and we are collectively invincible here.

In Conclusion of the Beginning ....

My mother was M.E. affected in the 1970s and I was affected in the 1990s like Cynthia Sue Larson (author of *Reality Shifts* and *Quantum Jumps,* and *High Energy Money*), even though there was no official name for it yet. I know now it has always been here, but most could not see matter constantly shifting in response to collective consciousness for very good reasons – continuity, paradigm consistency, and sanity. I believe all the "timelines" are accessible from the here-now, but in layers within the holographic multidimensional universe. All is consciousness and consciousness is all. Usually you can only see one dimension, or one layer of the hologram at a time. The New Human is fast becoming able to see many layers at once, but probably not *all* of the dimensional layers for obvious reasons. The residue from the old timeline in the new timeline proves that both are right here right now. Our consciousness is expanding within the hologram into multiple layers or levels, so we think we are seeing multiple timelines, when we are just seeing multiple dimensions or layers of reality from one place - the eternal here-now. One reality, one matrix, one God, one us (including extraterrestrial life) within infinite levels of reality. Picture a holographic onion without end. We never move to a new reality. Reality (the matter matrix) constantly moves around us in response to collective feelings, beliefs, and actions. Better to make those feelings and beliefs as true to you as possible, instead of an auto-response to human elite programming. The material world is an external expression of the you inside – better to make it as good as it can be.

This is why I think mainstream authorities are silent on the Mandela Effect so far: because they cannot figure out how to explain possibly millions of people misremembering something in exactly the same way. That in itself is miraculous, or a statistical impossibility without a hivemind. There should be as many different versions of the so-called false memory or confabulation as there are people falsely remembering them, but there is not. There is only one so-called false memory of something with residual proof of how it used to be. There are usually only two, or rarely a few, as things flip-flop between different versions of itself. Some corporations are presenting their name both ways now in a single online listing. Until they can figure out how to explain this phenomenon, they are staying largely mute on the subject. But not to worry – the next generation will not buy into organized deceptions. They call a spade a spade and the see the Mandela Effect and are not afraid to say so. And the Mandela Effect is spreading so fast it will not be long before the majority of humans see it – making it the new normal, while those who do *not* see it may be classified as abnormal (not part of the norm or majority). When the proverbial shift hits the fan, we will be the ones standing strong saying, "You are not crazy, things *are* changing, and we can prove it with reality residue." The best thing we could all do is to save as much Mandela Effect residue as possible completely offline, so online A.I. cannot wipe it out with the click of a keystroke.

The so-called "NPCs" or non-player characters may be us, because we cannot be programmed any more to play the game the way the programmers intend. Or we are a glitch in the matrix that can see the matrix-boundaries and the matrix-programming the programmed game players cannot. Truthers are the virus or the glitch in the program. If the aggressive, greedy programming of daily survival on Earth upsets you, you can stop placing so much importance on the collective screenplay. Become the conscious director of your own life, then a superconscious director of the whole; and when enough of us do this, we will create the cooperative compassionate world we are fully capable of having here now. Wherever and whenever you encounter suffering do all you can to help, but do not fall into despair over things you cannot change. Be loving enough to change what you can, patient enough to accept what you cannot change, and wise enough to know the difference between the two. One of my favorite prayers is "The Serenity Prayer" by the American theologian Reinhold Niebuhr:

"God, grant me the serenity to accept the things I cannot change,
Courage to change the things I can,
And wisdom to know the difference."

Random Thoughts on the Subject

No fear here - only LOVE. You are a sovereign being, and as such, no one and no thing can take your energy, but you can give it away willingly through fear, sadness, uncertainty, resentment, hate, anger, and jealousy. Do not give your energy away - stay in a state of love, compassion, and joy as much as possible where you become impervious to everything but LOVE! That is the State of Grace so many religions teach.

What we believe becomes. What we feel becomes even faster.

If it can die it is not real. All is Love. Love is everlasting. Love is real. Everything else is fake because it is temporary.

True you cannot solve a problem unless you first see there is a problem to solve, but what you focus on grows. This is the Law of Attraction: like attracts like. Studies show happy people who focus on the positive, attract happier people and events to them. While sad or angry people who focus on the negative, attract like-minded people and events into their lives. If you look at toroidal energy fields you will understand why this happens in a self-perpetuating way, creating constantly growing feedback loops.

There is no such thing as New Age or Ancient Wisdom. There are only your thoughts and they are both wise and mundane.

Perfect definition of the "beast system" - the few humans who are smart and greedy enough to enslave the rest of humanity to their exclusive benefit. They prefer we blame this on Satan, demons, Archons, Anunnaki, lizard aliens called Reptilians.... anything but humans, because that makes us feel weaker than them. When you realize all evil here stems from humans, then seven billion decent people throwing off the shackles of a million oppressive humans is not so hard to imagine or achieve.

Interesting how humans hang everything unexplained or scary on something outside of themselves. Remember when people thought volcanic eruptions were caused by fire demons living inside? Same for hadron colliders and quantum computers that are expected to open demonic portals.

Those who prefer you think and feel *their* desires into reality - would prefer you thought matter reacting to consciousness is a crazy idea.

Earth is not a prison planet. There is nothing to escape here except your own feelings and beliefs, and you sure cannot run far from those! This is a beautiful but challenging here-now, where we learn to act compassionately in cooperation within a group matrix.

Is the Bible just another religious book written by men who walked the Earth fairly ignorant of scientific process thousands of years ago? I believe there are pearls of wisdom in all human religious texts, but I feel most religious text is dogma construed by human ruling classes for control of the masses through their belief.
We are the programed-players in our world, but the elite currently write the code we gobble up and spit back out for them – until we are mature enough to write our own code (which is now).

The increased cosmic energy coming in now due to our scattered magnetic shield may be causing us to *see* the Mandela Effect by scattering our changing our brain waves. It could be that simple (See Vannessa VA's section in this book.)

I think the top controllers of the system here are human and visiting lifeforms are just observers waiting for us to play nicely. They obviously think we are capable of this or they would have left by now.

We do not need someone other than ourselves to run the reality matrix here - our collective subconscious is powerful enough to do that ... but the "creator" of the "collective us" – that is something more.

Do not kill evil or in the process you become the evil you are attempting to kill, but rather heal all suffering whenever it crosses your path: The no-harm principles of collective well-being propels collective evolution of a species.

No black holes, no gravity, no dark matter needed with toroidal fields of infinite cold clean abundant free energy.

Air is not empty space. It is filled with energetic plasma, though still invisible to the current human eye, connects us all to everyone and everything. When we see this we will become extremely altruistically powerful.

Drop the Standard Model of the universe - it cannot possibly work in our holographic multidimensional reality.

Historically, the idea of a Shift or the Event transporting the goodies somewhere good and the baddies somewhere bad (heaven vs hell), has been written into human consciousness and human religious mythology for at least six thousand years. Probably longer if we could find their stories. In fact, I think it is coded into human DNA/RNA.

I too have found that there is divine intelligence and sovereignty involved in everything and everyone, and I may always lovingly ask for healings for others, but I may not command them for others. However, for myself, *I Am* the sovereign divine being in charge of my experience here in matter. God made it this way. Therefore, I am free to command the matter I have been given in ways that affect me.

If feeling good gives you a good life, then I suggest turning off msm except for comedies and love stories.

When you lucid dream, you explore with consciousness and power (like the director of a movie) a world of your own subconscious creation. Very safe. When you astral project and leave your body, you consciously explore worlds not only of your own creation - which is why it can be scary for first-timers. But when you realize these are only the dreams of other lifeforms - then it's not so scary anymore to enter worlds that are not entirely of your own creation.

When you successfully astrally project you will know because you lose all boundaries (even the sense of a personal body) and you lose all sense of time.

From my research I have learned all humans have the innate capacity to manifest in matter. Some choose to evoke their power (emotional charge to items or events) through negative harmful ritual ... while others choose to invoke their power (emotional charge to items and events) through positive loving feelings. Both work.

Lucifer the light bearer (and I'm no fan) is considered the snake who offered the Apple of Enlightenment or Knowledge (Gnosis) to Adam and Eve, but the Babylonian God of War from the Old Testament cursed them and all humanity for self-awareness. The Old Testament God clearly loved nothing more than to plague, smite, and drown his greatest creation here – people. Not the same loving, forgiving God Jesus introduced to us as a correction to the faith of the Old Testament (Hebrew Bible) with a New Testament. Why these two very different religions with very different Gods are presented in one holy book is a mystery, unless they are recreating the good god vs. bad god, Enki and Enlil, from the Mesopotamian/Sumerian/Babylonian myths, where they also borrowed the Genesis and Flood stories.

You save you. And when enough of us do this then We save Us.

Since collective feelings and beliefs lead to collective actions, that means we can change things here quickly - as soon as we start directing our own beliefs feelings and actions instead of responding to fear programming.

Why does this holographic timeless multidimensional simulation of infinite information in waveform plasma collapsed into matter respond to collective human consciousness? Because God is universal consciousness acting here through us.

Earth politics is the Hegelian Dialectic of repeated crisis-solution-crisis consolidating power over humanity through separation and fear. It is that simple. At-One-Ment ends this.

Your consciousness is more powerful in a multidimensional holographic plasma field than any machine made by man or woman can ever be. Saying hadron colliders and quantum computing are more powerful than your consciousness - is like saying humans are more powerful than God.

We can't trust monkeymen and monkeywomen to self-govern fairly or justly - yet. *Do Not Let Them Off Earth* would be my SOS back to my alien nation, if I was a visitor here.

Flat Earth vs Spherical Earth has gone back to an unsettled position because the masses can believe nothing their rulers tell them anymore. And it will remain so until each of us rises high enough to see for ourselves. In a holographic matrix it can be all shapes or none.

Fear not death immortal souls - study toroidal energy fields instead.

Thank you I love you.

Part One Endnotes:

1. Lucasfilm Ltd., The Empire Strikes Back, 1980.

2. Famous Logos, Volkswagen Logo, https://www.famouslogos.net/volkswagen-logo/, accessed 5.16.2019.

3. Wikipedia, Adriaan Vlok, https://en.wikipedia.org/wiki/Adriaan_Vlok, accessed 5.16.2019.

4. Dorell, Oren. "Winnie Mandela Controversial Ex-Wife of Nelson Mandela Dies at 81", USA Today, 4.0.2018, https://www.usatoday.com/story/news/world/2018/04/02/winnie-mandela-wife-nelson-mandela-dies/477898002/, accessed 5.16.2019.

5. Larson, Cynthia Sue. Reality Shifts: When Consciousness Changes the Physical World. Reality Shifters, 2012. Larson, Cynthia Sue. Quantum Jumps: An Extraordinary Science of Happiness and Prosperity. Reality Shifters, 2013.

6. Atwater, P. M. H. Future Memory. Hampton Roads, 2013.

7. Than, Kerr. "Sun Blamed For Warming of Earth and Other Worlds", Live Science, 3.12.2007, https://www.livescience.com/1349-sun-blamed-warming-earth-worlds.html, accessed 5.16.2019.

8. The Electronic Text Corpus of Sumerian Literature, Faculty of Oriental Studies, University of Oxford, http://etcsl.orinst.ox.ac.uk/, accessed 3.12.2019.

9. Sitchin, Zecharia. The 12th Planet: Book 1 of the Earth Chronicles. HarperCollins, 2007

10. Rowling, J. K., and Andrew Davidson. Harry Potter: The Complete Collection. Bloomsbury, 2015

11. Clery, Daniel. "Colliding Stars will light up the night sky in 2022", Science, 1.6.2017,

https://www.sciencemag.org/news/2017/01/colliding-stars-will-light-night-sky-2022, accessed 5.16.2019.

12. Zyga, Lisa, "Detection of mini black holes at the LHC could indicate parallel universes in extra dimensions", Phys.org, 3.18.2015, https://phys.org/news/2015-03-mini-black-holes-lhc-parallel.html, accessed 3.12.2019.

13. ETOTv , "Inuit People on Pole Shift", 7.4.2011, https://youtu.be/_HZ_Dvkxi-8, accessed 3.12.2019.

14. Phys.org, 3.14.2011, "Quake Moved Japan by 8 Feet", https://phys.org/news/2011-03-quake-japan-feet-usgs.html, accessed 5.16.2019.

15. O'Connor, Tom. "Fukushima's Nuclear Waste Will Be Dumped Into The Ocean, Japanese Plant Owner Says", Newsweek, 7.14.2017, https://www.newsweek.com/fukushima-nuclear-waste-dumped-ocean-japanese-protests-637108, accessed 5.16.2019.

16. GSM, "What is a Grand Solar Minimum", https://thegrandsolarminimum.com/, accessed 5.16.2019.

17. 3 CBS Philly, Space Agency: "Weakening Of Earth's Magnetic Fields Could Indicate Pole Reversal", 11.25.2013, https://philadelphia.cbslocal.com/2013/11/25/space-agency-weakening-of-earths-magnetic-field-could-indicate-pole-reversal/, accessed 5.16.2019.

18. Pradervand, Pierre. The Gentle Art of Blessing: A Simple Practice That Will Transform You and Your World. Cygnus Books, 2010.

19. A Course in Miracles. Foundation for Inner Peace, 1992.

20. Treybig, David. Life Hope & Truth, "144,000", https://lifehopeandtruth.com/prophecy/revelation/144-000/, accessed 5.16.2019.

21. Investment Watch, "Will Trump Reinstate the Smith-Mundt Act Obama Repealed And Once Again Ban State Sponsored Propaganda?" 1.18.2016, https://www.investmentwatchblog.com/will-trump-reinstate-the-smith-mundt-act-obama-repealed-and-once-again-ban-state-sponsored-propaganda/ , accessed 5.16.2019.

22. Imus, Deidre. "Who Does the Childhood Vaccine Injury Act Protect?", Children's Health Defense, 12.12.2017, https://childrenshealthdefense.org/news/childhood-vaccine-injury-act-protect/, accessed 5.16.2019.

23. Pope, Sarah. "It's Time to End the Monsanto Protection Act", The Healthy Home Economist, 5.16.2019, https://www.thehealthyhomeeconomist.com/its-time-to-end-the-monsanto-protection-act/, accessed 5.16.2019.

24. Resnick, Jordan. "How Fluoride Affects Consciousness and the Will to Act", Waking Times, 8.22.2014, https://childrenshealthdefense.org/news/childhood-vaccine-injury-act-protect/, accessed 5.19.2019.

25. Jacobsen, Annie. Operation Paperclip: The Secret Intelligence Program to Bring Nazi Scientists to America, (Little, Brown & Company, 2014) 575 pp., endnotes, bibliography, index. Central Intelligence Agency, Intelligence in Public Literature, Reviewed by Jay Watkins, https://www.cia.gov/library/center-for-the-study-of-intelligence/csi-publications/csi-studies/studies/vol-58-no-3/operation-paperclip-the-secret-intelligence-program-to-bring-nazi-scientists-to-america.html, accessed 5.16.2019.

26. Children's Health Defense, "US Water Fluoridation: A Forced Experiment that Needs to End", 1.9.2019, https://childrenshealthdefense.org/news/u-s-water-fluoridation-a-forced-experiment-that-needs-to-end/, accessed 5.16.2019.

27. Bovsun, Mara. "German spies nearly blew up Statue of Liberty in 1916, closing torch to tourists forever", New York Daily News, 6.25.2016, https://www.nydailynews.com/news/crime/german-spies-blew-state-liberty-1916-article-1.2687925, accessed 5.16.2019.

28. ZeroPointNow, "JFK Release: Second Shooter, UK Tipoff, CIA Media Infiltrations, and LBJ Fingered in Coup", 10.27.2017, https://www.zerohedge.com/news/2017-10-27/jfk-release-findings-second-shooter-uk-tipoff-cia-media-infiltration-and-lbj-fingere, accessed 5.16.2019.

29. Moorjani, Anita. Dying to Be Me: My Journey from Cancer, to near Death, to True Healing. Hay House India, 2015.

30. Vitale, Joe, and Len Haleakalā Hew. Zero Limits: The Secret Hawaiian System for Wealth, Health, Peace, and More. Wiley-VCH, 2015.

31. Das, Subhamoy. Learn Religions, "Hinduism's 4 Yugas", or Ages, 11.4.2018, https://www.learnreligions.com/the-four-yugas-or-epochs-1770051, accessed 5.16.2019.

32. Marc The Arcturian , "EARTH: A – Z"; Part II – How Earth REALLY Orbits Our Sun; Photon Belt; Time Collapsing; Re-Release", 3.21.2017, https://www.youtube.com/watch?v=hoDvrq1B__Q&list=PL_YoV9P RAMjwMvcIgbKxTy2C8PVdn9_gS&index=5, accessed 5.16.2019.

33. Grossman, Lisa, "Solar system caught in an interstellar tempest", New Scientist, 9.5.2013, https://www.newscientist.com/article/dn24153-solar-system-caught-in-an-interstellar-tempest/, accessed 3.12.2019

34. Hernandez, JD, MCP, Rey, et al. Beyond UFOs. the Science of Consciousness and Contact with Non-Human Intelligence. Academic Research Foundation (The Dr. Edgar Mitchell Foundation for Research into Extraterrestrial and Extraordinary Experiences {FREE}), 2018.

35. Talltanic, "Mind Blowing Discoveries in the Last Year", 11.1.17, https://youtu.be/D2urVCLIcA4, accessed 2.28.19.

36. Brennan, Pat, "The Super-Earth that Came Home for Dinner", 11.4.17, NASA Jet Propulsion Laboratory California Institute of Technology,

https://www.jpl.nasa.gov/news/news.php?release=2017-259, accessed 2.27.19.

37. Cynthia Sue Larsen, "Physics Experiment Challenges Objective Reality", 4.1.2019, https://www.youtube.com/watch?v=xrZotcsJjA0&t=241s, accessed 5.16.2019.

38. ThunderboltsProject, "Wal Thornhill: On the Black Hole's Non-existence, Space News", 4.19.2019, https://www.youtube.com/watch?v=Dk2-lH9ewuA&t=87s, accessed 5.16.2019.

39. David LaPoint, "The Primer Fields" video series, Part 1, 12.17.2012, https://www.youtube.com/watch?v=9EPlyiW-xGI&t=409s, accessed 2.28.19.

40. Geoengineering Monitoring, Stratospheric Aerosol Injection (Technology Factsheet), 6.11.18, http://www.geoengineeringmonitor.org/2018/06/stratospheric_aerosol_injection/, accessed 7.21.19.

41. ZEG TV HIDDEN FROM THE PUBLIC, "These Sumerian Clay Tablets Reveal the BIGGEST Secrets of the Solar System", 9.2.2018, https://youtu.be/BDTHFXDF9G0, accessed 2.17.19.

42. BinaryResearchInst, "The Great Year", 5.4.2019, https://www.youtube.com/watch?v=l3ZDcj0kF_0&t=19s, accessed 5.16.2019.

43. Nield, David, "New Bright 'Star' Could Appear in The Night Sky in 2022", Science Alert, 1.10.2017, https://www.sciencealert.com/here-s-why-a-bright-new-star-could-be-appearing-in-the-night-sky-in-2022, assessed 2.27.19.

44. CIA.gov, Declassified in Part – Sanitized Copy Approved for Release 2013/06/24 : Chan, Thomas. The Adam and Eve Story. Bengal Tiger Press. CIA-RDP79B00752A000300070001-8, https://www.cia.gov/library/readingroom/docs/CIA-RDP79B00752A000300070001-8.pdf, accessed 5.16.2019.

45. CIA.gov, Declassified in Part – Sanitized Copy Approved for Release 2013/06/24 : Chan, Thomas. The Adam and Eve Story. Bengal Tiger Press. CIA-RDP79B00752A000300070001-8, https://www.cia.gov/library/readingroom/docs/CIA-RDP79B00752A000300070001-8.pdf, accessed 5.16.2019.

46. Sepehr, Robert. 1666 Redemption Through Sin. Atlantean Gardens, 2015.

47. Booth, Mark. The Secret History of the World. The Overlook Press, 2011.

48. David LaPoint, "The Primer Fields" video series, Part 1, 12.17.2012, https://www.youtube.com/watch?v=9EPlyiW-xGl&t=409s, accessed 2.28.19; www.primercube.org.

49. ThunderboltsProject, "Wal Thornhill: Black Hole or Plasmoid? Space News", 4.16.2019, https://youtu.be/J4NffTr_GMk, accessed 5.19.2019.

50. Veritassium, "Is This What Quantum Mechanics Looks Like?", https://youtu.be/WlyTZDHuarQ, accessed 7.9.19.

51. 101 SRPHD – Truth Exposed channel, "Mandela Effect – Carl Sagan Remembers The Sagittarius Arm/Carina Cygnus Spiral Arm", 9.1.2016, https://www.youtube.com/watch?v=IcnV2wu99mw&t=85s, accessed 5.16.2019.

52. Richard Tarr, "Neil Degrasse Tyson remembers we are in the Sagittarius Arm", 11.30.2016, https://www.youtube.com/watch?v=BRYupzzLFBE, accessed 5.16.2019.

53. Ra, et al. The Law of One. Whitford Press, 1982.

54. Vannessa VA, "Mandela Effect Dolores Cannon New Earth", 6.8.2017, https://www.youtube.com/watch?v=B2rnHXrkh_U, accessed 5.16.2019.

55.   Gayle, Damien. "Near-death experiences occur when the soul leaves the nervous system and enters the universe, claim two quantum physics experts", The Daily Mail, 10.30.2012, https://www.dailymail.co.uk/sciencetech/article-2225190/Can-quantum-physics-explain-bizarre-experiences-patients-brought-brink-death.html, accessed 5.16.2019.

56.   Pradervand, Pierre. The Gentle Art of Blessing: A Simple Practice That Will Transform You and Your World. Cygnus Books, 2010.

57.   Slatter, Jean. Hiring the Heavens: A Practical Guide to Developing a Working Relationship with the Spirits of Creation. New World Library, 2010.

58.   Barrie, J. M., and Jan Ormerod. Peter Pan. Puffin, 1988.

59.   Atwater, P. M. H. Near-Death Experiences, the Rest of the Story: What They Teach Us about Living, Dying, and Our True Purpose. Hampton Roads, 2011.

60.   A Course in Miracles. Foundation for Inner Peace, 1992.

Mandela Effect Testimonies: Beyond Fear

Testimony 1

This is DEAD GPK, channel producer on YouTube, and I have been experiencing the Mandela Effect since August of 2016. In the past, I have always researched or looked into fringe type topics, such as UFOs, cryptids, time travel stories, and anything I found to be mysterious or interesting. I had just come across videos on John Titor and other time travel videos in the summer of 2016. Jumping back and forth between topics, I kept seeing thumbnails for videos that had Nelson Mandela or the Berenstein (Berenstain now) Bears images. I had no clue what it was, or why it was coming up on my searches, but I decided to watch them. The first video I saw had a robot voice and made no sense to me at all. I decided it was probably just clickbait and moved on.

Now for a long time I had already started to document changes I was seeing in the sky. The sky had been looking very strange to me starting sometime before 2012. The Sun had turned a blazing white color during high points of the day, and the clouds were very low with strange shapes and colors. I would post photos on social media hoping someone would comment, or agree that it was different. No one ever did, or even noticed what I was noticing. At the end of August 2016, I watched a video on the Ford logo changing and I was completely floored by what I was seeing. I had owned two different Ford Escorts for more than fifteen years, and the logo never looked the way it is now. The F had a very strange curly line on it now. That was the video that made my hair stand on end and get that WTF moment that many have tried to describe, but really there are no words for it. I must have watched it four or five times in a row trying to make sense of everything I was now noticing that had somehow changed without being officially changed, and probably happened long before I noticed the changes.

The big ones for me were the creator of the Peanuts cartoons Charles Shultz always being Shulz now; the curly pig tail on the Ford logo F now; Fruit Loops being Froot now; and many more. The way they are now and have supposedly always been is not how I remember them being in the past. It felt like information overload at the time.

I did what I am sure many others may have done too, try to debunk it or find a logical explanation. But the more I looked for answers, the more I realized it was something that could not be explained. Looking back, it now seems that I saw the changes way before, but just passed them off as new branding or product changes. By the end of 2016, I had found many other channels that shared the same experience not only in changes, but the physical effects too. There was ringing in the ears, time passing faster, and time slips/glitches being reported by many. I joined groups and was participating in the chats of many Mandela Effect livestreams. In February of 2017, I posted my first video of a collection of sky photos on YouTube under the user name DEAD GPK (GPK stands for Garbage Pail Kid). I have since posted many more videos, and have become a supporter of many channels. I have also collaborated with many others, passing information or sharing sky photos from other sky watchers. I even discovered a few changes myself that others passed along to their subscribers on their channels. You can always see me around here, there, and everywhere. I could probably go on forever recounting some awesome times chatting with everyone in the M.E. and sky watching community. The community has become very important to me and I have learned to listen, but in a non-judgmental way.

I do feel the changes have made me more aware of everything around me. At times it can be very shocking and sometimes scary, but overall I feel it is not a bad thing at all. I do get this overwhelming feeling of being "homesick" sometimes, like that feeling when you have been gone away from home and you are ready to get back. I cannot say for sure what I believe is causing the effect - my perspective is always changing on what it could be, and I do entertainment many theories on this. I do truly feel that it is a smaller piece to a bigger thing that is starting to happen all around us. There is a bigger plan or picture forming, and for me personally something spiritual and supernatural is happening, but in a good way. I hope I have shared my perspective the best way I could and feel nothing but love for everyone.

Juan, DEAD GPK YouTube channel

Testimony 2

Everything changed around 2015 for me, but I do not like to blame CERN for the Mandela Effect. I think it is more of a natural phenomenon – an evolution in spiritual consciousness. When I first looked into spiritual awakening, around 2015, I was sick and was hospitalized with double pneumonia. I did not feel like I was going to die, but family members were worried. This is when I started to see Mandela Effect videos like the Berenstain Bears et cetera. As an artist myself, when I saw Mandela Effect changes to the Thinker statue and the Mona Lisa, I knew the phenomenon was real. I knew for sure they had changed several times. I saw the original Thinker statue in Mexico at a special exhibition, so I have no doubt about the changes since then.

Once awake and able to see the M.E., I started getting involved on Shane's channel doing shows in the early days, but it triggered my partner, and that was something we had to work through. I started my own channel, Josee, where we could just hang out and talk about anything at all on my Lightworkers Hangout livestreams. The Mandela Effect is part of it, but not all of it, but it is what initially brought us all together.

I think the M.E. is just a tool to wake people up to the fact the world is not what we thought it was - the world is changing and evolving. Where there is deception or lies about reality I think we have to go within and change ourselves (our beliefs and feelings). It is not going to come from without, because it is not out there to find. I think the M.E. is a good thing. I think we created it to wake us up - like our future selves created it to wake us up now instead of later. Why some of us wake ourselves up and others do not? I have no clue. And if we force it on others who are not ready they freak out and get scared and angry. So I let people wake up when they are ready, not when I am ready for them to see it. I think some of the angriest people are the most "religious", but those with the most "faith" feel safe. Some people give their power away to one person or book, and if it changes, they get scared and angry because they are no longer saved by that person or book - they have to do the work themselves for ascension.

I never felt any fear. I thought it was exciting that matter could shift and change. Before that I had the feeling something was coming. I would watch the sky and look for changes. I told my partner I can feel it - something new and important is coming. I am not religious, but I *feel* more than I think, so I could feel that something was brewing. I am Native Algonquin and live in

Canada, but I was raised in the Catholic religion. Still, I got bits and pieces of our traditions from my grandparents, and throughout my life I connected with my native roots, so being in and with nature is very important to me. It is here that we get closer to God than in buildings made by men. Nature changes all the time, nothing is static if it is alive. Maybe that is why the changes of the Mandela Effect don't scare me. Change is natural and change is good – change is necessary for life.

I think it is also about seeing it for what it is, and not engaging emotionally with it. Getting emotional is not always good. I'm not saying ignore the feelings seeing the Mandela Effect brings up, but feel them, and let it go so you can move on to the next realization about your reality. This keeps you growing instead of getting stuck in one feeling or the other about this phenomenon. Easier said than done, I know, because I'm still working on this myself!

Josee YouTube channel

Testimony 3

I came across Shane on his Unbiased & On the Fence channel on YouTube through a reference from Allison Coe's channel. I was blown away by his research and videos about the Mandela Effect. I have read the Bible through numerous times and have memorized so many scriptures. The biggest goosebump Spirit flowing synergy for me is the Bible verse Isaiah 11:6: which for me and many used to be, "The Lion shall lay down with the lamb." That is how I memorized it. Now it states a WOLF shall dwell with the lamb. I was weak at the knees and just laid flat on my back to take this in. My first thought was a scripture reference to be aware of wolves in sheep's clothing in Luke 7. What or who could change the Bible?! Revelation 22:19 warns us, "And if any man shall take away from the words of the book of this prophecy, God shall take away his part out of the book of life, and out of the holy city, and from the things which are written in this book." Isaiah 40:8 states, "The grass withereth, the flower fadeth: but the word of our God shall stand forever." Scripture upon scripture about the word of God kept flowing through my mind.

I must say I had no fear, just a knowing that this is part of a huge energetic shift. I called in to Shane's Friday night livestream and we discussed the changes in the Bible. It was in that discussion that Shane triggered an awakening of spiritual truth in me. The Living Word is Alive! Peter 1:23, "Being born again, not of corruptible seed, but of incorruptible, by the word of God, which liveth and abideth for ever."

Finally, I now know that God is bigger than the Bible. The God I knew was the God of the Bible. Now I embrace the expanded Living Word! I no longer feel guilt for searching, reading and studying anything outside of the written word! Having the freedom to put it all together has allowed me to integrate spiritual knowledge, wisdom and understanding. I am in gratitude for the Mandela Effect and the awakening it has triggered.

April

Testimony 4

I remember questioning my memory as early as the 1990s, as things like celebrity deaths seemed to reverse themselves. When I saw the Mandela Effect change video about the *Berenstain Bears* books, I was hooked! It had a name now – the Mandela Effect, and I must have watched every M.E. video on YouTube I could find for at least a month. I felt exhausted and excited by the new possibilities of consciousness controlling matter and reality. I had always been taught it's mind over matter, but never saw it demonstrated so obviously before! I was a little surprised to see others dismiss it as nonsense, or ask me not to talk about it because of fear when I tried to show people examples of the phenomenon, so I just let them be. I figured they will see it when they are ready to see it. I was lucky to have one close family member affected, so we could discuss them as they occurred. For more information and community support, I turned to YouTube, where I found Unbiased & On the Fence and a loving supportive community of people there who were also affected by the Mandela Effect. Many of them were fellow artists, musicians, poets, philosophers and deep thinkers like me. They also seemed more kind and open-minded, less strict with religious dogma, and way less fearful than most people commenting on most other channels Mandela Effected or not! I felt so happy to find such an amazing group of people it was like coming home to a new old family. Sure, there is plenty of fear on the Mandela Effect out there, saying it is caused by aliens, demons, atom smashers, quantum computing, the Antichrist, or even the end of the world ... but it sure does not feel that way to me. I guess you have to be afraid of these things BEFORE you see the Mandela Effect to be afraid of them after you see it. Otherwise it just shows how powerful we really are. How our consciousness collectively affects the matrix all around us. How we are the masters of our reality here, and how God put us here to figure this out, and become the masters of our own material world in a cooperative and loving way.

Maybe our human rulers figured this out a long time ago and scared us away from everything – even our own destiny as spiritual cocreators in physical matter. We sure don't need reptiles or demons to do that much. The future seems brighter now, like we can band together and save this planet and ourselves from ignorant greedy human governing destruction. To me the Mandela Effect is a wake-up call and a lifeline to positive change here and now, not just in the nebulous future that never quite arrives.
Susanne

Testimony 5

When I first noticed the Mandela Effect videos on YouTube they seemed strange and funny, like Jiffy peanut butter becoming Jiff, Berenstein Bears becoming Berenstain, and Tom Hanks saying, "Life *was* like a box of chocolates" in the movie *Forrest Gump*, instead of life *is* like a box of chocolates. So I thought it was an internet meme, hoax, or just a joke. As I looked further into it, there seemed to be more and more evidence that this was a real thing – that some things in our world were suddenly changing in mysterious ways. Nothing was immune from it - books, movies, TV shows, famous movie lines, car logos, company names, food product names .... None of that seemed to really matter until it got more serious with changes to well-known passages in the Bible, geography, history, and the scariest of all – changes to the human body and animals.

I wanted to figure out how and why things were changing, and a lot of the videos I found about the Mandela Effect were indicating this was a sign of the end of the world (like the Biblical Apocalypse), even though here were no direct references to the Mandela Effect in the Bible. Other frightened people were claiming particle colliders and quantum computing was ripping holes in our matrix, or creating portals for demons to enter who apparently had nothing better to do but take the dash out of the Kit-Kat candy bar and change a lot of car logos. These doom and gloom videos scared me at first, until logic crept in and I realized there was actually no evidence to support the fear. I just couldn't take any of the "fearporn" seriously. It went against all logic, all facts, and my natural instincts. Some even claimed that time travelers were messing everything up, or we were living in a simulation like a computer game that had gotten glitchy or broken. Again, without much evidence. So I kept looking and found only a few channels looking at the Mandela Effect without dark-colored glasses on, who took a more balanced, logical, scientific, or spiritual approach to it. I felt a sense of relief in these online communities where people could see things changing around them, but still feel safe like the world was not actually ending. Some even saw hope in the phenomenon that it was a sign of increased awareness or an upward evolution of consciousness to see how matter works.

Where does matter come from? What made all of these particles that make up our physical world from the clothes we wear to the mountains we climb in the first place? I never even thought of that before, so in that way the Mandela Effect had a very positive affect on me, by making me think more about reality. I never felt lonely, scared, or sad. I guess because I showed it to family members and some could see it right away like me, while others could not and just laughed at me. One asked me not to talk about it because it scared her to think matter could just up and change like that. But a few of those who initially laughed when I showed them have come around to seeing it too now, so I think it's just a matter of time before everyone sees it and experiences it.

Once you see it you can't unsee it and there is no escaping it. Matter is a part of our world and it is doing some unexpected and unpredictable things, but hasn't our world always surprised us? Things change and we adapt. That's the story of evolution. I think this is part of human evolution too, so I don't see it as the end of the world - just the beginning of seeing the world differently.
Elizabeth

Testimony 6

I think the Mandela Effect is interesting because it's still a mystery. Why do things suddenly change - what is causing that? It doesn't scare me because most of my friends see it too. We're young (my

friends are 18 – 26) and it has been around most of our lives, so it seems normal to us, but we do remember things that were different when we were younger. I was raised in a family that looks for UFOs and thinks mental telepathy should be normal - so how could this scare me? Honestly, we don't give it much thought, but it is fun sometimes to be the first to see a change before your friends do. I have no idea what is causing it – maybe the same thing that causes life.
Stacy

PART TWO

PAULO M. PINTO

YOUTUBE CONTENT CREATOR:

SPIRITWALKER CHANNEL

www.youtube.com/Spiritwalker

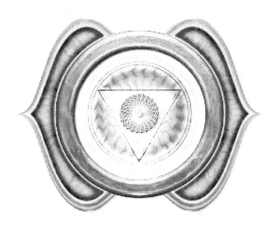

Trouble at the Limits of Reality

Sex in the City? Yes. That is how I personally remember the title of the popular sitcom. The show debuted in 1998, the same year I moved to Australia from my native Brazil. In that year, everything changed in my life, everything was new, exciting and special. My memories of that time are as vivid as it gets. I remember thinking that the "in the city" was somewhat peculiar – that the whole title was a little odd, but wasn't that the main point of a sitcom title? Should it not be quirky and make people do a double take? I remember asking myself whether the show was going to be about how people have sex when they are in the city, as opposed to when they go back to the suburbs … Or perhaps the premise was that it is easier to find sex when one is in the city, and not out in a rural area somewhere. As that was my first year living in an English-speaking country, I also remember questioning if the reason I found "in the city" odd was because my grasp of colloquial English was still imperfect. Perhaps the title was a reference to slang I had not yet learned. I remember thinking about the "in" over and over, as if it were part of my assimilation process. Then sometime in 2015, I came across cascades of videos on the internet where befuddled fans claimed that the title of the show had somehow changed to Sex and the City. Actually, it had not changed. According to all available records – old tapes, promotional material, websites, magazines, you name it – the title had always been *Sex **and** the City*. All available evidence showed the title had always had the "and" in it since its inception. Everything I looked up showed there never was a show called *Sex **in** the City*. (1)

Initially, I wondered if the confusion could be due to a geographical or market-specific foible. Perhaps the show was launched in Australia with a different name from the US original? Digging deeper, however, I found that was not the case. US folk were as stumped as us down-under. Brits, Canadians and Kiwis also reported remembering the "in". People in social media and internet chatrooms were perplexed, because, just like me, the current title of the show was not how they remembered it.

I would have happily forgotten about this issue, had I not come across an entire library of memories that somehow no longer matched existing evidence. My memories of certain company logos, song lyrics, album covers, commercial product names, movie titles, catch phrases and names of places ... no longer matched existing historical records. Of course, initially I thought my memories were false. Somehow I had fantasized about things that never existed; but I soon found a large number of people on the internet complaining about the same alleged false memories. What is more, their supposedly false memories corresponded *exactly* with my own. Could all these be made-up memories? How could different people, of different ages, and in different parts of the world hold exactly the same false memories?

Particularly disturbing to some people were perceived changes to Biblical verses. When it comes to the Bible, as in movies to some extent, people tend to memorize certain passages or scenes. Some of them become iconic in the process. They have studied them over and over, and the memories usually hold for them an intense emotional charge as well. As we know, emotional memories are vivid and lasting, and collective emotional memories are usually considered reliable. This threw a monkey wrench on sceptics' arguments that the whole thing was just false memories of a particular group or culture. Besides, it was happening everywhere: befuddle comments from Germany, confused observations by Americans, Canadians and Brits going crazy, mystified Australians and baffled Brazilians ... what could possibly explain this? Ladies and gentlemen - welcome to the Mandela Effect.

Stranger Than Fiction

In this and the following sections, we will consider what the Mandela Effect could be, according to possible theories about our reality. But before that, it is useful to take a step back and acknowledge we have no flipping idea about what reality truly is! Is it a simulation of some sort? A four-dimensional slice in the cake of the multiverse? Is it a hologram? All of the above?

Of course, we can never experience reality itself. The only thing we can experience is the information purportedly sent by reality to us and transduced into electric pulses by our senses and nervous system. We cannot know reality; we only know the tail end of a chain of electrical stimuli, which allegedly started 'out there' somewhere. There is no way to know what 'out there' is, or even if there really is an 'out there' - a material world sending us information to be decoded in our minds and with our senses.

When my eldest son was four, he claimed he did not need to go to school. His argument was that he already knew all there was to be known: he could run, he could jump, he could speak, and he could throw things around. What else was there to be learned? Why should he bother going to school? Humanity often acts the same.

By the late twentieth century, humanity claimed to know everything there was to be known. We displayed the same cute simple-mindedness as a toddler trying to weasel his way out of starting school. We had learned all physics, all mathematics, we had gone through all possible social and historical upheavals, tried all possible forms of government … We often felt we knew everything about ourselves, our biology and everything about the universe. There were talks, books and papers naively proclaiming the end of physics, the end of history, and so forth. However, a few pesky issues remained. These issues were brushed aside as nonsense by an overly confident scientific establishment. But open-minded and careful examination shows that these issues cannot be dismissed so easily. They challenge our understanding, experience, and appreciation of reality. Some of these issues could be directly linked to the Mandela Effect, and understanding them could help us figure out why our collective memories seem to be changing. For other issues, the link with the Mandela Effect could be more peripheral. What is important is that when we open our minds and decide to investigate metaphysical phenomena, we never know where the road will take us. Once the cat is out of the bag and we accept that materialistic scientificism does not describe reality, an exciting world of weird phenomena opens up. Let us briefly look at a few.

Synchronicities

Swiss psychiatrist Carl Jung noted that some of his patients would often experience what he called "meaningful coincidences", which he termed synchronicities. (2) Jung conjectured that synchronicities were generated by some causal connecting principle. Situations may sometimes be connected in a meaningful way, even if we do not understand the nature of the connection. The classic example is one of Jung's patients having a dream of a golden scarab. The patient was rational and logical and many of her psychological difficulties stemmed from this inflexibility. In one session, she was recounting to Jung the dream in which she was presented with a golden scarab jewel. Like most materialists, she thought the dream was meaningless and had no connection to the real world. At one stage, they both heard a gentle tapping on the window. Jung stood up, and saw that the tapping was caused by a small bug outside. He opened the window and a gold-green colored scarabaeoid beetle flew in. Jung captured the insect with his hand and he handed the beetle to his patient saying, "Here is your scarab."

If you have enough metaphysical curiosity to be reading a book like this, then you have probably already noticed many synchronicities in your own life. You may be asking yourself about their meaning and causes, but unfortunately there is no consensus. Synchronicities are very personal experiences. Some argue that they could be signposts from one's own Higher Self to arouse curiosity – a gentle nudge alerting us to look beyond the veil of our physical reality. Others suggest that synchronicities are 'glitches in the matrix' – small bugs in the code of reality. Whatever they are, synchronicities exist and they cannot be explained away by statistics or probabilities. They are real events that suggest our current understanding of reality is either wrong, or at least incomplete.

Some people wonder if the Mandela Effect and synchronicities are not somehow related. Both phenomena challenge our materialistic view of a reality governed by random physical interactions. Both phenomena suggest that the human mind perceives and perhaps influences reality in ways we do not yet grasp. Both phenomena conflict with our conventional assumption of linear and sequential time. Could it be possible that by studying the Mandela Effect we will shed light on the mysterious phenomenon of synchronicities? Conversely, can our intuition or the new science of consciousness tell us anything about synchronicities that will help us understand the Mandela Effect? Both synchronicities and the Mandela Effect are consistent with the hypothesis that our reality could be a type of simulation. Synchronicities could be messages or signposts placed by those in charge of the simulation to guide us towards certain objectives or experiences. The Mandela Effect could be a glitch in the matrix, whereby the simulation changes our perception of the past and present, but some people with more sensitivity may still be able to recall residuals of the 'old' reality (reality before the changes). We will discuss this more throughout this book.

UFO Phenomena

The phenomenon of Unidentified Flying Objects (UFOs) currently being changed to Unidentified Aerial Phenomenon (UAPs) hardly needs an introduction. I myself saw lights in the sky pulsating and changing position very rapidly when I was a teenager in my native town of Recife, Brazil. A group of about ten terrified people experienced this with me. The next day, one local newspaper gave us the typical "nothing to see here" excuse. It said the strange moving lights had been military rocket tests. So, we learned that the whole town had also seen the weird phenomenon, and many had contacted the authorities. Because of this we can easily discard the possibility of hallucination. Unlike the US and other advanced countries, the Brazilian military is underfunded and cannot even keep up with the latest military technology officially available. The suggestion that they were involved in advanced technology testing was rather hilarious. Besides, later in life, I learned that Brazil is a hotspot for UFO sightings.

UFOs have been seen by all cultures, social segments, countries, and at all times. There are descriptions of UFOs in ancient Sumerian texts, ancient Egyptian hieroglyphs, and even in the Bible (Old and New Testament). At this stage in our civilization, there are only two types of people who do not believe that non-terrestrial intelligent life exists and is visiting us: the clueless and those with vested interests. Without meaning to be insulting the clueless tend to be those individuals who are perfectly content to believe only what mainstream media tells them to believe. Those with vested interests usually have two motivations. The first is the concentration of power. The Illuminati, cabal, deep state, shadow government, (whatever you wish to call the small group of human ruling elite) controls the information allowed on mainstream media, and they wield it to keep oppressing the rest of humanity, whom some report they call 'useless eaters' or 'the dead'. (3) The second motivation is hubris. A lot of individuals not necessarily associated with the elites or the cabal will ignore UFO evidence to protect their reputations. They wonder how they can keep their jobs and status as respected police officers, doctors, politicians, scientists, theologians or scholars if they acknowledge having seen something so ground-breaking and unconventional.

Some materialists, most of whom have vested interests in the suppression of this kind of information, would say that UFOs are simply mass hallucination. Yet they do not give any explanation for what mass hallucination is, or how it works. If someone showed evidence that things such as mass hallucinations do exist, that would in itself be a fascinating metaphysical phenomenon – proving the existence of a shared subconscious or 'hivemind'. How does one hallucination transfer itself non-locally from one person to another, across regions, cultural backgrounds, languages, religious inclinations, and levels of education like Mandela Effect observations do? Alas, instead of addressing these questions, materialists just put their heads in the sand and call anyone that is not doing the same 'crazy' or 'conspiracy theorists'.

This is precisely the same approach most people take on the Mandela Effect. It is far too convenient to ignore something that challenges your comfortable view of reality. UFOs are scary stuff for a lot of people. It may challenge our notions of religion, who we are, and where we came from. Many people may not be ready to take that jump yet, and the information should not be forced upon them. However, for those of us who are trying to understand what is going on, open-mindedness is essential.

Some researchers have connected the Mandela Effect to UFO phenomenon, suggesting that non-terrestrial beings could be altering the way humans perceive reality. Many in the truth-seeking community associate UFO's with time travel. According to them, the so-called aliens could be humans from the future who came back in time to assist the development of their ancestors. Proponents of this theory suggest that it is possible that the interference of beings from the future in our current timeline could have caused it to splinter and change. In the minds of some, this possibility opens up a big can of worms associating the Mandela Effect to UFO phenomenon. Are the perceived changes in our timeline the result of deliberate manipulation by beings from the future to make sure humanity evolves in a certain way? Could these changes be accidental by-products of timeline manipulation? How did Mandela Effect experiencers manage to preserve residual memories of the original timelines before manipulation?

Superluminal Matter, Entropy, and the Law of Attraction

Einstein's theories of relativity suggest that nothing in the universe can move at speeds above the speed of light. This is a fundamental rule in physics and has been accepted as gospel for a century. However, this may very well be another dogma accepted by the scientific community - despite being false. In truth, there is no impediment for a particle to become superluminal (accelerate beyond the speed of light), as physicist Fred Alan Wolf and many others point out. (4) *The Law of One* material argues that the astral or metaphysical reality is made up of the same subatomic particles that constitute our physical universe, except that these particles have gone superluminal. (5) Physicist Fred Alan Wolf also argues that a subatomic particle that is accelerated beyond the speed of light would exit our physical universe. (6)

Every massive object in our universe has a certain amount of energy. As the object moves - its energy changes. The interesting thing about moving faster than light is that you may end up with negative energy. The technicalities are not essential for our discussion here, but those mathematically curious can check out a few ideas about this in the chapter endnotes. (7)

It is difficult to imagine what negative energy could possibly be, but there is a direct implication to our discussion about entropy and time. The Fundamental Thermodynamic Relation suggests that under certain conditions there is a direct relationship between the energy and the entropy of a system. If you increase the energy in a system, you will also increase the entropy of that system. Entropy itself is a difficult concept to understand, but it could be broadly defined as the degree of disorder or chaos in a system.

This makes intuitive sense. For example, in an ice cube, water molecules are neatly packed together. If we increase the energy applied to this ice cube by heating it up, the ice will melt, and the molecules will no longer be neatly stacked. Instead, they will be moving and sliding over each other, which is the characteristic of liquid water. Because the molecules will be sliding over each other, the degree of the disorder of this system (entropy) is higher than if the molecules were all stacked neatly and statically on top of each other - as they are in the state of ice. If you give this system even more energy, the water will become vapor and the molecules will be flying and bumping into each other – meaning the chaos, or entropy in the system will have increased even more.

Physics shows that the entropy of a system is either stable or increasing as time goes by, but it never decreases. This result is known as the Second Law of Thermodynamics and can be visualized by simple examples. For instance, you cannot unscramble an egg once it has been scrambled. The egg system when scrambled is in a more chaotic state, which means high entropy, than when it was in its whole original state. Left alone, the scrambled egg, as a system, would never unscramble itself with time. That just never happens. Another example: an apple on the ground is a relatively orderly system. All molecules have a precise location and form a very specific orderly structure: the stem, the peel, the seeds etc. If you leave the apple alone on the ground, it will rot. Eventually bacteria, air and moisture will rot the apple so much it will no longer be an apple - just an unstructured mush of organic goo. That shows that the system went from a low entropy state (the orderly apple) to a high entropy state (the rotten apple mush).

You can also see how entropy works if you open a bottle of perfume in a room. Initially, as soon as you open the bottle all molecules are still close together inside it. This is a low entropy state. If you leave the bottle open for a while, the scent of the perfume will fill the whole room. What happened? The molecules of the perfume dissipated among the molecules of the air: a high entropy (disordered) state.

As we saw in the example of ice to water to vapor, if you apply energy to a system, its entropy will increase. If there is a positive relationship between energy and entropy, could it be that negative energy could be associated with negative entropy? If positive entropy is a tendency for a system to become more and more disorderly as time goes by, negative entropy would be a tendency for a system to become more and more orderly as time goes by. In the perfume bottle opened in a room scenario, perfume molecules dissipate through the air and eventually saturate the entire room. This happens because this system, like all material, physical systems, is endowed with positive entropy. If the system operated with negative entropy something weird would happen. The state of the system would develop inversely. The molecules could start saturating the entire room, but would progressively concentrate until they all agglutinated together somewhere. Does this happen? Of course, it never happens in our material universe, but it may very well be how astral (metaphysical) energies operate.

People who have the power of clairvoyance often discuss how thought forms attract other thought forms of similar vibration. In addition, we have all heard of the Law of Attraction, whereby like attracts like: positive thoughts, beliefs, feelings and actions attract positive outcomes or results. The Law of Attraction has been proven in real life and experiments. There have been examples of people that changed their lives, their careers and even healed themselves from incurable diseases using the power of feelings and beliefs with the Law of Attraction. There are so many books, videos, talks and websites dedicated to the Law of Attraction that we could not possibly reference them all here.

So, what is the point of all this discussion? What is the link between negative entropy, the Law of Attraction, and the Mandela Effect? Well, if we do have the capacity to shape and reshape reality using the power of our minds and hearts (thoughts, beliefs and feelings), as the Law of Attraction suggests - could it be that the Mandela Effect is an example of humanity unconsciously changing our collective past? Is it possible that a shift in human thinking could have changed not only our present reality, but our entire timeline? These are tantalizing questions and will be discussed in depth in the next sections.

The 100th Monkey Effect

Also known as the Law of Critical Mass, the 100th Monkey Effect is the proposition that individuals belonging to a group may unconsciously intuit knowledge that has been learned by a minimum number of group members. (8) For example, if you belong to and have strong mental links with a society, you may unwittingly and effortlessly learn skills that have been mastered by other members of that society – so long as the number of those knowing it has reached a critical level for it to automatically spread to the whole group.

The concept was proposed in the 1950's by scientists studying populations of Japanese snow monkeys. They noted that when a certain number of monkeys in an isolated island of the Pacific Ocean learned a new skill (such as washing food with sea water instead of eating it coated in sand), other monkeys on their island would also develop the same skill. The unexpected finding was that the new skill would also spread throughout several groups of snow monkeys on different islands, even though these groups had no contact with each other.

The phenomenon suggests that a group (or a species) could have something akin to a collective mind to which individual members are all somehow connected. Once a new skill, idea or concept reaches critical mass in a species, it is uploaded to the collective mind, becoming instantaneously available to all members of that species. Of course, materialists scoff at this concept. Wikipedia (at the time of this writing) derides the 100th Monkey Effect as a hypothetical phenomenon. However, the effect has been documented in many experiments, and is consistent with the metaphysical view that individual minds are non-locally interconnected. (Non-locally means outside, or beyond time and space, instantaneously and without physical interaction.) This is coherent with Carl Jung's notion of the superconscious mind shared by members of a species. It is also consistent with Rupert Sheldrake's notion of the Morphic Field that connects all individuals of a species, and guides their development in a harmonious and coherent way. In addition, the 100th Monkey Effect is consistent with Erwin Laszlo's concept of the Akashic Field (A-field) connecting individuals and availing non-local transfers of information between them. Finally, the concept is consistent with the *Law of One* book series notion of a Social

Memory Complex, whereby members of a social group share the same collective mind that exchanges information and feelings to all members non-locally. While these complexes are usually fully formed in societies of very advanced beings, it is possible that a rudimentary group mind could form even among so-called irrational animals. For instance, ants and bees act in coordinated ways while building, feeding, and protecting their nests and hives.

If real, the 100th Monkey Effect is one possible explanation for the explosion of Mandela Effect examples that took place around the mid-2010s. Around that time, all of the sudden, people were finding Mandela Effect residuals (records, photos, footage et cetera) that corresponded to their cherished memories of how things were before the M.E. changes took place. Of course, the expansion of communication through the internet contributed to the sharing of Mandela Effect ideas and residuals, and whole communities of Mandela Effect experiencers began forming. But the internet had been around for a long time and there is still no convincing explanation for the rapid dissemination of M.E. testimonials suddenly appearing only around the mid-2010s.

With all of these unknown quirks of our reality, can we really dismiss something like the Mandela Effect as mass hallucination? Note that the very concept of mass hallucination is in itself fascinating metaphysics. How could a person catch a hallucination from another like you catch a cold? In the next few chapters we explore some exciting theories that could help us understand what reality is, and how the Mandela Effect could be explained as a by-product of each possible scenario.

Do We Live in A Simulation?

The idea that we may live inside a computer simulation has been around for a long time. So long in fact, that it has already left the realms of academic speculation and conspiracy theories to reach the mainstream. Most of us have seen the blockbuster movie series *The Matrix*, which gives this topic a very gloomy treatment. In 2016, a report by Bank of America Merrill Lynch argued that there was a 20 to 50 percent chance that we are living in a simulated matrix. (9) This possibility is also supported and promoted by entrepreneur Elon Musk, and Oxford philosophy professor Nick Bostrom. (10) The argument is that any civilization advanced enough to create computers would eventually create simulations so perfect that it would be impossible for people to distinguish simulation from reality. Programmers have been creating computer games that are more and more realistic with each new update. Elon Musk predicts, "If you assume any rate of improvement at all, then the games will become indistinguishable from reality." (11) Why would an advanced civilization create computer simulations? For the same reasons that we on planet Earth create games – for fun; to experience and learn with challenging situations; to live exciting adventures, or difficult conditions without risking life and limb. One of the strongest arguments supporting the possibility that we are living in a computer simulation - is basic probability.

Imagine that there was the flesh and blood civilization A out there in the universe that became advanced enough to invent computers. This civilization would grow and develop its technology and create ever more realistic computer simulations. These simulations would grow so realistic, that at some point, an entirely simulated civilization B would be created inside the computers of the original flesh and blood civilization A. (Think for example about how today we have games like The Sims, whereby a player can create an entire society and an entire civilization just for fun.) For the simulation to be perfect, artificial civilization B would be forced to stay in character, that is, would not be allowed to figure out it is simulated. In this way, civilization B would proceed in its own mental and technological progress, much in the same way as civilization A did. The technological progress of civilization B would mean that it too would at some point develop computers and computer simulations. As these simulations become more complex and autonomous, a third civilization – let's call it civilization C – would be created inside of the computers of simulated civilization B.

You can see where we are going with this. There would be only one flesh and blood civilization A, and an endless string of simulated civilizations B, C, D, E et cetera. Thus, it is far more probable that our current civilization on Earth will turn out to be one of the many simulated civilizations, than the single original flesh and blood civilization that started the whole thing.

Another argument supporting this theory is that we can only experience reality through our senses (smell, taste, vision, touch and hearing); that whatever reality is, humans cannot experience it directly, but only through the filters of the five senses. And this is the problem, because all our five senses do is to produce electrical signals that are interpreted by the nervous system to the brain. In theory, there would be no difference if these electrical signals were produced by something 'real out there', or by some type of machine. If we were living in a simulated reality there would be no way of knowing it, because it would seem to the senses to be real at all times.

As we are going to see below, the Mandela Effect is perfectly compatible with the theory that we live in a simulation. In fact, the Mandela Effect even seems to corroborate or reinforce this theory, and this validation happens in the most remarkable way. But before we delve into it, we need to investigate the simulation theory a little more closely.

The Limits of Reality

The simulation theory of the universe could possibly explain some of the puzzles we struggle with regarding the limits of reality.

One curious example is déjà vu, in which an observer has the strong sensation of having already experienced the current situation. In the context of a simulation, this could be explained in a few different ways. Every simulation follows a plan, a preconceived set of situations that a simulated character could be subjected to. When computer programmers are designing a simulation, they plan every little detail. Before simulating, say, a castle on top of a mountain, they have done a lot of planning and design. The programmers have tried different textures for the walls, researched the types of plants that would prevail in that climate or region, played around with lighting and shadows et cetera. The same is true if the programmers are planning a scene where two characters meet and go on a quest. The designers plan everything beforehand: the vegetation, the clothing, the surroundings, the weather. If a player was also in some way part of the design stage, they might have some strange recollections of the programmed places and situations they planned before and are now experiencing.

Psychic abilities may also be explained with the simulation theory. If we live in a simulation, it is possible that what we call psychic abilities could just be the players somehow seeing beyond the code. Let me explain. Suppose we live in a simulation and my character is at a given point of the map. If the map is two-dimensional, it would have two coordinates. Therefore, let's say that my character called A in the simulation is currently located at point (10,10), that is, ten units of width and 10 units of depth from a certain reference point in the simulated map. This information could be stored in the computer's memory as something like "A[10;10]". Your character, called B, is situated very far away from mine. Let's imagine that your character's coordinates were one thousand units of width and three thousand units of depth from the reference point. So, the location of your character would be stored in the memory of the computer as something like "B[1000;3000]". In the same way, the location of all other characters C, D, E et cetera would be stored in the program memory. In the simulated map, your character would be a very long way away from mine, in fact, there could be a mountain range, or an entire ocean between these two points. There is no way that our characters could know of each other or interact with each other because of the (simulated) distance and all of the geographical hurdles between them.

However, in the memory of the computer, the coordinates of character locations would most likely be stored physically close to each other. Computers tend to store information in lists or tables, and very often (if memory has not been fragmented) a list will be stored in a contiguous physical area of memory. That is, the list of all the character locations is likely to look something like: A[10;10] B[1000;3000] C[456;6590] D[0,2] and so on.

Now imagine for a moment that the computer accesses this list to read the location of my character A, but the reading device is faulty or not properly calibrated, and reads the entry for A and also the entry for B, which is next in the list and therefore very close in the physical memory mapping. This could mean that my character knows his own location, but he now also knows the location of character B. Without having any simulated interaction with character B, my own character would receive what would appear to be a flash of consciousness informing him of the location of that character. This 'flash of consciousness' would be nothing more than an error or poor calibration in the memory reading device. But to the characters immersed in the simulation it would feel like remote viewing, or a telepathic connection.

This logic could explain why we tend to be more telepathic with those we love or know. It could be that all the information about the family and friends of our character in the simulation is stored in contiguous quick access lists physically stored close together to accelerate retrieval. When accessing these contiguous lists, the memory reader device could more easily err and access info about other characters close to us in the simulation and in the physical memory - leading to a more psychic connection between those characters. Psychic phenomena (including déjà vu) in the simulation could also be generated by other types of malfunctions, such as compression errors, transmission glitches, and other anomalies.

The simulation theory also suggests some interesting new ways to think about some scientific puzzles. For instance, the existence of an absolute reference grid (the Ether) that would permeate the entire universe is solved when we think that reality could be a computer simulation. When a simulation creates a synthetic universe, it needs to create synthetic space (the reference system of coordinates we discussed above). When your character in the game moves around the simulated environment, this movement is simply a change in coordinates being recorded in the computer. This system of coordinates must be consistent for all characters regardless of where they are in the game. Therefore, the simulation needs to start from a reference grid that encompasses and underpins the entire simulated reality.

The simulation possibility also helps us understand the enigmas of quantum physics. As we discussed previously, quantum physics states that reality does not exist until and unless it is observed. This is entirely consistent with a computer simulation. Think of a simulation computer game like so many available these days. When you log into the simulated reality to play, the computer must create that reality for you. Nothing really existed before you logged in, because if no one was playing the game there was no need for the computer to generate any simulated environment. It is only when a player logs in – to observe and interact with the simulated reality – that the computer starts generating that environment.

Proponents of the simulation theory would suggest that the reason quantum physicists say that nothing exists without observation is because nothing is being simulated if there is no one experiencing the simulation. Quantum physics states that when a subatomic particle is not being observed, it exists only as waves of probabilities. These probabilities could just be the range of all possible ways the computer could simulate the particle if there were someone logged in to experience that particle. Without a user logged in to the game, there is no need for the computer to manifest that particle or create that environment, even though the possibility for it to do so always exists. It is like a rich invisible landscape just waiting for a player or observer to bring it into existence just by looking at it.

The simulation theory could help us understand the complex interaction between destiny and free will. Many believe that destiny is set and there is no escaping it. What is 'written' to happen will happen. Others hold that humans all have free will and can change their lives and destiny through their own choices. The simulation theory offers us a way if reconciling these two ideas. You will remember that in some games (especially the older ones), the characters only have a limited number of actions they can take: jump, duck, run, or punch. This menu of possible actions may even be rather long and complex, but it is certainly finite. The action that your character will actually take at a certain moment will be decided by your free will, but the choice will be restricted to that particular menu. Here we see an example in which a player is relatively free to decide on an action to take (free will), but the set of possible action choices is pre-determined (destiny). This type of interaction may help us understand the dichotomy between these two concepts. The understanding that reality, if it is a simulation, is intrinsically dependent on whether there is someone experiencing it or not - is very important for our understanding of the link between the Mandela Effect and the simulation theory of the universe. But before we go there, we need to discuss who could be responsible for the simulation itself.

Who Is in Charge?

The issue with the simulation theory is that a computer simulation would necessarily require a programmer or programmers. So, if we live in a computer simulation, who or what is programing it? There are many people out there who think humanity is under the yoke of a nefarious group of beings that control the simulation. This has been portrayed in many ways from the Gnostics' discussion about Archons, the Sumerian Tablets' description of the Anunnaki, the general lizard-human hybrid the ruling elite are sometimes accused of being (Reptilians), to the intelligent machines in the Hollywood movie series *The Matrix*.

I tend to think that indeed humanity is under the thumb of some perverse group. However, if we are in a simulation, I do not think this group is controlling it. My intuitive suspicion is that the negative groups are as locked into the simulation as we are. The only difference is that we are trying to get out of the simulation, while they are trying to accumulate power and wealth inside the simulation. Jesus's words, "My kingdom is not of this world", and Biblical references that Satan "… is the god of this world", are consistent with this view. [2 Corinthians 4:4] Think about it, if Satan is the god of this world, it may very well mean that he is also locked into the simulation. This could be why Illuminati Satanists seek money and power from this world. If they had access to the greater reality outside of the simulation, why would they try to accumulate simulated money and simulated power?

For example, certain global banking families are widely touted to be key Illuminati families. It is known that they accumulated their money by funding both sides of many wars since the Napoleonic times. They also made great profits by manipulating stock markets and industry price-fixing. What they did was immoral and today people outside of elite circles are prosecuted for this type of activity, but it was not magic. They just saw opportunities and profited from them, while being bound by the same laws of space, time, and matter that you and I are.

Think about it. If these wealthy banking families were part of the group that controls the simulation, why would they need to make money through simulated mundane activities like market manipulation? If they controlled the simulation couldn't they just materialize piles of gold bars in their backyard by simply adjusting or tweaking the program? Couldn't they just transform themselves into god-like super villains with superhuman powers like Thanos, Galactus, or Lex Luthor from comic books, and take over not only Earth but also the Galaxy, or Universe? Why don't they do that? This would suggest that *all* humans, no matter their position, are simulated characters.

I think another trick used by the Illuminati under the thumb of the Archons is to use economic power to further increase their material wealth. This is a well-trodden track in the negative path. A person or a group of people has economic power, but instead of using it to improve the condition of humanity, they wield that power in a way that further oppresses their sisters and brothers. A clear example of this may be found when big pharmaceutical companies acquire the commercial rights to a drug and then increase its price by as much as 5,555 per cent (which actually occurred)! (12) This is just one sad example of how many of the elites operate on this planet. They use petty tricks and malicious con-jobs to generate money and power for themselves. Why do they need to resort to lowly actions that harm others for their own personal profit if they, or their Archontic overlords had full control of the simulation? Wouldn't they just materialize the wealth they are addicted to out of thin air by manipulating the code?

The reason I believe this does not happen is that the Illuminati (and whoever is controlling them) is as bound by the rules of the game as we are. They do not control the simulation. They, as well as we, must operate within the parameters of what is possible as material bodies in space-time. If Satan is the god of this world, then Satan may be the toughest kid in the playground, but only inside the simulation. So, if the Illuminati and their Archontic controllers are not the programers - then who is coding the simulation?

My intuition tells me that we are. Every person on this planet is both a game player and programmer. The game player is the part of our consciousness, possibly the conscious mind, which experiences the simulation from inside the simulation. The conscious mind is the portion of our being that is fully immersed in the illusion and cannot exist outside of it. On the other hand, the programmer is the part of ourselves that calls all the shots. This may very well be what psychiatrist Carl Jung called the superconscious, what metaphysical people call the higher self, or what the *Law of One* books and the books on *Seth* by Jane Roberts call the Oversoul. This is the part of you that exists outside of the simulation, and is already connected with every other game programmer. The objective of the game programmer, or Higher Self, is to promote the evolution of the conscious mind just so the whole you can eventually escape the simulation. The whole you - being the higher-self programmer plus the lower-self player.

The superconscious mind would act like a parent supervising their young child (the conscious mind) through primary school years. The parent wants the best for the child and knows that the child's destiny is to graduate and leave school behind, but the parent also knows that this will only happen when the time is right and the child is ready. Not one second sooner. This ties well into The Event, The Shift, Ascension, or Rapture theories that will be discussed later.

A lot of people on the surface of Terra are now ready. The 'glitches in the matrix' that some of us observe almost daily, such as the Mandela Effect, synchronicities, déjà vu and psychic phenomena, are very strong indications that we are busting out of the simulated matrix. The matrix can no longer confine the power of human consciousness – at least for some of us. There are many people more than happy to remain locked in the materialistic cycle of eat-work-sleep, but if you picked up this book, you have a bee in your bonnet. That bee is your superconscious telling you that it is time to grow up and leave elementary school behind.

The Simulation and the Mandela Effect

The Mandela Effect also fits remarkably well inside of a simulated universe. The cognitive dissonance that we experience when we remember one thing that does not exist in our observed reality - very often feels like a glitch in a computer program.

Again, let us think of computer games in which you build civilizations. In these simulation games, the player needs to develop their own civilization, which includes building cities, acquiring resources, growing a population, and defending their territory from attacks by other players. In some cases, as it happened so often with me when I was playing, the attacks can become quite vicious and a player may lose most of their important cities and resources. At this stage the player may decide to stop playing and go back to a saved version of their game *before* the attacks started. Kind of like a computer reset or restore. By doing this, the player will be able to prepare better for future attacks, build more defenses, and divert more resources to cities that are more vulnerable. This way, when the attacking forces eventually show up at their border, the entire situation will be re-played, but this time with a better outcome because the player was better prepared through the previous negative learning experience.

Some of the defeats the player incurred the first time around will not be repeated in the re-play. The player, as a real being outside of the simulation, will have memories of those defeats, even though their new simulated population in their new reality never experienced them. This sounds remarkably like the Mandela Effect. There is a part of us that remembers some things in certain ways that are different from what our physical senses (which are completely immersed in the simulation) perceive them to be. There is a part of me that remembers the name of the popular TV show as *Sex in the City*, even though my physical eyes trawling through the internet, or through old VCR tapes can only see *Sex and the City*. I have vivid memories of Darth Vader in a Star Wars movie saying, "Luke, I am your father," despite my senses insisting that in the current reality he never said that. Instead he said, "No, I am your father," in all of the available film recordings. In addition to these personal impressions, a staggering number of articles, testimonies, blogs, videos and papers posted on the internet suggest many people feel the same way. (13)

According to this theory, those experiencing the Mandela Effect have some residual memory of something that cannot be confined to the simulation itself. Recall that the gamer remembered the old events, but their simulated population did not, because for them these events never took place. They were erased through the program reset or restore to an older setting before those game events took place. So those experiencing the Mandela Effect must have tapped into some higher form of awareness that was not erased when the simulation was backtracked, erased, and restarted. But not everybody manages to do this. A lot of people, the vast majority in fact, have not noticed anything unusual at all, and are very happy to continue playing the game of life - taking their cues from their environment. If for example, all *Star Wars* movie footage available shows the droid C3PO with one silver leg, then it must be true, even though many recall both legs as entirely gold in color. If someone has memories of it being entirely golden, that must be a false memory, even if tens of hundreds or tens of thousands of people share the *exact* same memory. Because those firmly in the simulation or matrix cannot fathom anything outside of it, therefore as soon as a change occurs, they immediately assimilate it as always having been that way – just like the characters in the re-set game.

Time, Parallel Realities, and Crossing Timelines

The idea of parallel realities does not need an introduction. It is all over the place, from science fiction to religious texts; from art and poetry to philosophy. What is perhaps less known is that the hypothesis of parallel realities is also a serious scientific proposition. For example, string theory is the best attempt so far to find the elusive integration of relativity and quantum mechanics: a 'theory of everything'. The problem is, string theory only works if the mathematicians assume that our world exists in no less than 11 dimensions. That is, in addition to the well-known three spatial dimensions (width, depth, height) and a fourth dimension of time - there would still be *seven* other parallel dimensions out there. If this blows your mind and you cannot visualise how you could possibly live in an 11-dimensional reality, don't worry - I don't think anyone can.

Parallel realities are also presented as a theory in quantum physics. Quantum mechanics is a very strange field of study that holds that a subatomic particle could be in two places at the same time. The mathematical treatment of quantum mechanics works very well and has never been debunked. The theory correctly predicts what physicists see in their experiments every time, but at its core, quantum mechanics does not explain the nature of reality. For example, it can be used to correctly predict that an electron could be *simultaneously* in two different locations, but it does not discuss why it is possible for any object to be in two places at the same time. Some speculate that this is the nature of a wave, so the particle must therefore also be a wave, but nothing in the quantum world is certain. We are still exploring the world of the particles that make up the atom.

Some physicists suggest that their role is to calculate matter, and that pondering why the universe is this way, or that way, is best left to philosophers. Other physicists disagree and have taken on the task of proposing explanations for the strange behaviour of subatomic particles. One such explanation is known as the Many Worlds Theory. According to this, our reality is constantly splitting into many parallel realities. This is happening all the time with every observation and decision we make. For example, an electron may be simultaneously at two places, A and B, while it remains unobserved. When a scientist, say Alice, observes the electron, she finds it to be in place A. But what happened with the electron also being at point B? The Many Worlds Theory suggests that at the time of observation, reality forked out into two parallel realities. In reality 1, the observer Alice 1 found the electron in position A. In reality 2, observer Alice 2 found the electron in position B. From the moment that the observation was made and reality split, Alice 1 no longer had any contact or interaction with Alice 2. Both will continue their lives independently and separated for ever more. This would eventually lead to a nearly infinite number of Alices living a nearly infinite number of lives. Not surprisingly it is not the most popular theory of the universe, but with the Mandela Effect gaining in popularity, and the consequent discussion of timeline (or dimension) hopping with each new perceived change in matter – that could soon change.

What Is Time?

Let's be honest. No one has the foggiest idea about what time is. What you will read in this and the next few sections are speculation, but speculation based on the study of physics, psychology, metaphysics, and mysticism.

The simplest starting point is to see time as a rate of change between two states of being in the three-dimensional universe. In this sense, time is intrinsically associated with motion within the three-dimensional state, and this is a very interesting result in itself. If nothing in the universe could move or change, the concept of time would become irrelevant. Thus, time is intrinsically linked with the concept of mobility or change in the three-dimensional space.

A key step towards understanding the nature of time was taken by physicists studying thermodynamics in the nineteenth century. Scientists noted that thermodynamic, and indeed all physical systems, always tended to go from a state of relative order towards a state of relative disorder energetically, and never the other way around. Left to their own devices, in the absence of any external forces, physical systems always move towards chaos.

The typical example is a sandcastle on the beach. When you build a sandcastle you are organising the grains of sand in a very specific order. After you finish building, you go home and return to the beach the following weekend, only to find that your sandcastle has disintegrated. This is because the sandcastle, along with the wind and the waves, form a physical system. As such, the action of the waves and the wind will be such that order in the system will decrease. That is, the grains of sand that were neatly and orderly arranged will be moved into more and more chaotic arrangements.

Biological systems seem to throw the proverbial monkey wrench into the entropy argument. Biological or organic life always does the exact opposite moving from random chaotic states towards organised arrangements. Like the world of the protozoa or single celled organisms into the extremely organized and highly specialized complex cells of the human body. For survival or energetic efficiency, single cells begin collecting together into larger and larger communities, in which they can specialize into brain cell functions, kidney cell functions, et cetera. Going from a disorganized single cell community, into a highly organized body state. These observations have led a few brave scientists such as Robert Lanza and Rupert Sheldrake to propose alternative theories that govern the development of 'live' biological systems, as we will see later in this section.

Even traditional scientists are not sure how entropy applies to lifeless physical systems. There is no law of physics preventing the wind and the waves from randomly shifting the grains of sand in such a way that they end up forming a sandcastle. This accidental movement *towards* order would be completely consistent with the laws of physics. It just never happens in practice. Because of this puzzle, scientists came up with the idea that entropy, which is the degree of chaos or disorder in a physical system, always increases over time.

To some extent, this idea of time-increasing entropy can be explained through mathematics, or more specifically probability. Consider one grain of sand being moved by the wind. There is a very large number of places where this grain of sand could land if the wind gusts are random. It is possible that this particular grain could fall exactly into a place as to complement the wall of the castle, but there are many more other spaces where the grain could fall that would not contribute to the composition of the castle. Therefore, it is far more likely that the grain of sand will end up in a place where it does not contribute to the composition of the castle than in a place where it will. This leads us to the mainstream physics conclusion that the entropy (degree of chaos) of a system without any conscious force of intervention will always increase in time.

Scientists are so sure of this result that they ended up defining time as a function of entropy. In fact, it is not really time, but the *direction* of time. If you are observing a physical system and entropy is increasing through successive observations, then these observations must be taking place going forward in time. If your observations show that entropy is decreasing, then you must be going backwards in time. This concept is called the 'arrow of time'.

The question that materialist scientists have doggedly refused to answer is: if systems without interference always move towards greater disorder, then how could organized life have arisen without any external interference? They want you and I to believe that atoms of oxygen, hydrogen, nitrogen and carbon randomly bumped into each other repeatedly until they could randomly combine in such a way with exactly the right amount of energy (from the sun or a lightning strike) just so they would form the first molecules of protein. What is more, this would happen billions of times over with the same astoundingly improbable result. Then the first molecules of protein would combine randomly again to form the first bacteria, and so on and so forth, until the most complex and varied lifeforms existed in one place. What is miraculous to some is considered an accident of merging molecules by others.

To me, what is most astounding, is that scientists claim this has happened even despite the science itself: even though the law of entropy and the arrow of time firmly state that *this should not happen* in forward moving time. The law of entropy suggests that early energy on this planet (and in the universe) should have disorganized over time into weak energetic chaos, instead of organizing into strong complex lifeforms - be they plant or animal. Again, we find materialistic science contradicting itself. A system that generates self-contradicting propositions must be internally incoherent and therefore meaningless.

One of the few serious attempts to resolve this inconsistency has been proposed by scientist Robert Lanza's theory of Biocentrism. (14) His theory proposes that the universe is biocentric, in other words, that consciousness creates the universe and not the other way around. (15) In addition, Lanza demonstrates that modern (e.g. materialistic) science cannot explain why the laws of physics are so precisely balanced for animal life to exist. Also revolutionary is PhD biologist Rupert Sheldrake's hypothesis of the morphic fields. (16) He suggests that simple fragments (such as protein molecules) can and do assemble into more complex structures (such as a cell), because they are simply following a template, a mold. For this revolutionary contribution, Sheldrake was fiercely attacked by the establishment - even to the extent that some of his TED talks were banned. (17)

Time as an Expression of Consciousness

There has been a growing trend among mystics and researchers alike to consider time as some type of illusion. Or more precisely, time as one of the manifestations of the four-dimensional matrix illusion in which we live. I am attracted to this line of thinking, because it would provide a possible answer to what could be the real nature of time.

If the physical matrix illusion in which we live is a holographic world created by the beings we know as our Higher Selves, then it is only plausible that time is also an illusion. This line of thinking suggests that time is somehow subject to consciousness, and this is where things get interesting. There are multiple examples in our everyday activities that indicate time is subject to consciousness. In fact, we experience this very frequently. For instance, the notion that, 'time flies by when you are having fun', suggests that the rate at which time passes for a given person is a function of their state of mind in the moment. If you are bored, time crawls, and if you are excited, time flies.

Materialists will try to twist the argument around and say that time itself did not change − it continued passing at the same rate, but the psychological perception of time changed. So nothing really happened with the rate at which time passed, but the appreciation of that rate by the person involved in the fun or boring activity changed. I believe this type of argument no longer holds any water. Quantum physics proved that consciousness does collapse the wave function of subatomic particles, that is, the behaviour of a subatomic particle-wave changes whether there is someone observing it, or not. Multiple scientific experiments have shown that subatomic particles behave in a way (as particles) if the experiment is being observed (by a conscious observer) and in another completely different way (as waves) when the experiment is not being observed. Scientists are befuddled about this, some are beginning to accept what mystics have known for millennia: consciousness influences reality. The argument (that materialists like to use) that the human mind is just a passive internal observer of a static external world - has lost its credibility.

If human consciousness can affect matter, why would it not be able to affect time as well? The sensation of time speeding up when you are doing something enjoyable, or slowing down when you are doing something tedious, could very well be an actual distortion of time itself. Or at least a distortion of the portion of time, or the time cocoon, around you.

Famous healer and author Barbara Brennan suggests an interesting experiment in her book, *Hands of Light*. (18) She describes how altering one's state of mind through meditative practices can alter a person's perception of time. One experiment is simply to meditate while looking at a clock. Try to use the hands of the clock as an object to fix your focus on and reach a meditative state, where you feel serene and have fewer random thoughts so common in the normal awakened state. Brennan claims that while doing this exercise, she felt changes in the rate at which time passed for her, or in other words, she could see the hands of the clock speeding up or slowing down. I have personally performed this experiment more than once, and have seen the hand of the clock that marks seconds get stuck at one point and not move for what appeared to be more than one second. Again, some may argue that what is changing is not time itself, just our perception of it. This may be true. But if consciousness can alter the state of subatomic particles thereby changing matter itself, it is not a big stretch to consider it can also alter time.

Two-Dimensional Time

Time is usually treated as one additional dimension to the three spatial dimensions that we are living in: width, depth and height. In this sense, time would be represented as a line connecting two different states of the same three-dimensional universe. For example, you - reading this book right now in a room, represent a three-dimensional framework in which all objects and spaces have width, depth and height. There is another state within the same system in which all objects are essentially the same, but the coffee mug on top of the desk has already gone cold, and your body is one hour older. The line connecting these two states of the three-dimensional world is a line that necessarily sits outside of the three-dimensional world: it is a line in what many are calling the fourth dimension, or time.

So the arrow that connects all states of our three-dimensional universe, and progresses towards the future, is a one-dimensional representation of changes in our physical universe. However, many theories suggest there could be a multitude of parallel universes, in which all alternatives of choices, actions and developments are taking place at the same time in different spatial but nearby places. As we discussed above, the idea of parallel universes is the critical feature in the Many Worlds interpretation of quantum physics. In addition, parallel universes could represent just different sets of parallel dimensions to which we do not (normally) have access. And the idea of dimensions parallel to those we normally perceive - is proposed by mathematicians and physicists working in String Theory.

We could think of another timeline representing all possible states of another three-dimensional universe. For instance, in one timeline you could have chosen to drink coffee, and as time progressed, your beverage cooled down slowly on the desk. In a parallel timeline you chose a milkshake instead, and your drink warmed up. This alternative timeline could be parallel to our own timeline (as in diagram A below), or it could cross our timeline, depending on the decisions and actions of the sentient beings of both universes (diagram B).

Diagram A   Diagram B

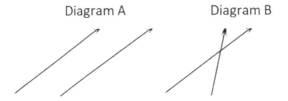

For simplicity, let us consider only those cases of parallel lines. We could depict our four-dimensional (space plus time) universe as an arrow marked A in the diagram below. We could also consider another parallel four-dimensional universe denoted as B. This universe could be relatively similar to ours, which is the reason why the B arrow is relatively close to the A arrow. For instance, the parallel universe B could have an exact copy of you, your family, and your house, except for minor details such as your car being red instead of blue. There could also be completely different universes, with more substantial discrepancies from our known universe. These universes could still follow the same general laws of physics and morals as ours, but the details of life, history and society could be considerably different. In some of these, you could be the President of Uganda, or an astronaut. Or the Earth could still be in the middle ages, or maybe the planet would have never have existed in the first place. We depict such a universe as an arrow C with the same orientation (direction of time) as our original universe A's arrow, but situated at a considerable distance from it.

A   B   C

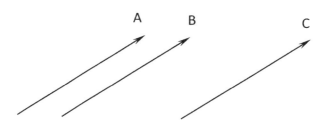

If you keep adding new aligned arrows towards infinity, the system will no longer be a disjointed collection of one-dimensional arrows of timelines, but a plane. From this, we draw an interesting insight. Time could indeed be two-dimensional (as in a plane), as depicted in the figure below. Or more specifically, time would be one component of a two-dimensional time-reality plane. The time-reality plane, as opposed to a single timeline, would contain all possible different ways in which parallel universes with the same laws of physics to ours - could evolve. Direction T (time) in the diagram below shows the direction of the passage of time, and direction R (reality) shows the different realities, or parallel universes that could exist and would be subject to the same rate of the passage of time (T). Note that the different timelines could cross – they are just being depicted as parallel for simplicity in the figure below.

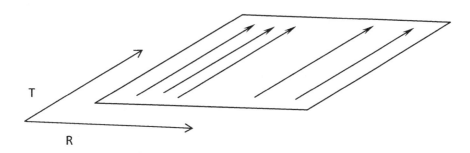

In the example above, the timelines are aligned, but as I said before, the timelines do not need to be parallel and in the same direction as the dimension of the passage of time (T). For instance, imagine a reality in which Earth is riddled with war and corrupt politicians. Let us call that reality A in the figure below. Imagine also another reality in which the populations of Earth have decided to abandon all forms of armed combat and demand the highest standards of morals from their politicians, bureaucrats, officials, and business leaders. Let us call this reality B. Reality B exists and is as 'real' as reality A. This is one of the most remarkable and exciting conclusions coming out of quantum physics: all possible states of the universe could exist in a very real sense within parallel realities.

We do not know why we are in reality A, while reality B seems so much more desirable. But in the spirit of making the most of the hand you are dealt, let us suppose that humankind in reality A decides to improve their situation. Then imagine that we all decide that through the power of our actions and intentions we will make our world a better place. We will no longer accept manipulative lies from leaders. If a politician wants to start a war, the people should demand that he or she go to the battlefield himself, instead of sending innocent young members of society. How many wars would there be then? If we decide to meditate and to visualise a world in which violent conflict, poverty and corruption no longer exist, and as we do this, the combined power of our consciousness starts exerting an influence on our timeline A. We will see that this timeline then veers towards the other timeline, B, that already contains the world we imagine; and the two merge into one with attributes of both timelines.

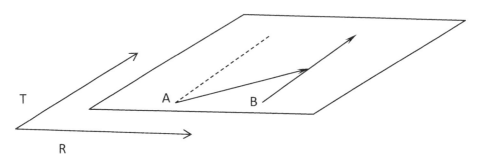

My suspicion is that this type of diagonal movement is happening all the time. We are the result of our decisions individually and collectively. At every day, every hour, every minute, and second, we are making decisions, acting, thinking, feeling and visualising (desiring and rejecting) things. These decisions, feelings, actions and visualisations inevitably take us across realities – sometimes towards better realities, and sometimes towards worse ones. So, diagonal movements in the time-reality plane should be the norm, not the exception. Which would mean Mandela Effect type changes to reality are the norm and not the exception. What is exceptional here is that we never noticed it before the recent upsurge in 'Mandela Effect awakened' individuals who see most if not *all* of the constant changes to the reality structure around them; based on the collective decisions, thoughts, feelings, memories, expectations, actions and visualisations of the group.

This is the sense in which time could be (at least) two-dimensional. Or to be more pedantic, time could be one of the defining components of a two-dimensional superstructure, in which parallel realities exist and evolve. These realities exist in parallel, but they may also cross each other, because of the actions, thoughts and choices of the sentient beings in each reality. We will see below, in the section Parallel Timelines and the Mandela Effect, that we seem to have confirmation that time behaves like a two-dimensional structure.

Drifting from one reality to another would be very common in such a way that diagonal movements such as that in the picture above would be the norm. Movement along the T direction would always involve some sideways drift in the R direction. In reality, T and R would be inseparable. Because of this, it sounds reasonable to conclude that time could very well be a two-dimensional structure including a dimension of *time-flow* (T) and a dimension for *time-reality* (R), as drawn above. This takes the flat space-time fabric diagram from Einstein, and in superposition across multiple dimensions, changes it to more of a hologram of light-wave-particles dancing and merging in all directions at once.

Parallel Timelines and the Mandela Effect

So far, we have discussed briefly some possible views on the nature of time and the characteristics of a timeline, which is a one-dimensional structure marking how time passes in each reality. We also discussed the possibility that different realities may exist following the same underlying structure (laws of physics and societal organization). Proving that time is multidimensional is most likely beyond the scope of the current state of our science. Nevertheless, we can discuss evidence, however circumstantial, that time could indeed be multidimensional, and that multiple parallel realities may not only exist, but may also be accessible to us and in many cases intersect our own reality. If this was not possible, then why would they be investing in D-Wave Systems quantum computers to compute or access information - interdimensionally?

Interestingly, the Mandela Effect itself could help us understand this multidimensionality of time. The Mandela Effect is entirely consistent with time being at least two-dimensional: comprising of a *time-flow* (T) dimension and a *time-reality* (R) dimension. To understand this better, consider the two parallel timelines in the diagram below. One departing from the past of timeline *A* and progressing towards the future within timeline *B* of the same universe. A'B' offers another timeline that is different from the first, but sufficiently similar to it, so that most of the details would be the same across the two worlds. This similarity would be along the lines of physicist and quantum computing pioneer David Deutsch's statement, "… but some [parallel universes] differ only in some minute detail like the position of a book on a table, and are identical in every other respect." (19) These two similar parallel timelines are depicted below.

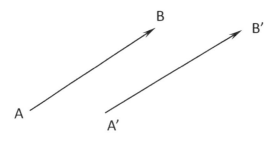

As we discussed above, human consciousness has the power to shape the universe around it. In fact, many already believe we are constantly shifting and pushing our timeline towards those parallel realities in which we focus our attention and expectation in a strong and persistent way. I believe this caused our original timeline *AB* to shift towards the parallel reality *A'B'*, and intersect the new reality at some point (*C*) in the recent past (as per the figure below).

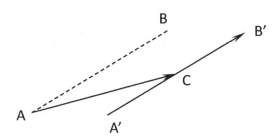

Those of us who migrated from reality *AB* will find themselves in a strange situation where many of our memories will hark back to point *A*, while everything around us will indicate a slightly different past *A'*. While at the same time for many individuals who always lived in timeline *A'B'* - nothing would have changed for them; those from the *AB timeline* (the so-called Mandela Effect experiencers) would have slightly different memories and the past that would seem at odds with the memories of the original inhabitants of the *A'B'* timeline before the merge. Any residual evidence found simply supports the merging realities theory.

The fact that the Mandela Effect even exists, and people are experiencing, discussing and trying to understand it - suggests that time could indeed be at least two-dimensional, and it could be accessible to us through parallel realities merging, and through the steering power of our collective consciousness.

Holographic Reality

The possibility that reality is a hologram has been suggested by academics such as Ervin Laszlo, (20) Michael Talbot, (21) Jude Currivan, (22) Brahma Kumari Pari, (23) Gregory Friedlander, (24), as well as many others. The idea is truly fascinating because, if correct, it changes our understanding of the universe and who we are. In short, a *hologram* is a lower dimensional representation of a higher dimensional object. For example, when you look at certain types of pictures (a two-dimensional print) and you have the impression that you are seeing a three-dimensional object, you are looking at a hologram. A form of holograms is commonly used on credit cards now, where you see a three-dimensional object.

Holography is the science and technique of producing holograms. The YouTube channel *One (Eileen Colts)*, also a contributor to this book, makes a very good point that the widely used expression 'holographic universe' is a misnomer. (25) A more descriptive term should be 'hologramic universe,' or perhaps 'the hologram universe'. However, I think that because the word 'hologramic' is not defined in Standard English, the proponents of the theory expressed it this way. The Oxford Dictionary defines the term 'holographic' to mean "produced using holograms" as opposed to holographs. This is still inadequate because in theory something could be produced using holograms, but not be a hologram itself. In any case, the term stuck, and there are different types of holograms, but the most interesting ones (often called transmission holograms), have at least two defining properties: parallax and self-similarity.

Parallax

In a conventional (non-holographic) two-dimensional image, we often represent three-dimensional objects using perspective. This is done, for example, by reducing the size of distant objects relative to near ones; or by fading the image of distant structures (such as a mountain range far off on the horizon), while sharpening the colors of closer ones (like a house across the street from the observer); but these are just optical illusions.

In a hologram, information about objects is recorded without illusions. The height of a distant object is recorded as the same as a similar sized object nearby. The reason our eyes perceive depth in a hologram is not because of tricks of perspective, but because of a property called parallax. According to this property, the representation of an object or scene changes with the angle used by the observer to see the picture.

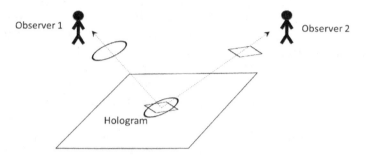

You can see this in the most basic holograms that if you change the angle of observation – the picture changes. This is what gives the impression of three-dimensionality on an otherwise flat picture.

Parallax is an effect created in holograms through very complex techniques, and we do not need to discuss them in this book. However, a simplified example may help us understand the principle. When cartoon designers are creating a moving image and they want to give it a sense of depth, they change the rate of movement according to the relative distance to the observer of objects in the frame. For instance, to simulate the camera (observer) moving to the right, the designer moves all objects in the frame to the left. The sense of depth is achieved by making distant objects move more slowly than near ones. This is the essence of parallax.

In a hologram, objects are not moving by themselves, therefore we cannot use the exact technique described above to achieve parallax. Instead, it is achieved through a complex process that has to do with the property that every point of the hologram contains information about the entire hologram. The critical point here is that there is an interaction between the observer and the hologram. In a conventional image, if the observer changes the angle of view, he or she will continue seeing the same image, only a little slanted. However, in a hologram, changing the angle of view results in a different image being perceived by the observer.

This is entirely consistent with the latest discoveries in the study of human consciousness. The way you *decide* to observe everything around you will *change* what you see. For example, a very negative person will tend to see the negative side of everything, and overplay its importance. This will lead to the observer developing a sense of negativity and hopelessness. In turn, these emotions will make them feel worn-out and seem unpleasant to others, causing them to have less success in relationships and at work. When this observer receives rejection because of their negative projections that others avoid, it serves to reinforce their negative view of the world, and so forth, in a closed feedback loop. Therefore, they have perceived what they *chose* to perceive, and they have experienced what they *chose* to experience - whether they know it or not. The universe showed them a picture that was largely influenced (if not dictated) by the angle they used in their observation. Their negative views, creating negative actions - created a feed-back loop with others reacting negatively towards them, and so on.

Sometimes these dynamics are called 'self-fulfilling prophecy' or the 'Law of Attraction', and have been extensively discussed in psychology and esoteric literature. Most people tend to think of the Law of Attraction in the purely psychological context. However, I believe it is more complex and deeper than that, and involves actual transfers of astral (superluminal) energy. The Law of Attraction may represent the mechanism whereby our conscious (or even unconscious) intention can change reality. As we will see, this framework could be behind the Mandela Effect, which after all, appears to be a change in reality governed by thoughts aka memory.

Astral and mental energy are made of superluminal particles. This means that your thoughts are real things floating around the place. Some clairvoyants can actually see them, and researchers call these objects thoughtforms. Even more important, these thought-forms are self-organising or self-attracting. This property is a direct consequence of negative entropy associated with superluminal systems, as we discussed before; and could explain the feelings of astral entity attachment.

If someone spends a lot of time thinking about negative possibilities, they may attract astral entities, or thought- forms from themselves and other humans; as well as physical events associated with their negative emotion. For example, if someone is angry and holds onto this anger, cultivating and feeding it in their daily actions, their astral body will emanate thought-forms of anger in the same way a transmitter emanates electromagnetic signals for another antenna to receive. The thought-forms of anger in their astral field could attract angry people, astral entities (similar thought-forms), or events wherever they go. Angry people 'pick up' on the anger of other people around them. (They even draw them to themselves.) This means that they walk through their day carrying a nefarious mist of heavy, dark, astral energy about themselves. Because of negative entropy, this negative cloud attracts negative things back: a computer will lock up; spilled coffee on their shirt; the neighbour's dog barking at them; and so forth. It can even take them much longer to heal minor illnesses like a head cold, than happier more positive people.

I experienced an interesting example of the Law of Attraction in early 2018. I had just published a YouTube video describing an involuntary astral projection I had the previous night. The video did not have many views, but I was later contacted by a viewer – let's call him Bobby – about his own astral projections. Bobby was concerned because he was involuntarily, astrally projecting at night, and in the process, thought he was being harassed by some demonic astral entities. He was stressing out and losing sleep over the astral stalking. Why was he attracting these entities? We agreed to talk, and I asked Bobby to arrange to contact me directly by email. In the meantime, I wondered what I could possibly do to help Bobby. I knew nothing about his life, his personality, his relationships, his karmic debt ... nothing. So, I sent him an email. A few weeks went by and there was no response from Bobby. I emailed him again to ask if everything was OK. His curt response was: "I am on vacation. Don't bother me." So, right there and then, the whole mystery was solved (at least in part). Bobby was such a bad-tempered person that even on his holidays (when you're supposed to be more relaxed) he would lash out at the person whom *he* had contacted for help; and who was trying to help him free of charge to free himself of negative attachments while astral traveling. Is it any wonder he is attracting negative energies while his consciousness is outside of his physical body?

In fact, this mechanism is in part, but not entirely, responsible for what a lot of people call karma. Whatever you focus on, comes back to you, and it will keep coming back until you change your thought patterns - which changes your actions. The negative entropy of astral energies and thoughtforms could also help explain a phenomenon that Carl Jung called synchronicity. For example, you are thinking about whether or not to buy a blue shirt - only to realize that you are now 'seeing blue' everywhere. You may notice blue cars passing by, people with blue shoes on, someone in a sitcom saying that he is "feeling blue" …. Of course, most of these instances can be explained by your focus or attention. You could reason that the quantity of blue things around you is the same as before – only now you are paying more attention to them. However, there are some synchronicities that are extremely difficult to explain away. I have pages of material with bizarre synchronicities that happened to me, and I am sure you have some startling examples of your own. A lot of these examples are not coincidences. They are just a response from the universe to your own thought patterns. You are thinking specific things and the universe is answering in the same specific ways. If you keep thinking positive things, you will attract positive thought-forms, people, and events back to you. You will surround yourself with positive astral energies. Many call this the 'Armor of God' – they *feel* invincible and this feeling repels negative astral energies.

Two people can see the same scene completely differently. For example, one person might focus on the rain that is cold and annoying, the truck that brings noise and pollution, and the high price of the subway fare. They may go home feeling miserable. This person has made a choice to see the negative side of things and the universe will respond according to their focus. Another person experiencing the exact same scene might be thankful that the plants are getting some water, that the passing truck driver has employment, and that their fare helps maintain the transport system for so many. They go home feeling energised and grateful. The universe responds to this person according to the paradigm they chose to see and feel. This example of the same reality looking different to two people at the same time (because they choose to perceive it from two different viewpoints or angles) is the essence holographic parallax in our reality. Does this sound familiar? Two different people perceiving the exact same thing differently? Yes, the Mandela Effect could be related to this holographic feature of parallax, as we will soon see.

Self-Similarity

Every part of a hologram contains information about the whole. For example, if you cut a transmission hologram of a flower in half, you do not get two half flowers - you get two smaller *whole* flowers. If you proceed to cut this hologram into a thousand pieces, you will obtain a thousand little whole flowers. (Most common holograms that we see in printed money and books etc. are reflection holograms, which are cheaper to make and do not have self-similarity.)

In a transmission hologram, self-similarity is obtained through a process of bouncing laser beams off the target object and making the beam from the whole object converge to record the information on a single point of the holographic film. So, if you did this using a vase as a target object and converged all laser beams into a very small area (say, a millionth of an inch by a millionth of an inch) you would have a whole picture of the vase in one millionth of an inch - but you would need a microscope to see it. You just repeat the process around contiguous areas until you fill the entire film (let's say, ten inches by ten inches) with multiple points containing the whole – which is blowing it out. This way a larger image is created out of the information contained in a large number of smaller images coming together. (In theory, it should be information contained in an infinite number of punctual images, but this cannot happen in practice.)

The concept of self-similarity is far reaching. It is such a powerful concept, and so common in nature, that it lends credence to the universe indeed being a hologram. Self-similarity means that every single component has information about the whole (much like every cell in your body contains the information of your whole body through DNA in every cell). Some people even see God this way – as the collection of all, or the sum total of everything in existence. Conversely, the whole is present in each component. Homeopathic, Herbal, Chinese and many alternative holistic medicinal therapies are based on this philosophy – treating the whole person instead of treating the one symptom.

From a metaphysical stance this is a tremendously powerful proposition. This is equivalent to saying that the Infinite Creator is within each and all of us; because we are the components of the whole Infinite Creator. This is at the core of the teachings of many major religious and spiritual traditions – particularly native traditions. Many traditional spiritual philosophies teach that the Infinite Creator is in each creature. Jesus, for example, constantly identified himself and God in every human being: "… and the King shall answer and say unto them, verily I say unto you, inasmuch as ye have done it unto one of the least of these my brethren, ye have done it unto me." [Matthew 25:40] In Hindu tradition the creator God, Brahma, identifies divinity inside each person, albeit in a veiled form: "… we will hide their divinity deep into the center of their own being, Humans will search for it here and there, but they won't look for the divinity inside their true selves." (26) The native beliefs of Aborigines in Australia and original Americans even saw spirit or God in all animals, trees, mountains and streams.

Self-similarity is so pervasive in our universe that it was found in our quest to describe nature: fractal geometry. To understand this, we need a broad-brush introduction to fractals: what they are and how they are created. A fractal is a geometric object that has fractional dimension. This may be a bit hard to wrap your head around, but the discussion below should help.

You will remember from high school geometry that a line is a single dimensional object. There is only one dimension associated with it: length. Similarly, if you imagine a plane, you will have pictured a two-dimensional object: a plane has length and width. Picture a cube and you will see that the cube has length, width and height, or in other words - three dimensions. You will soon notice that the dimension number of objects is always an integer: 1, 2, 3, et cetera.

This was the state of geometry until Benoit Mandelbrot, a Polish-born French mathematician, discovered there can be geometric objects that flout this rule. As mind-boggling as this can be, Mandelbrot discovered that some objects could have fractional dimensionality, such as 0.5 dimensions, 1.2 dimensions, and so on. To help us visualise this, let us build a fractal ourselves. The fractal we will make is called the Koch Curve, and it is disarmingly simple to visualise. Imagine that you have a simple (one dimensional) horizontal line of length L.

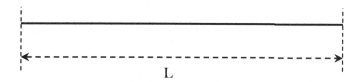

Now divide this line into three segments of equal length (that is L/3) and remove the middle one:

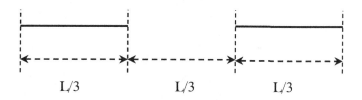

The missing segment in the middle will be the basis of an equilateral triangle in which all sides are equal to L/3.

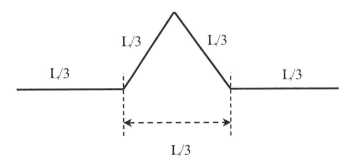

Now you have four segments each of length L/3. If you repeat the steps above, (dividing each individual segment into three equal parts and making a triangle with the middle segment), you will have a progression that will look like the picture below.

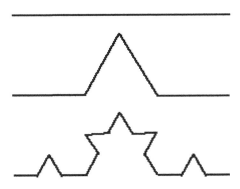

Now you have a total of 16 segments (you can count them to confirm) and each will be of length L/9 (that is, one third of the original L/3).

    To build the Koch Curve, you just have to keep repeating the process *ad infinitum*. Each of the 16 segments you have in the previous picture will be split in the same way to form new triangles, and so on, and so forth. As you continue repeating the steps over and over, you will notice that the length of each individual segment will approach zero, and the number of segments will approach infinity. The curve will start to look like the bottom panel curve in the diagram above. (There are some beautiful examples of Mandelbrot Fractals videos on YouTube.)

There is a mathematical way to calculate the dimension of the Koch Curve. If you use it, (readers can research the formula independently), you will notice that the Koch Curve has dimension approximate to 1.26 – which is between 1 and 2. This is a rather curious result. What does it mean to have dimension between 1 and 2? It means that the Koch Curve is no longer a line (which has dimension 1), but it is not yet a plane (which has 2 dimensions) either. The Koch Curve is something in the middle between a line and a plane. It is a completely different class of geometric objects altogether. It is as if the Koch Curve has been defined by a single-dimensional line, but this line has been shaken up and broken with infinitesimally small fractures, and eventually this line becomes kind of fuzzy. Being a little bit fuzzy, it is as if the original one-dimensional line had gained a certain area, which is a characteristic of a two-dimensional plane. The fact that the dimension of the Koch Curve is a fraction is what gives this object the name 'fractal'.

Fractals are self-similar. This means that observers can zoom into any part of the fractal object and the image they see will be identical to the original fractal in the first place. In the Koch Curve it is easy to understand why this happens. If you have subdivided all the segments in the smaller segments, following the same order *ad infinitum,* it will not matter which scale you choose to see the object in: you will always see the same subdivision and geometric pattern.

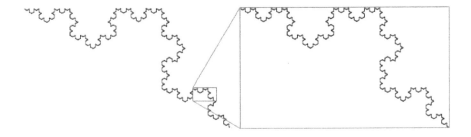

Fractals have been used all over the place to help calculate the length of coastlines, the amount of water in clouds, and certain properties of plants. Also, to understand and describe patterns of soil erosion, branching tracheal tubes, blood veins, leaf growth on trees, disturbances in air, water flow, and the density of matter in the universe … the list goes on and on! The more scientists and mathematicians look into our reality, the more they find fractal-like patterns. German scientist Tino Kluge summarizes this with, "One can argue that everything existent on this world is a fractal." (27)

Our universe exhibits some very compelling examples of fractal-like self-similarity. As we discussed, parallax and self-similarity are the two defining ingredients of a hologram. If we have already found strong indications that our universe exhibits both, the case for a holographic universe is extremely strong, and this comfortably includes the Mandela Effect phenomenon.

The Holographic Possibility of the Mandela Effect

If our reality is indeed holographic, the Mandela Effect could possibly be explained as an extreme case of parallax. How would that work? For millennia mystics and philosophers have said that human consciousness evolves; that the way we perceive reality changes over time. This is not very difficult to verify. The way that children perceive the world when they are three years of age is quite different from how they see the world at age ten. They now have more knowledge, have gone through more experiences, and have a wider array of emotions with which to perceive everything around them. They will find new meanings that were beyond their perception when they were younger. Despite being the same child, their consciousness has changed – so their observation of the universe is what is different.

Something similar seems to be happening with the entire human species, but some who cannot see it or understand it yet tend to deny it. History shows human consciousness has always evolved at glacial speed, but something has changed in the past few decades that indicates the pace of consciousness development now appears to have increased dramatically.

I do not pretend for one second to know *why* this acceleration of human consciousness evolution (or Quantum Awakening) is happening. Perhaps the acceleration of time, that we discussed in a previous section, is part of this phenomenon. Some mystics say that Earth is being bombarded with different (or more intense) cosmic and astral radiation from the center of the galaxy, or a photon cloud, or photon belt. Others say that the acceleration is caused by our own higher selves who concluded that we (or at least some of us) have learned everything we could from this primary class (called Life on Earth), and are now ready to graduate to middle school (another planet, another universe, another dimension of Earth). Still others say that Earth (Mother Gaia, Sophia) is a sentient being that is responsible for changes in human consciousness. The Hindus have the Yugas in which consciousness rises and falls cyclically over a period of twenty-six thousand years (which fits nicely with Nemesis our twin sun's hypothesized orbit around our Sun). To me the jury is still out, and it is conceivable that the true answer could have all of these ingredients - plus some.

However, knowing the reason or the exact nature of this change in conscious (quantum awakening) is not essential in order to experience it. In fact, it could even be counterproductive. We could spend days debating what is happening and concentrate all of our activity on the rational part of the brain, and in doing so completely neglect our task: to learn to go inwards for guidance from higher self; to develop love and compassion for all; to see the Creator in all beings including ourselves. All inward sight.

What is essential is to acknowledge that a shift is going on and that you are not going crazy. That other people are feeling as bamboozled as you are (you will find some welcoming communities in the comment section of some Mandela Effect channels like ours in this book). And that is OK! No one hops onto a roller coaster for some peace and quiet! If you are down here on Terra in these critical and exciting times, it is probably because you either needed to change your thought patterns, or you volunteered to help others expand theirs while on this ride with them.

The Mandela Effect could be a by-product of this shift – often called 'The Event' now. If the universe is a holograph (or a hologram), it is conceivable that a change in the angle of our observation could change what we see. If our consciousness is now operating in a different way, it is only natural that our perceptive senses – vision, touch, hearing, taste, smell, (magnetism and non-local perception), could start picking up different signals than before.

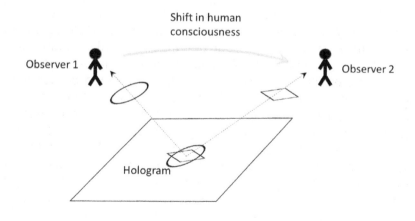

A holographic reality could have all possibilities encoded in one single data point. Let me give an example. When you watched the *Star Wars* movie series in the seventies and eighties you, like me, were probably fascinated with the droid C3PO. You probably memorised that C3PO was golden all over and that became a very firm and emotionally charged memory, because as a true fan you probably saw each movie countless times in the movie theatre and then bought them on video and DVD. But if reality is holographic, perhaps all possible renderings of C3PO were encoded in the hologram of reality. In one rendering, C3PO was blue; in another, it was green and seven feet tall; in a third rendering of reality C3PO was a girl robot – and so on. The fact that C3PO was male and all golden was *not* hard coded in the fabric of our holographic reality, because all possibilities or dimensions are in it. Perhaps, what made C3PO look male and all golden was a combination of the information encoded in the hologram *plus* the way in which we chose to experience the hologram collectively at that time., or due to our position in the multiverse. Had humanity chosen to watch the original *Star Wars* movies with a different mindset, perhaps C3PO could have been perceived as female, blue, or any color.

So, today some of us, (the Mandela Effect affected), look at the old footage of Episodes IV, V and VI and shudder to see that C3PO (now) has a silver lower right leg. Is it possible that this silver leg was always there, but we somehow chose collectively not to see it before? If all potential renderings of C3PO were encoded in the fabric of the hologram, and you must choose one at a time for continuity, this possibility cannot be discounted.

This theory is fascinating, not because of a fictitious movie character from decades ago, but because of what it could mean for the future - what it could represent for the ascension or Quantum Awakening of humankind. Ascension could be achieved through a shift in humanity's perception of reality, because that perceptional shift could put you in an entirely different nearby place within the whole. A lot of people expect that ascension will be a grandiose, Earth-shattering event. For instance, religious Christians may think of ascension more along the lines of the 'Rapture', whereby the physical bodies of the saved will be lifted from the ground and taken up to heaven somewhere in the sky to meet with God and the angels. Another more modern interpretation is the catastrophic annihilation of society due to war, climate change, or a comet hitting the Earth, with the survivors establishing a new and improved human civilisation in the aftermath. Others expect massive UFO disclosure with 'aliens' (non-Earth non-terrestrial beings) announcing their presence and handholding us into a better place and kinder social order. This is pretty much how people describe The Event now: with a rainbow cloud transporting us to 5-D Earth, or New Earth which offers compassionate cooperation as a social order. People still predict exact dates for this event, even though past predictions have failed miserably. Many expected this rapture during 1987's Harmonic Convergence when many planets aligned, and again in 2012 with the end of the Mayan Calendar.

What if non-Biblical ascension or rapture is something else entirely? What if it is a subtle shift in human consciousness, just like the Mandela Effect, which would give us more time to adapt and adjust to it (like Dolores Cannon always said)? What could it look like? Perhaps you would wake up one day, have breakfast and learn from the morning news that crime in your city has fallen remarkably for no apparent reason. You would walk around familiar streets on your way to work and notice that people are happier, lighter - more compassionate. You would reach for your phone to call that friend of yours that is always negative or materialistic, and you would find that his number strangely is no longer in your contacts list. Reaching out to a common acquaintance, you might be told that friend had moved somewhere else and indeed you would never be able to reach him again. You get to work and your boss is suddenly more considerate, and you cannot understand why ... did you previously misremember your boss as a psychopath? Were you hallucinating before? Or are you hallucinating now? How could such dramatic changes in your reality occur so suddenly?

After a day of work, you head home, take a shower and sit in front of the TV (or computer) to catch up on the news. Your jaw drops when you learn that Congress or Parliament is studying bills to close corporate tax loopholes, bring billions of dollars from black budgets back into the government's books to fund healthcare and university programs for all, drastically reduce military spending, close unused bases, and double the minimum wage. You shake your head in disbelief and exclaim, "I don't know what the heck is happening, but I like it! I have these weird memories of everything being so gloomy, so bad for so many of us. I have these bizarre recollections of the government being controlled by lobbyists for the benefit of corporations and banks only – the one percent... where has all of that gone? What is happening to the world? Why is everything now so nice now, society so benevolent, the government so caring and accountable?"

All over the world people are now striving to resolve their issues without violence, through negotiation, and mutual understanding... Most people no longer care about personal financial gains – their focus is now on the best possible outcome for all concerned. People are perusing their passions too now - they are taking acting lessons, learning to play musical instruments, spending hours studying how to paint with oils and watercolour, learning how to bake, traveling more, studying more, meeting up and interacting more .... People are checking with their neighbours to see if there is anything they could help them with. Yet, you have these bizarre memories of the world being a place of selfishness, materialism, and war.

How could all you see around you now *be* the complete opposite of what you remember? Everything is peaceful, society is supportive and cooperative, and politicians are transparent, honest and well-intentioned... Medical research companies de-list from exchanges to be able to research new treatments and medication without being tied to profit. The entire medical profession is only concerned with treating the sick, not birthing billionaires. Yet you have these nightmarish reminiscences of big-pharma being callous and money-hungry where they actually harmed people instead of healing them ... Where did all that go? Did it really exist? Or did you just make that up? Why is everything around you so cooperative, so meaningful, and so peaceful? In time, you will no longer pay much attention to the nightmarish memories of a frightening world where money ruled everything and everyone. Where greed truly was considered good and was gluttonously rewarded with power, as the suffering of the many produced the profit for the few. Perhaps they were just fantasies (nightmares) or false memories which do not correspond to the reality you see all around you. Slowly you will start forgetting those recollections. One night, you sit down to watch some old TV shows to reminisce about your earlier years. The old re-run is called *Sex and the City*. A strange feeling grips you: Hang on, didn't this show use to be called *Sex **in** the City*?

The Mandela Effect and Ascension Theory

Ascension is a term so loaded it is nearly impossible to have a balanced and dispassionate debate about it. Every established religion has a different name and blueprint for it. Every New Age guru has an authoritative description of how it will take place. Tele-evangelists dutifully lighten the wallets of the faithful, just so they are less encumbered to meet the Lord when they are ready. 'Preppers' stockpile ammo to blow out the brains of those not ready to share in the love and compassion of the New Earth. The UFO community, gazing towards the Pleiades, sighs while picturing Earth being invaded by armies of tall, anorexic, oxygenated super models. Everybody, or at least those with some practice or concern with personal spirituality, is expecting some type of decisive, Earth-shattering, or catastrophic event that will bury the old world and lift the remaining humanity from confusion and moral degradation. Then, some of us have the Mandela Effect.

This unsettling phenomenon teaches us that reality could be more fickle and more malleable than we first thought. The reality you know and trust today may simply be different tomorrow when you wake up. Changes may be gradual, subtle, and nearly imperceptible at first. In fact, some people may not even detect them at all, and will claim that you, who are noticing the inconsistencies, are just suffering from false memories.

What if this is how ascension takes place, or at least starts? Small, discontinuous jumps in reality accruing moment by moment, year by year, taking us gradually further from the timeline we used to know. Little changes that make us doubt what we are seeing at first, then ignore them, until their accumulated effect is so noticeable, we no longer understand reality. In this chapter we will explore some ideas about ascension and discuss some implications of the Mandela Effect to humanity's transition into higher consciousness. It is divided into two parts: the first contains some ideas about what ascension could possibly be and feel like, followed by possible ways to prepare for it.

What is Ascension?

Ascension means different things for different people, and of course, no one has the foggiest idea of what it really means, because we on this planet have not gone through such an event on the global scale that we know of. Some describe their personal ascension experiences to heaven-like places during Near Death Experiences (NDEs). However, there are a few commonalities among most religious and metaphysical groups of a single ascension knowledge that we can all hang our hats on. Here are just a few that I find particularly sensible.

Firstly, ascension involves the idea of humanity somehow becoming better in some type of quantum leap or short period of time. By short, I mean relative to the usual millions of years it takes for a species to evolve naturally. Better in what sense? Most religious and metaphysical groups would contend that "better" means more compassionate, more caring towards one another and towards nature, more patient, more loving, and more tolerant. This alone makes ascension, whatever it turns out to be, a very enticing proposition after all of these millennia of Luciferian domination of Terra. This is the moral dimension of ascension that dovetails with the Christian belief in the coming of the Kingdom of Heaven on Earth, or the Golden Age; and Biblical scripture about the Rapture when the righteous of us are instantly taken up into heaven en mass - creating a group ascension.

In addition to the moral dimension, there will most likely be a physical dimension as well. It is likely that ascension may involve changes in our DNA. Some expect these changes would give us extra durable bodies, immunity from (or at least greater resistance to) disease, perfect memories, longer life spans, telepathic and telekinetic skills, precognition, the ability to perceive and contact interdimensional or spiritual realities and beings ... and many more upgrades to our current state of being. "Humanity 2.0", as some put it, or the New Human. The current status of humanity is commonly referred to as third density or 3D (also used to describe the third dimension). The ascension process, with its moral and physical implications, would take us into the fourth density (4D) according to Ra: The Law of One material. Whereby 4D is not considered as time. (28)

Many traditions from Hinduism to Theosophy, from Spiritism to the Law of One, state that ascension (regardless of the different names given to it) represents nothing more than a natural punctual evolution of sentient energy in this universe. These traditions state that consciousness (or sentient energy) begins its infancy inhabiting mineral bodies. This is usually taken to be the first density (1D) stage of consciousness, where sentient energy learns, for lack of a better word, how to simply exist in a physical form of matter. Rocks have a certain degree of consciousness, although this would not be recognisable to us now in the human state. Water also has some degree of consciousness. As the sentient energy inhabiting these mineral bodies is refined, more advanced containers are needed to allow for further development. Sentient energy then begins to inhabit vegetation. Plants are conscious and anyone that ever spoke or sang to a favourite plant only to realize that it had grown a little faster in the following days - will attest to this. Numerous studies have concluded that plants can "feel" or respond to other plants, or human emotion. While the mineral realm allows sentient energy to experience existence in physical form, the vegetable stage takes consciousness to the next level of yearning for growth and development.

The next level, as you guessed it, is the animal realm. Here, sentient energy learns the lessons of self-preservation and individuation or self-identity. By individuation I mean the fledgling realisation that one is different from its surroundings. (Do not confuse this with Jungian Individuation, which has a different but not altogether unrelated meaning.) For instance, a dog somehow knows that it is different from the tree it pees on. A cat sees a mouse not as a part of itself, but as something separate from itself that requires chasing.

Interestingly, the Law of One lumps the plant and animal realms together as second density (2D), which is the stage where sentient energy experiences the urge to self-sustain, grow and reproduce. This may sound very strange for most of us, who think of animals as far more intelligent and responsive than plants. Should not animals have a separate density for themselves? The fact that the Law of One uses 2D for both plants and animals suggests that plants may have an advanced, albeit still irrational, consciousness. Perhaps as advanced as dolphins, or dogs. Maybe we like to think of plants as dumb, because they do not move far, or appear to communicate, but that is a silly non sequitur. Late physicist Stephen Hawking, afflicted with Amyotrophic Lateral Sclerosis, could barely move in the later years of his life. Yet his physical body housed one of the most powerful minds humanity has ever seen. Sufferers of Locked-In Syndrome, or pseudo coma, are also in a state of complete or near complete paralysis, but they retain consciousness and are aware of their surroundings. A simple internet search of "plants communicate" will bring up all kinds of research findings on how plants communicate with each other, and by that definition, must be considered as aware.

When consciousness has inhabited 2D containers for long enough, the next step is taken into humanity, or third density (3D). This is the realm of deeper self-awareness, of the differentiation of the ego, of the pursuit of that which goes beyond mere survival. Beyond "I am different." Into "How and why am I different?" The artistic sense is born; an appreciation for beauty, as well as logical thinking and planning. This is the stage where self-awareness discovers time through the perception of a future and a past. A sense of life as part of a community and a desire for deeper meaning - all of these define third density.

So, here is the first kick about ascension. We have done it before! Many times over. We have ascended from the mineral realm into the plant or animal realm, and finally into the human realm of existence. Ascension as a process is a constant in the universe. We have done it many times and will likely do it many times more. Not that this will help us much now. Each ascension-jump is completely different from the previous one. Even if we could remember our last ascension, from 2D to 3D, that memory would not necessarily serve as guidance for what is about to happen to us now.

Before we proceed, it would be useful to clear a few things about nomenclature. The Law of One describes the densities as a function of the stages of consciousness development. As we saw above, this body of knowledge holds that the process of ascension that humanity is experiencing now - involves a shift from 3D to 4D. Hypnotherapist and author Dolores Cannon, as well as other spiritual and metaphysical scholars, prefer to think of ascension as a shift by humanity from 4D into 5D. So, which one is correct, are we shifting into 4D or into 5D?

The '5D' that Dolores Cannon and others refer to is the fifth *dimension*. This school of thought takes into consideration that humanity currently lives in the physical universe – the three physical dimensions plus time, which is the fourth dimension. As humanity grows in consciousness and begins to perceive higher realities, we will start to sense the fifth *dimension* – which is sometimes taken to be an astral, or spiritual non-physical plane. This is totally consistent with the Law of One material, which states that our next jump in consciousness will allow us to perceive and contact interdimensional or spiritual realities. Therefore, whether you prefer to say that humanity will shift into the fifth *dimension,* or if you prefer to state that we will ascend into the fourth *density* - either way, you will be correct. For clarity and consistency, we will continue using the Law of One definitions in this chapter.

Are M. E. Residuals Messages About Ascension?

Filmmaker, author and gnostic scholar Jay Weidner has a fascinating take on what the Mandela Effect could mean to humanity at this time, which many consider a time of ascension. Weidner proposes that the Mandela Effect is not an epiphenomenon of parallel realities colliding, or a time loop gone awry. He thinks it is an intentional message to humanity from a higher intelligence. One of the examples that Weidner uses is a famous line from the movie Forrest Gump. He recalls, as do I, that Forrest said, "… life *is* like a box of chocolates. You never know what you are going to get". This is what he and many of those aware of the Mandela Effect remember. However, the line in the actual movie is (in this current reality), "… life *was* like a box of chocolates." But this is the whole problem with the Mandela Effect: in the reality where we find ourselves now, nothing has changed. The movie line always said "was".

Regardless, Weidner suggests that this perceived change from "is" to "was" is in fact a message to humanity from a higher universal intelligence. In the past, life used to be uncertain. This past corresponds to humanity's third-density, pre-ascension status on this planet. As the process of ascension has already started and humanity finds itself well into the crucible of the 3D - 4D overlap, that uncertainty about the human condition will no longer apply. Ascended, fourth-density humanity will be able to see through the veil of materiality. We will be able to transcend the physical illusion and have a direct experience of our undying spiritual nature. We will understand our role in the multiverse, our weaknesses, our strengths, our objectives, and the lessons we still need to learn. Everything will be crystal clear. In that sense, ascended humanity will no longer live in uncertainty. Life on Planet Earth will no longer be like a box of chocolates. This, claims Weidner, is the deeper meaning of that specific Mandela Effect residual line. (29) There are a number of other examples of Mandela Effect residuals, each of which could carry its own hidden meaning as a message from higher consciousness to lower consciousness.

Fattening Tails

In these last days in 3D, duality has come back with a vengeance. Duality refers to the notion that some people prefer to follow the positive path predicated on love, compassion, wisdom and unity. Others prefer the path of separation, control and enslavement. You may have noticed that the extremes are drifting further apart. Those willing to make this a better planet are working harder and harder on improving conditions for society, helping the environment recover from the impact of corporate greed and urban sprawl, contributing to improvements in medical and engineering technology. Those hell-bent, if you excuse the pun, on controlling and exploiting others for their exclusive benefit are becoming more remorseless, depraved and dissolute. The extremes are getting more extreme. Humanity's moral bell-curve – with a few selfless light workers on the right, a few egotistical psychopaths on the left, and a crowd of undecided 'sheeple' in the middle – are growing fatter and fatter tails. But the good news is, as the extremes become more extreme – the ones in the middle finally see it and are forced to choose – which tips the balance of the scales one way or another.

I do not believe this is an accident: it is all planned by the higher governors of human evolution on Terra. As it turns out, people who have had the authorization to incarnate on Terra since the 1970s are those who have a chance to ascend into fourth density. Those people who have chosen the path of love and compassion, and have worked hard to develop their consciousness through multiple incarnations, have received the authorisation to reincarnate now, expunge their remaining karma, and try to make the cut for ascension into the fourth density positive reality matrix (Law of One). Similarly, those negative people who have chosen the path of selfishness, and have worked hard to develop their consciousness along the negative path, also incarnated now in an attempt to proceed to the fourth density negative reality matrix. It is this growth at the extreme levels of humanity that gives us the feeling now that 'the good are getting better and the wicked are getting worse'.

Many claim that the wicked are getting worse in the final days is the true manifestation of a cryptic passage in *Revelation,* 20:7 and 8, "When the 1,000 years are finished, Satan will be free to leave his prison. He will go out and fool the nations who are over all the world. They are Gog and Magog. He will gather them all together for war. There will be as many as the sand along the sea-shore." (30)

The 'sheeple', those who only care about consuming and do not care about their moral or spiritual growth, are most likely the ones as numerous "as the sand along the sea-shore". These folks will be deceived by the evil forces (those who have chosen the negative or service-to-self path) and may continue to be enslaved by them - at least until the next round of ascension opportunity. It is the 'sheeple' that mock those experiencing the Mandela Effect, because the 'sheeple' do not have the acuity of consciousness to perceive that reality has changed, and is continuing to change around them. They are the ones that describe the Mandela Effect as a "false memory syndrome", or confabulation.

Worlds Collide

The 2013 movie *Star Trek – Into the Darkness* opens with a rather unsettling scene for those with eyes to see. (31) Most people have not deciphered this, but the attentive students of metaphysics (Gnosticism and Spiritism) would have felt a chill go up their spines right in the opening drama. The opening sequence is definitely an instance of disclosure: someone who knows their stuff and is schooled in metaphysics was trying to give humankind a not-so-subtle message about what is happening at this time of ascension for our species.

The movie starts with a young Captain Kirk and his First Officer running through a very bleak and primitive planet. They dash through the thick red vegetation in a nightmarish scenario. The viewer learns that they are trying to escape from a large group of humanoid-looking creatures. These beings appear to be somewhat intelligent, but in a very primitive state of technological development. The humanoids act and look like primitive people still going through their Stone Age.

Dr. Spock manages to prevent a volcanic explosion from obliterating the village of the primitive humanoids. However, something goes wrong and Spock, stranded inside the crater of a gigantic volcano, needs to be rescued by the Enterprise. The ship is hiding under water just so the primitive inhabitants of the planet have no inkling that a vastly technologically-superior human species is covertly visiting them. However, in order to save Spock, who is running out of time, the Enterprise has to abandon its cloak and fly off towards the crater in the volcano. The sight of the massive spaceship taking off astonishes the primitive humanoids, who fall down on their knees to worship the craft. All this takes place in the year 2265 (in our future). What is the name of the bleak primeval planet where all this drama takes place? Nibiru.

Since the 1970s there have been multiple and consistent channellings (from independent sources) on this topic. Brazilian medium Chico Xavier frequently spoke about the astral 'purge' that a *cleansing planet* will cause when its highly magnetic astral atmosphere attracts the souls of those who have not developed their being in love and consciousness. The messages state that human souls who do not make the cut for ascension by the time Terra shifts to a planet of regeneration - will be transported to a primitive orb where they can repeat this third-density stage of evolution. Spiritist mediums and researchers state that this planet is Nibiru (which is also known by a variety of other names as presented on page 59 in this book). (32)

The Bible refers to this planet as Wormwood - the "abomination that causes desolation". (33) Even materialistic mainstream science has started to understand this idea. In 2016, the scientific publication *Nature* discussed evidence of a giant planet on the fringes of the Solar System orbiting the Sun every 20,000 years or so. (34) Some believe this planet has a very strong magnetic field, and is currently at a developmental stage that is consistent with the Stone Age that we experienced on Terra hundreds of thousands of years ago. If so, life on Nibiru will be harsh and primitive and the migration of reprobate souls from Terra will kick start the glacial process of civilisation and technological development there. To me the prospect is almost terrifying. Most of us today live in a world of mobile phones, internet, life-saving robotic microsurgery, air travel, electric cars, flying drones and entertainment on tap. Repeating third density means that one's soul will be transported against its will to a planet where another cycle of primitive painful reincarnations will commence. These new lifetimes would consist of banging rocks together to try to make fire, terror of wild animals, being attacked by hunters from rival tribes, grunting and groaning to someone in the hope they will understand that you are hungry.

By picking up this book and reading so far, you have shown that you are concerned with the evolution of conscience and with higher metaphysical realities. Most people are not there yet. The 'sheeple' restrict their lives to materialistic pursuits – maybe to get more money, maybe to climb the corporate ladder, maybe to have more sex, or buy more meaningless stuff. A transfer to a primitive place to repeat third density is not a punishment from the Universe. It is simply a realisation by the oversouls and the teachers of humankind that some people are just not ready to take the next step in soul evolution or ascension – to a non-materialistic state of being, or better yet, a beyond-materialistic state of being. To force these people into a fourth-density positive environment in which telepaths cooperate in love and harmony to develop amazing technology and breath-taking works of art would be a violation of their free will to focus primarily on matter and material gains.

It does not seem to be a coincidence that the Mandela Effect and the approach of Nibiru are happening at the time of ascension. Is it possible that the approach of the Nibiru system, which could possibly comprise multiple celestial objects, has been disruptive enough to alter our reality thus causing the split or convergence in timelines? Take for example the telling of a world-wide flood wiping out most life on Earth, as told in many religions on many continents that had no direct communication with each other. Is that the cause of the Mandela Effect? An eccentric theory was proposed back in 2012, that Nibiru had indeed previously caused great devastation on Earth. Proponents of this hypothesis suggest that the only reason we are still here on Earth is that there may have been a timeline change in or before 2012 – the year of the catastrophe. The timeline we were in up until 2012 is different from the one we find ourselves in now. This, according to some, is the reason why some of our memories of what happened until 2012 no longer match the historical records in our current timeline. This could be the origin of the Mandela Effects that puzzle so many.

Accessing Intelligent Energy

Psychic abilities will be commonplace among the ascended. The use of these abilities is one example of what the Law of One cryptically refers to as accessing Intelligent Energy. In fact, such abilities are already common today and are becoming more and more usual over time. Most of you reading this book right now will have already experienced psychic ability episodes in your lives. Some people are full-blown psychics and have demonstrated remarkable abilities over time. Unfortunately, these individuals are still relatively rare. In addition, for every real psychic person out there, there will be one hundred fraudsters trying to scam their way through life pretending to have such abilities. This is very sad, but in a not so distant future these imposters will be out of a job, because real psychic abilities will be so commonplace.

Ascension will mean that humankind will move into a higher level of existence. The first thing that an ascended society will notice is that there will be no more deception, no more corruption, no more manipulation. All individuals will be united in the common goal of trying to make society work as a whole. Acting with love and compassion towards others and nature. It will really feel as if the Kingdom of God has descended on this planet. But it can still be very hard to imagine such a situation, because we have spent countless incarnations swimming in the muck of human greed and oppression. Everything that we have known on this planet so far, has been marred by violence, fakery, disrespect, greed and anger. It really is like trying to explain to the caterpillar how wonderful it will be when it finally morphs into a butterfly and gains access to the entire sky. The caterpillar may just ask, baffled, "What is the sky?"

There are some things about the post-ascension world about which we can speculate. One of these, is the new set of abilities that the average person may have. Many expect telepathy will be ubiquitous; everybody will instantaneously know what everybody else is thinking. We will be able to receive direct messages from our brothers and sisters of inner Earth and from the higher astral planes, who will continue to guide us. I do not claim to have regular telepathic contact with my guides – at least not yet. But the practice of meditation has produced some amazing circumstances that I have immediately recognised as a contact, or attempted contact. One such instance took place in 2016, while I was walking around Sydney's city center, going back to my office after a meeting in another building. I had been struggling with the notion of the *Bodhisattva* who, according to Buddhism, is someone who has ascended to a point when he or she can reach Nirvana, but refuses to do so because of the desire to remain on the planet helping others reach Nirvana. In other words, a Bodhisattva is someone who waits at the doors of paradise until more, or all, may go in.

I was struggling with this concept, which is something that I had been trying to figure out for a couple of years. On one hand, the goal of any Buddhist, as I understand it, is the dissolution of the ego, or the rise of one's consciousness to a state where the ego no longer calls the shots. My understanding of Nirvana would be to reach this state where the ego is no longer the focus – a state of complete reunification with the universal consciousness (or source energy, or God). My problem was that if anyone deliberately delayed entry into Nirvana, he or she would be delaying the dissolution of their ego. So, wouldn't this be tantamount to holding on to the ego? How could someone be considered an ascended Bodhisattva and yet be holding on to their ego – even if it were for a good reason?

This was driving me crazy and I could not get my head around this issue. Then while I was still strolling back to the office, I decided to do a quick walking meditation and ask for an answer from my spiritual guides. A few minutes later, I heard a voice inside of my head ask, *"Are you a Bodhisattva?"* That question unsettled me. I was looking for an answer to my previous question and not for yet another interrogation. So, I replied with a hesitant, *"No"*. The voice continued firmly, "*… then why are you wasting your time and mine with issues like this?"* I burst out laughing in the middle of the sidewalk. That brusqueness was unexpected, but somehow delightfully familiar. I knew my spiritual guides were frank and unceremonious. That is how I am, myself.

The End of Language

I think one of the most striking features of ascension will be the end of language. Both written and spoken language will become irrelevant and will eventually be relegated to only a few very specific uses. When Earth and its population are operating at the fourth-density level, the use of telepathy will be so prevalent that language will gradually fall into disuse. Perhaps language will not completely disappear from the face of the Earth, it will just not be the main game in town. It will not be the sole means of communication. This is similar to what happens to our technologies that gradually fall into disuse, and are relegated to very specific niche applications only. For instance, the horse and buggy technology was the main method of transportation over land for millennia. Today we use cars, trains, buses, helicopters and airplanes, but the horse and buggy did not disappear. You can still use this transportation if you wish: you can go for a ride in New York's Central Park, you can ride around your farm, or use it exclusively if you live within an Amish culture. But you will only use the horse and buggy for very specific reasons now. You will not use this technology during your daily life anymore. I believe the same will happen with written and spoken language.

It is not before time, either. Language has been fundamental to the evolution of humankind while in third density, but it is not without its flaws. Language is irreparably limited and intrinsically imprecise. How many times have you said, or heard something like, "I don't have words to express this", or, "'I don't know how to tell you how I am feeling"? These are genuine examples of the limitations of conventional language. It is not capable of expressing the range of human emotions we feel, or capturing the complexity of subtle human interaction. Language is also imprecise. It is very easy for someone to say one thing, and the listener to understand something else entirely. Sometimes intentionally, and sometimes unwittingly, we pepper our daily use of language with double entendre, puns, innuendos, ambiguities, equivocations, and drivel.

If that wasn't enough, language has also been at the core of much discord and disharmony. Throughout history it has been used as an excuse to invade, conquer and kill – such as when the Nazis decided to unify all peoples of Germanic languages. It has also been used to separate, and to create classes of oppressors and their oppressed – such as when language is used to dictate your social status. Much confusion and misunderstanding has resulted from our incapacity to create clear linguistic structures.

Philosopher Ludwig Wittgenstein wrote in his *Tractatus*, "Most of the propositions and questions of philosophers arise from our failure to understand the logic or our language." (35) Wittgenstein also argued that higher things, such as ethics and aesthetics, cannot be meaningfully expressed with language. This would still be the case even if we had a perfectly logical and precise linguistic structure, which we obviously do not. There are higher, transcendental things that he called mystical, that are beyond the reach of words: "There is indeed the *inexpressible*. This *shows* itself; it is the *mystical*." (36)

To be fair, the complexity and imprecision of our language merely reflects the quagmire that is the human mind itself. The problems of language are just a reflection of the confusion of a collective human mind caught between the old and intuitive ways of third density, and the angel-like modus vivendi of the fourth. Language is a mirror put in front of our faces. Language ambiguity and inefficiency reflect our own ambiguity and inefficiency of mind or intellect. Above all, they reflect our arrogance to think that the physical is all there is; we are merely physical creatures, and we are all there is.

As I mentioned earlier, when my son was three or four years old, he decided that he did not want to go to day care or school anymore. He told us that he already knew everything there was to be known: he could run very fast and he could draw! He considered these the only things he really needed to know about how to live on this planet. Humanity is a bit like that. Humankind's arrogance in thinking that we know everything, because we can now measure everything that is physical mathematically, is similar to my three-year-old thinking that he had learnt everything useful about life. Our arrogance is borne out of a childish naiveté that leads us to believe the silliest things sometimes. Little do we know how much about the universe, consciousness, and our part in it - we have yet to learn.

We have spent millennia in third density building our own egos and feeding off of it. Now this monster needs to be laid to rest, and it will have to be dragged kicking and screaming into a new fourth-density reality for humankind, which readers of Dolores Cannon books call 5D Earth, or New Earth. With fourth-density telepathy we will have meaningful and truthful exchanges. You will just feel like the collective. Ethics and aesthetics will arise naturally from the simple state of being part of this collective and wishing it to thrive. Words will no longer get in the way.

Is it any wonder that most of the Mandela Effect residuals we have today revolve around language? Changes in TV show titles; changes in movie lines; changes in Biblical passages; company and product names. The Mandela Effect itself seems to be telling us not to rely too much on language. In these times, when the process of ascension almost certainly has already started, the Mandela Effect is a sharp reminder of the unreliability of language. People had memorised certain movie dialogues and certain Bible passages, only to realize later (sometimes to their horror) that their memories no longer match historical records.

Little by Little Does It

Self-improvement can be a daunting task. This is because we have grown accustomed to doing things in a certain way, and any change means stepping out of our cosy comfort zone. There really is nothing wrong with having a comfort zone. In a crazy world like ours, it is gratifying to create a little bubble within which we feel in control. However, self-improvement requires stepping out of this zone. Ascension means stepping out of this zone. There is no other way in which this can be accomplished. The caterpillar literally needs to break out of its cocoon to morph into the butterfly. Besides which, when you are in your comfort zone, there is no need to do anything differently. Fortunately or unfortunately, most of our growth comes from being invited, pushed or stretched into new experiences; and some of these can be quite challenging. This is the reason many say their greatest challenges in life have held their greatest gifts – eventually.

The good news is that change doesn't need to be abrupt. Change can take place little by little. In fact, the best chance of changing something in our lives is to make this change gradual. When you decide to change something 'cold-turkey' you may meet a barrage of resistance – from those who had benefited from the old ways, and from the natural fear of failure in taking a new path. This resistance can be quite strong and may lead to discouragement, or quitting the attempted change. Remember that the laws of the physical and metaphysical universe we live in means that the reaction is proportional and opposite to the action. If the action is brisk and abrupt, the reaction will be brisk and abrupt. This serves some situations and personalities well. If you want the reaction to be gradual and smooth and more manageable in some way, the action needs to be gradual and smooth too.

A good example of this is the beautiful insight given to us by Buddhist practitioner Johanna Engwirda in her book *Digesting Life, Creating Awareness*. (37) This is one of the most remarkable books I have ever come across for its simplicity, beauty and value. Johanna tells us that at some juncture she was confronted with the need to make radical changes in her life. She was concerned and scared with thoughts of failure teeming through her mind, because the change she needed to undergo was so substantial and fundamental, that she could not envision how she could possibly pull it off. Then she had a beautiful vision during a meditation. The vision, which I paraphrase here, went somewhat like this:

She saw a massive wall stretching out as far as the eye could see. This obstacle seemed unsurmountable and discouraged anyone even considering overcoming it. One would need a gigantic wrecking ball to break through it, or a potent flying machine to go over it – none of which were available. Then she noticed tiny little pebbles flying through the air and hitting the wall. The pebbles were minute, but numerous, and were hitting the wall in frequent and regular intervals. She noted that every time one little projectile hit the wall it would make a small dent or cavity on the majestic barrier. She kept observing as millions of tiny pebbles continued their obstinate task of eroding the wall - little by little. She could see where this was going, and was happy that at least something was being done to demolish the wall. Something is always better than nothing, but she was also feeling frustrated by the slow rate of demolition. Nevertheless, she kept on watching it and never gave up. Every time a pebble hit the wall, a small chunk of the formidable barrier fell off, so the erosion grew. At some point, she noted the little cavities were getting larger and were starting to merge together. The merged cavities continued to grow into sizeable holes. Disenchanted, she continued to watch, thinking that by the time the job was finished - it would be too late for her. However, at some point she saw something remarkable that made her heart leap with unabated joy. The little cavities that had joined together into larger holes had continued to grow, until they started destabilising the wall. There was no need to wait an eternity for the wall to come down, because it was ready to collapse. Then it happened! The whole thing crumbled down with a mighty roar. The little pebbles did not have to do the entire daunting job. They just needed to get it started and persevere, step by step, until the sheer weight of the status quo of their activity brought eventual success.

I believe the gradual approach to inner transformation is a key lesson for those aspiring to be part of Humanity 2.0. Little by little, through steps almost imperceptible, we cause our own ascension, as well as the collective ascension. This is another unexpected lesson from the Mandela Effect. The first Mandela Effect residuals were noticed many years ago only by a few. Little by little, more started noticing M. E. residuals in their own lives, in their own countries, in their own languages. There has not been, at the time of this writing, a seismic, momentous event announcing to the world that reality has changed. In fact, our timelines are changing gradually - residual by residual. Many people won't even acknowledge or accept that things are shifting at all, if they don't notice these small insignificant changes along the way. Many so called 'sheeple' will happily ascribe the Mandela Effect residuals to the false memories of others. Yet those of us who have noticed and are puzzled by the Mandela Effect are receiving a wonderful lesson about patience, and the gradual nature of spiritual evolution. We need to understand that development and preparation for ascension is, at least at first instance, a gradual and continuous process.

Nurturing Untainted Love

Forgiveness and overcoming negative karma involves nurturing love. But there are different manifestations of love, and we should be mindful of their impacts on our consciousness. I wrote this section while I was half reading a book and half meditating. My mind was a bit high, literally, because I was in the middle of a flight between Melbourne and Sydney. Perhaps the feeling of light-headedness was just due to the low level of oxygen in the cabin. Taking advantage of this state of mind, I started madly typing away on my mobile phone, as if these ideas were being channelled through me in some way. It is an edited version of these notes that you are going to read now.

It came to me that the true value and power of Love is to create polarization towards service to others. As we develop love, we slowly start understanding that others are as important as we are, and they deserve the same care as we deliver to ourselves. I suppose this is a lesson that begins to be comprehended at some time while still in third density existence (the sequence of incarnations as sentient rational beings), as we begin to understand and value the presence of family, partners, friends, then like-minded individuals, then the community, and finally (hopefully) the entire human race.

Most of the forms of love have an element of self-love and self-service. When we love a life partner (*Eros* love from ancient Greek), we tell her or him, "you belong to *me*". This can also be the love of power, the love of domination, the love of greed. When we love our family members (*Storge* love from ancient Greek), we are saying, "I love you because you are the closest to *me*. You have *my* genetic material in you". When we love our friends and like-minded people (called *Phileo* love in ancient Greek), we are saying, "I love you because you think just like *me*. You have the same interests, graces and style that *I* do".

Storge love associates the red ray (survival) of the base chakra called Muladhara with the green ray (love) of the heart chakra Anahata. Eros love associates the orange ray (sexuality, reproduction, and creativity) of the second chakra Svadhishthana with the green ray of the heart chakra Anahata. Phileo love associates the yellow ray (social self-identity) of the solar plexus chakra Manipura with the green ray of the heart chakra Anahata. Have you noticed a pattern here? All of these things: Storge, Eros and Phileo are types of love, but they are all inward looking. They are *prototypes of love.* In all of these prototypes of love, the true love energy of the green ray from Anahata is present, but it is always tainted, and never pure. The green ray in prototypical love is always stained by the red, orange or yellow rays – the most basic rays of the ego and animalism.

Things are very different with *Agape* love, which is truly selfless. It is the type of love that involves sacrifice, abandon, wonder. It is non-egoic love that fills your heart chakra (Anahata) with the purest and brightest green-ray energy and vibration. It is the love of renunciation, humility, goodwill, charity, children, animals, humanity, Earth, God … it is the real engine that drives the creation of the Maia.

The Doorway is Not the Conscious Mind

Many people argue that the doorway to developing psychic abilities lies in the subconscious mind. An analysis of the human subconscious is well outside of the scope of this book, and way above my pay grade, but there are some things I would like to touch on here. Materialists regard the subconscious as simply a repository of instincts, hidden abilities and half-forgotten memories. I believe the subconscious is much, much more.

Let us start with a relatively prosaic example: when certain athletes are playing so well, they do not even notice it. Their passes are precision perfect, their catches make them look like they can foresee the future, and their stamina seems superhuman. Surely you have seen such displays. If fact, if you practise sports, you may remember experiencing such moments yourself. When everything is going just right, and you are not sure how it is all going so well. Through repetition, practice, or imagining success they are able to switch into a certain mode of doing things where they are no longer thinking. It is all automatic. They are 'in the zone'. Artists do this too.

In fact, there is a way to apply psychological sledging to an opponent that involves this knowledge. For instance, you could find yourself playing in a match: it could be golf, tennis, basketball, snooker, anything … and you notice your opponent is playing impeccably. This is a sign that your opponent has gotten into 'the zone'. It means he or she is now operating entirely from the subconscious mind (or some say the superconscious mind of higher consciousness). Their conscious, rational, objective mind has receded, and they are now operating in an automatic mode. When facing people in his mode, you could compliment them, or ask them, "How are you doing this? How are you playing so well?" This rather sneaky trick gets into your opponent's head - immediately taking them out of the zone. This is because the moment you ask them that question, your opponent must rationalise in the conscious mind to answer you. When that happens, the conscious mind tries to take over and it can only do this by pushing the subconscious mind back into a latent stage. When that happens, your opponent will get out of the zone, and will no longer be operating in an automatic way.

This happened to me one day in somewhat different circumstances. I was walking on my way to work when I saw a female beggar across the street from me. She was poorly dressed, although she had something to eat. I immediately felt a great deal of compassion for her going through such a difficult time; such a hard lesson of want and need. While I was observing her, I was also struck by a feeling of peace, acquiescence and comfort. It was as if I knew in that moment that everything that lady was going through was necessary for her own development; that she was not abandoned by her spiritual guides and her Higher Self; her suffering had meaning and purpose according to her pre-incarnation choices, her karmic debt and her own desire for spiritual advancement. I realized in that moment that I was in a kind of 'zone'. No one was saying these things to me; I just knew them. It was natural, it was automatic, and it was quick and beautiful. It was as if I had connected to a river of knowledge that would automatically contain all the answers. The Greeks called this Gnosis. I stayed there enjoying what I later realized was what the Law of One calls compassion with wisdom. I felt great compassion and love for that suffering lady, but at the same time, I also felt deep peace and acquiescence because I just knew that this was the pathway her Higher Self and her guides had chosen to foster deeper lessons.

At this stage, something strange happened. I asked myself, "This is a result of karma, this is the path that she chose in order to learn - but what is karma?" Then I started trying to define, compartmentalise, and deconstruct all I thought I understood about karma. The more I went down this route - the more anxious I became. I had this knowledge somewhere in my memory, and I knew I could tap into it, but at that moment it proved elusive and I could not verbalise any of the knowledge and feelings I had just had a few seconds before. I started feeling frustrated and empty. How is it that I had been studying and meditating for years, yet could not articulate what karma was? The more I pushed myself the more frustrated and anxious I became. Then I realized what was happening. By deciding to come up with a logical definition of karma, I had summoned the conscious mind, and it obeyed my command. It came to the fore and started working, but in order to do that, it had to push the unconscious mind out of the way. So the unconscious receded and became dormant again. The problem is the conscious mind does not have a link to infinite intelligence, and by summoning it, I had unwittingly cut myself off from the river of knowledge that had brought me the previous understanding and serenity. I had gotten myself out of the zone.

One of the weirdest examples of the connection between the unconscious mind and Intelligent Infinity can be seen in hypnotized people. The unconscious mind does appear to have the ability to break out of the physical illusion that some call Maya. I was watching people being hypnotised and some commands were the usual silly ones such as, "speak in a language no one understands", or "stay rigid like a plank of wood supported by these two chairs". The hypnotised people were obeying every command, and although the entire experience was very strange, it just suggested to me that they were in an altered state of mind where their bodies and their senses were operating from an unconscious level.

However, one of the orders completely threw me off guard. A hypnotised person was asked to imagine that another person was invisible and that she could see everything behind this invisible body. The person that was supposed to be invisible was given a small object to hold behind her back in a discrete way, just so the hypnotised person could not see what was hidden. There was no way the hypnotised person could have seen the object, and yet she guessed correctly what the object was. Could she really see through the other person because she was commanded from an unconscious level to do so? Do hypnotised people somehow gain Superman's x-ray vision? It is reasonable to expect that no one, hypnotised or not, can see through a solid object. What had happened?

That incident blew my mind, because it appeared that the hypnotised person had acquired superpowers. The best guess I have is that by hypnotising people you make them operate from the unconscious mind. And the unconscious mind has access to information that is outside of the physical illusion in which we live in - outside the prison of Maya. So, perhaps the unconscious of the hypnotised person did not need the physical sense of vision to understand or see what the other person was holding behind their back. Or perhaps the unconscious of the hypnotised person somehow melded with the unconscious of the other person holding the object, so they automatically knew what everybody else knew.

Psychiatrist, author and researcher Dr Karl Jung suggested the idea of the *collective unconscious*: which is the shared sum of all personal experiences of all members of a particular group or species. This collective unconscious – also known as the *superconscious* or hivemind – represents the totality of memories and experiences that a group shares. For instance, if I have a trauma of having been bullied as a child, and I tell you about that experience, we will now share the same trauma. Except that my experience will be more vivid, full of first-hand poignant memories, while yours will most likely be less emotionally charged. But in any case, the two of us now share this experience and it will influence our behaviour, even if we are not conscious of it. However, is it possible that the collective unconscious could contain the shared experiences of *all* individuals, even if those individuals never physically met? We are now talking about an extrasensory link between minds, sometimes called the human collective subconscious mind, or human hivemind.

It is also possible humans can attain certain states of mind where they gain access to a greater field of consciousness. Hypnotherapist and author Dolores Cannon reported that her hypnotized patients were able to tap into an "absolute power" and "the greater force in the universe" - that had the answers to all questions and could "heal anything". (38) The Monroe Institute has an entire training course on the superconscious and how to develop the abilities of mind that learn, among other things, "psychic sensing or knowing". (39) Biologist Dr.+ Lyall Watson found unquestionable evidence of a spontaneous transference of knowledge throughout a species, or a "mind-to-mind jump", which he called the 100th Monkey Effect. (40)

The difference between the conscious and the (personal) unconscious mind can also often be described in terms of the depth and appreciation of knowledge of which each type of mind is capable. The conscious mind specialises in *knowing,* while the subconscious prefers *experiencing.* In one of his fantastic philosophical lectures about the Law of One material, Dr Scott Mandelker discusses this difference with a simple, but brilliant analogy: You can study the effects of glycose, and understand all of the linguistic applications of the word "sugar" and its derivatives; but none of this will give you the experience of eating a sweet piece of fruit. (41)

I believe that the rise in human consciousness necessarily involves us learning to tap more into the unconscious mind than we have done in the past. That involves more experiencing and less rationalisation, less measuring and more enjoying. For example, those who attempt to rationalize the Mandela Effect will usually end up in a state of confusion. This phenomenon may involve forces and mechanisms that are outside our capacity to understand the universe. This is because our perceived universe is limited to the physical three-dimensional reality we see and touch around us, as is particle science and those who support the Standard Model of the universe – recognized science. The Mandela Effect is transcendent. It manifests in a greater reality, beyond our three-dimensional cage of matter. For this reason, I think the Mandela Effect is intrinsically linked with ascension. Ascension is the process of breaking out of our material cage, and the Mandela Effect appears like the first glimpses of light from beyond the broken bars.

Prayer

I believe prayer is the age-old catalyst of human consciousness development. It is a practice that has been adopted worldwide throughout all religions and cultures, and throughout the entire history of humankind. When I talk about prayer, I mean the true act of introspection and communion between a person and their most sacred inner space. I am not referring to those theatrical outward displays of piety and faux contrition that are so common among organized religious practice.

One key benefit of prayer has to do with the Law of Free Will that I discussed earlier. Higher spiritual beings, those who are full of love and compassion, have an immense respect for the free will of their human protégés. This means that they want to help you in more ways than you can imagine, but they can only do this if you authorise them to do so. They cannot prevent accidents, diseases, or conflicts if such things have an important role in your spiritual evolution, and if you chose them as situational learning events prior to coming into being. However, many believe there are a number of hazards that they can protect you from, but they will always ask first. They will never do something to you without your approval and consent. The Law of Free Will is sovereign and the strict observance of this law is a way for these higher beings to demonstrate their respect and love for humans and our independence. So this is the first spiritual role of prayer. Prayer is an official declaration authorising our spiritual protectors, guides, friends, and higher selves to help us and assist us in any way they can – once we have asked for their assistance. Prayer tells the Universe that these protectors are authorised to intervene in our lives without incurring karma for themselves, because they are only answering our call.

A second role of prayer has to do with the immense power of human thought. When we pray, we usually focus our attention on a specific issue, problem or conflict. We request and imagine receiving help and blessings from higher realms in response to our pleading. By doing that, we are imagining a world in which our problems have been solved or ameliorated. This imagination is extremely powerful, and the energy created by these thought forms helps shift our timeline towards an alternative reality that is closer to that which we desire. We are co-creators here, and we have the power to determine the world we live in with our thought, emotion and imagination. The self-denominated elites that rule (or ruled) this world do not seem to want humankind to wake up to and comprehend the immense creative power that each individual holds to effect change in this reality matrix. That is why these elites have created materialism, physicalism, scientificism, and consumerism. All of these doctrines keep communicating to us that nothing exists except the material – what can easily be measured and quantified. Materialism is an extremely effective thought-prison, and a number of us have fallen prey to it. The entire scientific community in a display of unbridled arrogance has determined they are the best and brightest at observing, measuring and defining reality for everyone; and anyone who believes in superstitions, paranormal gifts, and mystical knowledge is an inferior intellect stuck in the dark ages. This is exactly how the ruling elite want us to think in order to suppress the colossal creative power that humans naturally have over matter through their thoughts, feelings, imagination, visualization and prayer. This is also why they have been avoiding addressing the fast-growing phenomenon called the Mandela Effect, except to occasionally call it confabulation or mass miss-remembering. This ignoring is likely to remain, so long as residual proof of how things used to be still exists. If they are successful at removing all residual evidence of how things were before they changed, then they will be able to classify people experiencing the Mandela Effect as suffering from a new mental illness. It seems A.I. is clearing up as much residual evidence as possible through connection to the internet, but hard, physical, tangible, material proof of how many things used to be will likely always exist. If you find any – preserve it offline if possible. This could be a kind of safety net until mainstream thought catches up with the Mandela Effect affected who see matter changing in response to collective thoughts, feelings, imagination, visualization, expectations and prayer. In this way the people affected by the Mandela Effect represent an evolution in human consciousness, as their consciousness expands into awareness of how matter responds to consciousness.

A third role prayer plays in human development is as a catalyst for spiritual ascension. As we pray, we raise our vibration and shift our thought to emanations of love, compassion, forgiveness and gratitude. These are higher frequency energy called feelings or emotions, and by tuning in to them, we start to clean up our emotional and mental bodies, sometimes referred to as the astral and etheric bodies. The process is somewhat similar to placing a droplet of detergent on the middle of a small oil slick. The detergent breaks down the oil molecules, and the oil slick begins to disintegrate progressively from within. Without prayer, this cleaning would need to be done through other means, namely, karmic visitation in the form of disease, pain, cancer, sadness and depression. By praying, we bypass the need to use such drastic means of purification, and we decontaminate our astral bodies using the multiplicative power of higher frequency thoughts and feelings.

Meditation

It is said that praying is talking to God while meditation is listening to God. This is a lyric and simplistic description of the difference between praying and meditating, but it does appear to be very close to the truth for me. Meditation means different things to different people, but in a nutshell, I would describe it as giving your mind some time out to rest and regroup. Meditation is mentioned and recommended in many religious or spiritual traditions. The Bible discusses how we should sometimes just 'be' and just 'know' in order to reach Intelligent Infinity without being burdened by anything else: "Be still and know that I am God." [The Bible, Psalms 46:10.]

Buddha considered meditation so important that he placed it high in his recipe for ascension: mindfulness and meditation are the seventh and eighth steps in the Noble Eightfold Path to Enlightenment. In Hinduism, meditation is at the heart of the Yogic practices that seek to bring humankind closer to Divinity. Mystical philosophies employ Hermetic meditation techniques to expand the consciousness of adepts. The Law of One specifically mentions meditation as the channel to connect one's self with their Higher Self for guidance. (42)

Someone once asked me what were the benefits of meditation and what did I use meditation for? I just kept thinking about my inability to answer that question. It is like a baby asking a toddler what the benefits of learning to walk were. How could the toddler possibly even begin to explain this to the baby? If the toddler could exemplify they might say, "When you learn to walk, you are able to climb up on a swing and have lots of fun". To which the baby would probably reply, "What is a swing?"

Philosopher Ludwig Wittgenstein was aware there are some things that cannot be put into words. The highest order, the most important, the most fundamental questions in philosophy to him were essentially inexpressible in our limited language. When introducing his most famous book the *Tractatus Logico Philosophicus*, he stated, "My book consists of two parts, the one presented [in this manuscript] plus all that I have *not* written. And it is precisely this second part that is the important point … I've managed in my book to put everything firmly into place by being silent about it." (43)

To paraphrase this great philosopher and logician, perhaps the best way to discuss meditation is to be silent about it and the possible benefits it could bring you. I am certainly not in any authoritative position to provide the reader with an accurate description and discussion of the benefits of meditation. There are myriad books on the theme available, but I honestly doubt that even reading them all would do meditation justice. I will reserve the right to express all the magnificent benefits meditation can bring to you, the reader, by being silent about them. However, I can share with you my *personal* story. It is of course a reflection of my own relatively low state of development; my own inner demons and my *dharma* – my life contract for this existence.

I started meditating regularly in 2013. I had an hour-long, boring and relatively quiet train ride to work every morning in which a number of my fellow commuters dozed off. So I decided to start meditating during this ride. As I am writing this section early in 2019, I have clocked almost six years of daily meditation, and despite the priceless benefits received, I have not even begun to scratch the surface of what meditation can provide.

Before 2013, I had only dabbled in meditation, after having done a course on it in my early twenties. I remember in one session actually having a vision of an angel that instantaneously brought me to tears and interrupted that practice. But this incident had been a long time ago, and since then, I had become a religious Seventh Day Adventist who thought that meditation was ungodly. I left the church in the mid-2000s and was free from the dogmas and strict discipline imposed by the organisation.

After I started meditating, my train rides were extremely peaceful. I used earphones in the guise of ear plugs to get a bit of quiet, but did not use any music or binaural frequencies. Just silence. It is said that if you repeat something 21 times it becomes a habit, and my goal was to go through that threshold without giving up on the practice. I persisted and continued meditating, admittedly with the help of the lack of alternatives in a mind-numbingly boring train ride early in the morning en route to an even more boring eight hours in an office. Meditating soon became a habit, and I would automatically engage with it when I got my seat on the morning train; but much to my frustration, I had not had any transcendental experiences or visions. However, I noted that my anxiety would be dialled down and the whole day would be far more comfortable - due to my morning meditation.

Soon enough, I started hankering for my meditation hour in the morning. I started enjoying the feeling of quietness and reduction of the maddening mental clatter that assaulted my mind during normal hours.

Winter in Australia comes with its obligatory season of coughs and colds of which I am a perennial sufferer. I have a type of allergy that greatly increases the production of mucus when I catch a cold, and in addition to that, my immune system was so week that I would be among the first to catch a cold as soon as someone sneezed around me. I would catch a cold, spend two days in bed, get better, and then spend the next three weeks with chronic nasal congestion and sinusitis. By the time I finally improved from this ordeal and started to breathe normally, another flu and cold cycle would have started. Someone else in the office would fall sick with the next viral strain, and I would unceremoniously catch it. It felt like a state of continuous dis-ease. As sad and exasperating as it seems, it is absolutely true that during the cold season in Australia (which is the inverse of the Northern Hemisphere), I would catch a cold in April and get over it by late September.

I went to many doctors with no success. I could have recorded their response, "There is nothing you can do about this, take some (fill in the blank pain reliever), go home, rest, and get plenty of fluids." Well, as it turned out there *was* something I could do. It just did not feature in the menu of options our materialistic big pharma controlled allopathic church of medicine recommended. By June 2014, I realized I had not caught one single cold that winter, and the only thing I was doing differently was the daily meditation. I continued meditating, observing this possible side effect, and got the same results. Persistence with meditation had reduced the frequency and severity of my colds from 2014 to present. My office colleagues even noted that I was no longer the first one to call in sick. I was over the moon! Meditation had broken a lifelong pattern of cold and flu torture.

There were even circumstances where I went on holiday, and in the absence of my boring daily commute, stopped my daily meditation. Inevitably, I would fall sick either with a flu or an attack of sinusitis between one and two weeks after stopping meditating. It really felt like meditation had started a by-pass circuit whereby my body was eliminating toxic astral energies that were the trigger to my bouts of flu. By stopping meditating, for whatever reason, I was closing the faucet. The pressure would build until the toxic astral energies materialized in the form of mucus. Meditation appeared to have boosted my health.

Excited with this prospect, I did some research and indeed found many articles and books explaining how meditation lowers your blood pressure, boosts your immune system, and shortens your body's recovery time during ailments. You can find a plethora of material on this topic with a simple internet search, but I really think there was far more at play than this in my case. As it turned out, anger and pride are two of my most potent inner demons. And when these two nefarious emotions are cultivated in the inner realms of the astral/emotional body (as in holding on to resentment), they generate toxic stains that blemish the astral and possibly the mental bodies. There are fantastic descriptions of such processes in Barbara Brennan's amazing work. (44) I believe I have held on to this astral poison for millennia through a long sequence of incarnations. This stuff was festering inside my astral vessel like rotting etheric pus. It is not enough to stop being angry and to control one's emotions. The material that was already produced needed to be purged too. In its wisdom, my own body had commenced this purging through the mechanism of colds and flus. The suffering brought about by the never-ending stream of disease was slowly burning off the toxic etheric material and gradually cleansing my body. My disease would not happen only because I got in contact with the flu virus. The flu virus was merely the trigger.

The real cause for my disease was the need to flush-out the deleterious miasma accumulated over millennia that was weighing down my astral body and holding me back in my search for ascension. The amount of poisonous material I had accumulated in my astral vessel was not severe or toxic enough to give me something more serious like cancer, so, my wise body had determined that minor ailments such as constant colds and flus would be enough to purify my system. I think astral cleansing through disease is a welcome development. It is far better than no cleansing at all. However, it is a painful, inconvenient and sometimes a very, very slow process. Only heaven knows how long, or how many incarnations it would take for my body to expunge all of my miasma in this way.

I was absolutely delighted to realize meditation appeared to speed this process up considerably. Almost every day, when I meditated, I would feel stomach rumblings as if something was collecting around the area of the Solar Plexus Manipura chakra. I also realized that on many occasions when I was starting to feel sick and did meditation, I would experience diarrhoea and immediately feel better. As it turned out, meditation somehow allows Manipura chakra to suck up all of the poisonous material in your astral body and condense it for expunging it. After that process, Manipura will simply collect the condensed etheric material and merge it with your physical faeces. From this point onwards the material would be expelled from your body in the known way. When I realized that this was the process, I even started visualising during meditation an immense vortex in Manipura sucking up black stains that had attached to all parts of my body. I would visualise this vortex avidly slurping in all of the nasties from my astral body much in the same way as a black hole draws in any object in its vicinity. As I proceeded with this visualisation exercise, many times I would feel and even hear my stomach grumble. As a result, I stopped being a chronic flu sufferer. I have barely had any flus in years. Of course, I am *not* claiming that regular meditation will have the same effect for you. It will be most likely different, but probably no less amazing.

It was also meditation that allowed me to clear my mind in a way that I started receiving insights about issues troubling me. It is interesting that almost nothing seems to happen during meditation itself - but afterwards. For example, if something was bothering me and I decided to meditate to find an answer, absolutely nothing would be presented to me while I was meditating. It appears that the simple fact of expecting an answer while meditating may be somehow a hindrance to it being received right there and then. Perhaps because the act of expecting summons the analytical conscious mind, and this may impede communication with the subconscious. However, the constant practice of meditation meant that the answer would simply pop-up in my head when I least expected. This is usually the way in which information from the subconscious and the superconscious is bought to the surface: it pops up unannounced, unanticipated, as we go about our daily activities. This type of knowledge is usually called noetic, which means coming internally from one's own intellect through a mystical experience.

I started having noetic insights left, right and center all throughout my day. It was as if something or someone was trying to talk to and guide me, and after forty or so years I was finally paying attention. Throughout this section, I try to describe a number of insights and ideas that just came to me through this method of internal inspiration (the ideas presented here without acknowledgement or references). I credit meditation for opening a window into Intelligent Infinity. I do not know if meditation has strengthened the communication link between me and my Higher Self; if it has allowed my spiritual guides easier access to my intellect and communication functions; if it has provided our cosmic friends and inner-Earth brothers and sisters with a clearer communication channel; or if it has allowed me to tap into the Akashic Records. I do not know what really happened, but I am not the same person that I was *before* commencing my meditation practice. I am calmer, more aware, more attuned with Intelligent Infinity, a little bit wiser and healthier. As someone once told me: "prayer is when you talk to God; meditation is when you listen".

I believe those who meditate are also more open to the perception of subtle changes in our reality – such as the Mandela Effect. This is because regular meditation slowly attunes you to Intelligent Infinity – the universal field of consciousness from which all beings and things sprout. The same field artists draw their masterpieces from. It allows you to transcend reality and deepen your connection with your intuition, spiritual guidance, the universe, source energy or God. Of course, not all Mandela Effect experiencers meditate. But there are a number of other possible ways a person may begin seeing reality differently. Some of those awake and awakening now may not meditate in their current incarnation, but may have engaged with meditative or visualization practices in previous ones. There is a large number of old souls on the planet now – souls who have had a large number of previous incarnations as third-density humans living on 3D Earth. It is possible that these individuals at some point were taught meditation, contemplation or visualization in previous lives. If you are interested in material such as this book, it is most likely because you are one of these souls. So, it follows it is possible that individuals could naturally engage with meditation – even if they do not consciously know about it. One can dive into a meditative state while dancing, listening to music, playing music, drawing, painting, walking on the beach, watching a beautiful sunset, trekking through a forest, and so forth. So, it is very probable that you may have been doing quite a lot of meditating (at least in a shallower trance) even if you never sat cross-legged practicing mudras for hours.

Secondly, prayer is also a practice that elevates the vibration of your consciousness and leads you to transcend the physical. Prayer also opens up the channels between the individual and higher spiritual guidance, and allows the perception of realities outside the illusion of Maya. It is no wonder that a lot of the Mandela Effect residuals circulating on the internet relate to perceived changes in the Bible and other religious texts.

Thirdly, sincerity of heart is another causeway to higher realities. You may not meditate or pray, but if you truly and honestly seek to understand your role in the universe, or help others, that desire alone will open your soul to the mysteries of the reality behind perceived reality. Mandela Effect experiencers seem to be naturally more inquisitive, engaged, and intellectually and artistically inclined. In other words – creative thinkers. The pursuit of truth is what drives us, and the possibility of being wrong is not scary. We just forge ahead regardless of the scorn of the 'sheeple', the mocking by the mainstream media, and the venom of the vested-interest intellectuals and money-grabbers. Those who sell out their integrity and choke their genuine curiosity in order to obtain tenure, prizes, applause or research grants from the elites. These people are doing a disservice to humanity and themselves, by stifling genuine scientific exploration of consciousness and the nature of reality. In the words of Herman Hesse, "It is treason to sacrifice love of truth, intellectual honesty, loyalty to the laws and methods of the mind, to any other interests ...." (45)

This is what is so beautiful about the international community of Mandela Effect experiencers: the brave, often clumsy, but honest and uncompromising search for the Truth.

Part Two Endnotes:

1. Sex in the City, 1998 – 2004 HBO (Home Box Office).

2. Jung, C., G., Synchronicity – An Acausal Connecting Principle, Princeton University Press, 1960.

3. Deschamps, Justin, The Cabal Explained, Reptilian Aliens and the Council of the 13 'Royal Families, Stillness in the Storm, December 12, 2014 https://stillnessinthestorm.com/2014/12/the-cabal-explained-reptilian-aliens/ and Jay Parker and Mark Passio, Satanic Ritualistic Abuse, Truth Connections Radio, May 8, 2014.

4. Rosen, Eliot Jay, The Soul and Quantum Physics – An Interview with Dr Fred Alan Wolf, in 'Experiencing the Soul: Before Birth, During Life, After Death,' 1998.

5. Elkins, Don, Carla Rueckert and James McCarthy, The Law of One – The Ra Material, session 71.6, Unilaw Library, 1984.

6. Wolf, Fred Alan, Time Loops and Space Twists – How God Created the Universe, Hierophant Publishing, 2011.

7. Einstein's relativity theory suggested that mass and energy are related by the equation: $E = mc2 / (1\text{-}v2/c2)1/2$. When the speed v of the object is well below that of light, the equation collapses into the famous positive relationship between energy and matter $E = mc2$. But when v > c the equation simplifies to a relationship that shows that energy is proportional to minus mc2i, where i is the imaginary number the square root of -1.

8. Watson, Lyall, Lifetide: A Biology of the Unconscious, 1979, Simon and Schuster.

9. Furedi, Jacob, Bank of America Analysts Think There's a 50 per cent Chance We Live in the Matrix, The

Independent, 14 September 2016.

10. Wall, Mike, We're Probably Living in a Simulation, Elon Musk Says, September 7, 2018, Space.com, (https://www.space.com/41749-elon-musk-living-in-simulation-rogan-podcast.html), and Bostrom, Nick, Are You Living in a Computer Simulation?, Philosophical Quarterly, 2003, Vol. 53, No. 211, pp. 243-255.

11. Miller, Alan, The Illusion of Reality, NEXUS Alternative News Magazine, March 2018.

12. Johnson, Carolyn, What Happened to the $750 Pill that Catapulted Martin Shkreli to Infamy, August 1, 2017, The Washington Post.

13. To list just a few: The Mandela Effect – What Do You Remember? (https://mandelaeffect.com/); The Conversation, The 'Mandela Effect' and How Your Mind is Playing Tricks on You (https://mandelaeffect.com/); The Urban Dictionary, Mandela Effect, (https://www.urbandictionary.com/define.php?term=Mandela%20Effect); Unmuseum, The Mandela Effect: Are Alternative Universes Colliding?, (http://www.unmuseum.org/mandela.htm); Gaia, Is the Mandela Effect Changing Events in Our Universe?, (https://www.gaia.com/article/a-parallel-dimension-is-changing-people-and-events-in-our-universe); Entity Magazine, 50 Unbelievable Examples of the Mandela Effect That Will Make You Question Reality, (https://www.entitymag.com/mandela-effect-examples/); Forbes, The Mandela Effect -- Bad Memories Or An Alternate Universe? (https://www.forbes.com/sites/capitalone/2017/10/31/the-mandela-effect-bad-memories-or-an-alternate-universe/#2b1dc6612e5d); Buzzfeed, 20 Examples of The Mandela Effect That'll Make You Believe You're in A Parallel Universe (https://www.buzzfeed.com/christopherhudspeth/crazy-examples-of-the-mandela-effect-that-will-make-you-ques); Arapahoe Libraries, What's the Mandela Effect?

(https://arapahoelibraries.org/blogs/post/whats-the-mandela-effect/).

14. Robert Lanza, Biocentrism: How Life and Consciousness are the Key to Understanding the Nature of the Universe, Benbella Books, 2009.

15. Robert Lanza, MD, Biocentrism, http://www.robertlanzabiocentrism.com/.

16. Sheldrake, Rupert, A New Science of Life, J P Tarcher, Inc, 1981.

17. Video available on YouTube at the time of writing on the link https://en.wikipedia.org/wiki/Rupert_Sheldrake.

18. Brennan, Barbara, Hands of Light, Bantam, Reissue edition, 2011.

19. Deutsch, David, The Ghost in the Atom, ed. P. C. W. Davies and J. R. Brown (Cambridge: Cambridge University Press, 1986), 85.

20. Laszlo, Ervin, Science and the Akashic Field: An Integral Theory of Everything, Inner Traditions Bear and Company, 2007.

21. [Talbot, Michael, The Holographic Universe, Harper Collins Publishers, 1991]

22. [Currivan, Jude, The Cosmic Hologram, Inner Traditions Bear and Company, 2017.

23. Pari, Brama Kumari, Holographic Universe, Createspace Independent Publishing Platform, 2015.

24. Friedlander, Gregory, The Einstein Hologram Universe, Clean Water Books, 2013.

25. One (Eileen Colts), Holographic Universe for the Mandela Effect Community, YouTube.

26. Hindu Human Rights, Divinity Lies Within Us All, http://www.hinduhumanrights.info/divinity-lies-within-us-all/.

27. Kluge, Tino, Fractals in Nature and Applications, http://kluge.in-chemnitz.de/documents/fractal/node2.html.

28. Elkins, Don, Carla Rueckert and James McCarthy, The Law of One – The Ra Material, sessions 16.50, 20.36, 38.14 and others, Unilaw Library, 1984.

29. Sacred Mysteries TV, Kubric's Odyssey & the Brotherhood of Saturn, YouTube.
30. The Bible, Revelation 20:7,8.

31. Abrams, J.J. (director), Star Trek – Into the Darkness, Paramount Pictures.

32. Bezerra de Menezes, Herdeiros do Novo Mundo, 2009, Editora Ide] V. M. Rabolù also spoke about this in his book Hercolubus or the Red Planet. [Rabolù, V.M. Hercólubus ou la Plenète Rouge, 2002, Kendall Services Graphiques.

33. The Bible, Daniel 9:27, 11:31, 12:11, Matthew 24:15 and Mark 13:14.

34. Witze, Alexandra, Evidence Grows for Giant Planet on Fringes of Solar System, 21 January 2016, Nature, Volume 529.

35. Wittgenstein, Ludwig, Tractatus Logico-Philosophicus, proposition 4.03, 1921.

36. Wittgenstein, Ludwig, Tractatus Logico-Philosophicus, proposition 6.522, 1921, emphasis added.

37. Engwirda, Johanna, Digesting Life, Creating Awareness, Brolga Publishing, 2012.

38. The Bible, Psalms 46:10.

39. Cannon, Dolores, Dolores Cannon: What is the Subconscious?, YouTube.

40. Cannon, Dolores, Dolores Cannon: What is the Subconscious?, YouTube 14.
Watson, Lyall, Lifetide: A Biology of the Unconscious, 1979, Simon and Schuster.
41. Mandelker, Scott, The Law of One Podcast Series, https://thelawofonepodcast.blogspot.com/.

42. Elkins, Don, Carla Rueckert and James McCarthy, The Law of One – The Ra Material, sessions 17.40, 36.11, 49.7, 49.8. Unilaw Library, 1984.

43. McGuinness B.F. (ed), T. Nyberg (ed) and G.H. von Wright (ed), Prototractatus, Cornell University Press, 1971, as cited in Munoz-Suarez, Carlos, The Tractatus… Is It So Intractable?, Philosophy Now – A Magazine for Ideas, Anja Publications, Issue 103, July/August 2014.

44. Brennan, Barbara, Light Emerging, Bantam, 1993.

45. Hesse, Herman, The Glass Bead Game, 1943, Holt, Rinehart and Winston.

PART THREE

SHANE C. ROBINSON

YOUTUBE CONTENT CREATOR:

UNBIASED & ON THE FENCE CHANNEL

www.youtube.com/unbiasedonthefence

The Beginning

I want to start by defining exactly what the Mandela Effect is, where the name came from, and some of the terms that are commonly used to explain different aspects of this very strange phenomenon. In short, the Mandela Effect (also known as the M.E.) is when some people remember things in their past a specific way that current reality does not support. It is a mismatch between memory and history. This phenomenon has been observed in nearly every part of our reality - from art, books, movies, spelling, world events, company names and logos, et cetera. These changes number in the thousands, and the changes occur in a seemingly impossible way: meaning that when you go to the library, or look on the internet to research something, it appears that the way you remember it never actually occurred that way. Now you could think, as many initially did, that your memory is faulty, but then you find dozens, hundreds, thousands, and even hundreds of thousands who remember it wrong in *exactly* the same way you do. This leads many to believe the thing they remembered wrong *must* have changed, or the original way it used to be would not be remembered in exactly the same way by so many. There usually is still plenty of residual evidence (called residue) of how it used to be, across many different media platforms. Because of this, many now consider the Mandela Effect to be a change in matter, rather than a change in memory.

This phenomenon could easily be called a Quantum Awakening, or Quantum Shifting, but it received the title Mandela Effect because many people have a specific memory of Nelson Mandela dying in a South African prison in the late 80's, or early 90's; yet current history shows he was released from prison in 1990, became President of South Africa in 1993 and did not die until 2013. (1) This resulted in some people scratching their heads in confusion for quite some time. In a 2001 broadcast of "Coast to Coast AM", host Art Bell talked about receiving around a thousand emails from listeners saying they remembered Nelson Mandela dying, yet he was still alive at that time. (2)

It was not until around 2009, that the name Mandela Effect started being used to describe this phenomenon, as more of these collective discrepancies in memories and history began cropping up. The term is credited to paranormal researcher and author

Fiona Broome. On her website www.mandelaeffect.com she states:

"Many years ago, I was one of the people who coined the phrase Mandela Effect during a fun, slightly frivolous conversation in Dragon Con's 'green room' (www.dragoncon.com). ('Shadow', a Dragon Con security manager, was also part of the conversation. I have *no idea* which of us started using the phrase first. And, it's possible that my husband actually came up with the phrase.)"

"As an aside, Shadow mentioned that - like me - other people remembered Nelson Mandela's tragic death in a South African prison, prior to late 2009. (In this reality, Mandela died in 2013.) Suddenly, several others in the Green Room joined the conversation. It was a fascinating discussion that spun into weird and hilarious tangents ...."

"2009: Encouraged by one of my book editors, I started this website. A few people commented. Others emailed me with their insights. Most of the conversations were light and related to sci-fi concepts, and unusual memories."

"2010-2014: People began reporting memories *other than* Nelson Mandela's death in the 20th century. Visitors shared anecdotes and informal theories. Generally, we didn't take ourselves too seriously."

"2015: This topic abruptly reached critical mass. The Berenstein/Berenstain subject went viral, followed by other widespread alternate memories. Visitors were astonished to learn about others' memories with astonishingly *similar* details and points of reference by *multiple, unconnected* people." (3)

Commonly Experienced Mandela Effects

Let me provide a few other examples that are considered as some of the more well-known M.E. changes. Keep in mind, not all examples affect all people - that's another strange aspect of this phenomenon that we will go into later.

Film footage of the JFK assassination in 1963, was a big one for me and many other people. While growing up, it was the first graphic footage I had ever seen. What I vividly remember was a poor quality black and white film of the president and the first lady in the back seat of a convertible. The driver and Governor Connolly were in the front seat. There were a total of four occupants in the car: three men and one woman, as the fatal shots were fired. Take a moment to think back: how do you remember this footage?

As you read through this book, take note of your own memories and whether or not they seem to change as you hear about changes in matter and changes in collective memory. Do you have memories of both versions, or just one? There is something strange about how old memories seem to be replaced, as new information is taken in about the current state of those things in question. So pay close attention to how you initially remember some of the topics, and whether or not your memories shift to align with the current reality.

Back to JFK and the Zapruder film: If you research this topic, you will find that the Abraham Zapruder film (which is in color) was shown on television for the first time in 1975, and showed a much different scenario to the previous black and white footage. (4) In the Zapruder film there are now *six* occupants in the car, with three rows of seats in a longer convertible. Governor Connelly is still seated directly in front of JFK, but is now joined by his wife seated next to him in a middle row - directly in front of Jackie Kennedy. The driver is the same as I remember, but there is now another secret service agent in the front passenger seat next to the driver, where I remember the governor once sat.

While Jackie's reactions in the Zapruder Film are similar to how I remember them, there are some slight differences that can be noted. Current history shows the car they were riding in was one-of-a-kind, customized, and stretched to accommodate the extra row of seats. The history as I remember it matches the four-seater car that is still currently on display at the Historic Auto Attractions

Museum in Roscoe Illinois, with life-like figures of the president and first lady posed in the back seat. (5) Although they now say the car in the museum is *not* a replica of the original, you have to wonder why they would use a replica of the car from *my memory* instead of the historic version. These are the types of strange anomalies you come across when you find things that appear to line up with the history you and so many others remember, but do not align with actual history as reported today.

Since those days as a child viewing the graphic footage of the assassination of JFK, I saw the footage over and over again, almost yearly. I remember watching documentaries about the mysteries and conspiracies surrounding this major event in American history. One such documentary that probably no longer exists, explored the idea that perhaps the driver shot JFK - a scenario that is extremely improbable now that there is a whole new row of occupied seats blocking his line of sight; along with two extra witnesses, who would have surely seen the driver turn around and shoot the president.

While residue that matches your memories is helpful and seems like smoking-gun proof that reality *has* changed, it is typically seen as the reason people are confused and misremembering things. The old reality residue, many times, acts as a double-edged sword providing proof to support either reality one believes in, but this is not always the case. Think about how you remember the pose of Rodin's famous Thinker statue. For me, I had a lot of childhood memories of that statue. I remember being with my mom at a garage sale and asking her to buy a desktop-size replica of the statue. That statue sat on my desk while I was growing up, and I drew it quite a few times over the years. I have a vivid memory of being frustrated at how I could not get the clinched fist to the forehead to look quite right. In fact, those same frustrations returned while creating the comparison artwork below for this book, especially since no reference to how I remember it exists any longer.

Remembered (Recreated) Pose   **Current Pose**

Rodin's Thinker was even in the opening sequence to one of my favorite childhood TV science shows, "Mr. Wizard's World", but upon examining that shoe now, the pose has changed to match this current reality and not the pose I so vividly remember. Even stranger, the pose has now changed at least twice for me. In 2017, I first discovered the hand had moved from the clenched fist to the forehead, to an open back hand beneath the chin. Since that time, for me, it looks as if it has changed again to that open hand on the mouth, where he appears to be sucking on his knuckles. Each time I see a change in the statue's pose, every replica and photo of the statue changes too - to match the new pose in a seemingly impossible way. But not without leaving behind some pretty compelling residue.

There are photographs online of people next to the statue mimicking the pose as it was at the time the photo was taken. When the pose of the statue changes to a new, slightly different pose, the people in the photos *do not* change to match the new changes to the statue. In one photo, I saw at least 18 children posing next to the statue with their fist to their forehead (the original pose that matches my memory), yet the statue's pose had miraculously changed to the knuckles resting against the mouth. This in my opinion is not only some of the most rock-solid evidence of reality changing in a seemingly impossible way, but it destroys the theory that people are simply misremembering.

These strange pictures also provide some very important clues as to what the heck is really going on here, which I will discuss later.

The Mona Lisa portrait, by artist Leonardo da Vinci, is probably the best-known work of art in the world. As an artist, I remember staring at this portrait and wondering why it was so famous. What was it about the painting that captivated people so much? I didn't get it. Sure, it is good, but far from the *best* work of art I have ever seen. I remember having conversations about the mystery in the expression on the face of the Mona Lisa. Was she smiling, smirking, reserved, modest, or maybe a little shy? Was that enigmatic expression on her face what made the painting so popular? When I heard the Mona Lisa had been the object of a Mandela Effect change, I could not wait to see it. Although the M.E. change is subtle in one respect, it is like night and day to someone who spent as much time staring at it as I had. The change was a little startling at first, maybe even a little creepy when considering the seemingly impossible way this version (that was so foreign to me) came about. Mona Lisa was clearly smiling at me, as I sat looking at her in disbelief. Thank goodness I spent so much time looking at it before the change. As an artist it was not that hard for me to change it back in a computer art editing program to the enigmatic expression I once pondered so much. While my recreation is not absolutely perfect compared to the original I remember, it is certainly much closer than the current version with the more obvious smile (that supposedly has always existed). I posted a side by side comparison, and many others who saw it agreed my version was closer to how they remembered it too.

A few months later, someone left a comment asking me why I had not removed the hair net from the Mona Lisa's head. I was puzzled at first and re-examined my side by side comparison to see that both my recreation and the original now had a hair net. This is crazy, I thought. I explained that the hair net must have been added sometime after my recreation was made, because it was not there when I originally manipulated it in the art editing program. A few more months went by and I saw a video talking about how the Mona Lisa had changed again. They pointed out that she now has a bump on the bridge of her nose next to her left eye. I examined my recreation once more to find the bump was now on both my recreation and the original. While using the same computer program to alter the image, I had to zoom in so far to make changes that there is no way I could have missed this bump on the side of her nose, while her eye was the size of my entire screen. So, while I have updated my recreation of the painting for this book, I cannot guarantee something strange has not happened to it again by the time the reader gets to it. Just like Rodin's Thinker, I know of several different versions of the Mona Lisa now.

Remembered   Current

Rich Uncle Pennybags, the character featured on the board game "Monopoly", is no longer the way I and many others remember him. Growing up, I remember this iconic character as having a top hat, a monocle, a big mustache and a cane. Is this the way you remember him? If you pull out an old "Monopoly" board game now and take a look at it, you will see Rich Uncle Pennybags does *not* wear a monocle over one eye, and never has according to history. A little research reveals many people remember the character with a monocle, whether it is in Halloween costumes or clip art, or a direct reference featured in the movie *Ace Ventura: Pet Detective* in which the main character says, "you must be the Monopoly man", to an older man in a bow tie, with a big mustache and a monocle. (6) Do you remember him having a monocle?

I remember as a teenager learning that the term "city of angels" was a reference to Los Angeles from a 1991 song called "Under the Bridge", by the band Red Hot Chili Peppers. In the lyrics of the song, I remember him singing, "… the city I live in, the city of angels." However, when you listen to this song now he is saying, "… city of angel." If it was not for the discussion these lyrics spawned, I might be unsure as to whether or not it said city of "angels" in my past. But because I remember learning this phrase represented another name for Los Angeles, specifically from those lyrics, I have no doubts about my memory being accurate on this one. I am not alone. You can find many other people performing the cover version of this song still singing, "city of angels". You can also find lyrics online that are written this way too, even though the original recording appears to have always been "city of angel".

Another discrepancy in the memories of many people when compared with history - is the spelling of the children's television series and books *Berenstein Bears* versus the *Berenstain Bears*. (7) People remember specific conversations that took place as a result of the books being named BerenSTEIN - and whether it should be pronounced "steen" or "stine". These are conversations that would have never taken place if it had always been spelled "BerenSTAIN". How can this phenomenon be written off as simply misremembering? People typically do not remember an entire discussion about the pronunciation of a word that never existed, according to the history of the book and television series. It would not and could not have even been a topic for discussion. If it had always been spelled BerenSTAIN. Why would people debate if that was pronounced Stine or Steen?

Many of the changes are really small and easy to miss, or write off as bad memory, until residue comes along to reinforce your memory of the way things actually were. The 1960's hit song "California Dreamin" by The Mamas & the Papas is not the same now, as many remember it, in regards to one line in the lyrics. Many remember the lyrics in the second verse as follows:
"Stopped into a church
I passed along the way
Well, I got down on my knees
And I began to pray"
However, the fourth line of this verse now says:
"And I pretend to pray" (8)

While there have been many remakes of the song over the years that also say, "I pretend to pray", I did stumble upon two versions that still sing the original, "I began to pray". One by the

Carpenters, (9) And another by Nancy Sinatra. (10) Those who remember it the way it was *before* would consider this great residual proof that the lyrics have been altered, but in actuality, those who do *not* see a change will see this as *the reason* so many are confused about the true lyrics (the way they are now). This is another good example of why a lot of residue acts as a double-edged sword: supporting the beliefs on both sides of the issue.

In the 1994 Blockbuster movie *Forrest Gump* starring Tom Hanks, one of the most iconic lines in movie history from that movie is not the same as how I and many recall it having been said originally "My momma always told me, life is like a box of chocolates - you never know what you're gonna get". Is this how you remember the line? Now it appears to have always been, "… Life *was* like a box of chocolates …." (11)

I have seen some great residue for this one: a trivia game that has the line the old way I (and many) remember it; as well as some behind the scenes outtake footage from the movie itself, where Tom Hanks is clearly heard saying, "Life *is* like a box of chocolates", even though in the official released version he appears to have never said it that way. (12)

According to many testimonies on YouTube, another famous movie line spoken by Tom Hanks reportedly changed a few times, or flip-flopped. In the 1995 film, *Apollo 13,* Hank's famous line, "Houston, we have a problem," was reportedly changed to, "Houston, we've had a problem". (13) When I first found out about the Mandela Effect in March 2017, I thought long and hard about whether I recognized this change or not. Dual memories are not uncommon. I finally deciding that I just could not be sure about this one. But the strange thing is, a few months later, I witnessed that it had changed *back* to the original line, "Houston, we *have* a problem". In the Mandela Effect community this is called a "flip-flop", when something that changed for a while, suddenly changes back to the original. While I was not sure of the original change, I was most certainly sure it had changed the second time. I had heard about flip-flops before this, but nearly everything about this phenomenon is just too hard to believe until you see it for yourself - and with this flip-flop I finally had seen it.

I actually noticed a number of M.E. changes before I knew what the Mandela Effect even was, but I just assumed it had been changed by the producers or manufacturers, and that you could do some research to see when the change occurred. I just never felt the need to look into any of the changes I noticed, because who thinks the impossible has happened? It is not uncommon for brands to give their logo an upgrade, or try to be trendy by changing up the title or spelling. Other changes were a bit out of the norm, but I still did not consider these as something impossible that defied logic, or even given them much thought.

The Volkswagen VW logo was one that I noticed change, but I just thought the company had updated it. The reason it stood out to me, was because I had lived my entire life not realizing the logo was a V and W, until they separated the two letters with a little line or space between the top V and the bottom W. According to the logo's history, the logo has always had that horizontal line separating the two letters. There is no question in my mind about this particular change, because I would not have lived my entire life oblivious to the fact the logo was a V and W - if that line had *always* existed in my reality making the V and W separate.

Liquid Plumber is another one that I thought they shortened at some point to try and be trendy, but history shows it has always been Liquid Plumr. Many of the changes are so ridiculous that you have to wonder why people do not notice them happening, or believe you when you say they have not always been this way. But it is a difficult thing to wrap your head around, and some people just are not ready to accept the fact that things are happening that do not fit into the way they think the world and reality operate.

Even cartoons have been affected. I grew up watching what I remember as the "Looney Toons" television show, yet history shows it has always been ""Looney Tunes". The "Flintstones" cartoon has had a few changes and a flip-flop I personally experienced. In my early M.E. days, I came across videos discussing the spelling of the "Flintstones". There was a debate as to whether it was spelled Flintstones or Flinstones. At that time it appeared to have always been Flinstones, and I was leaving comments letting others know that I had a vivid memory of reading the Bible in my youth and learning about the Israelites circumcising themselves with flint knives. The thoughts that go through a boy's mind when reading something like this - have a lasting effect, firstly being thankful I would never have to endure such a thing, but also with the realization that flint was some type of stone. What would naturally follow was the ah-ha moment I had

225

at realizing that was why the "Flintstones" cartoon was named like that - after this type of rock. If you watch the cartoon, everything in the cartoon is cleverly named after rocks or things associated with the Stone Age in some way. After some time, maybe a few months, I realized the name had changed back to the original way I remembered it: "Flintstones".

This is when I discovered another change. Many people remember Fred Flintstone Yelling, "WILMA, I'M HOME!!!", in the opening or closing sequence, yet he never yells this in the television cartoon now. There are times when he says it in a conversational type voice, but never in the exaggerated yell so many of us recall.

My memory of Fruit Loops cereal is inaccurate, since it appears to have always been spelled Froot Loops. "Depends" disposable underwear has always been "Depend" according to product history. "Now or Later" candy I loved as a kid, now appears to have always been named, "Now *and* Later". "Funions", that I would always grab a bag of when I was traveling as a teen, appears to have always been spelled "Funyuns". "JC Penny" appears to have always been "JC Penney". JC Penney can be seen in the background of the movie *Back to the Future* when they are in the mall parking lot. When I watched that movie originally, I remember it was spelled JC Penny, but now that the spelling has changed from what I remember, you can check the movie and it has been updated to match the new changed spelling "JC Penney". Even if you have an old VHS tape in the attic stored in a dust-covered box that has been undisturbed for decades: -you can probably take it out now and see it has been changed too. It is simply unbelievable to many that the fabric of reality, the matrix, our shared material world could change in such a way. So, you can see how this has gone unnoticed by many for a long time, because the changes themselves are not a big deal, until you realize they are changing in an impossible way - changing and then appearing to have always been the new way.

Bible Mandela Effects

I heard about the Mandela Effect about a year before realizing it was more than just some far-fetched made-up theory going around on the internet. I am just not that observant, and I know how unreliable memory can be. But some things you just know, like your birthdate or eye color. It is not difficult to notice a change in important things, and is probably what is required to make a believer in the Mandela Effect for most people. Once you notice a change to something you are certain was one way, yet according to its history has never been that way - it really can rock your world.

Some of the most alarming M.E. changes for me personally, at first, were the changes to religious texts, specifically in the Bible. Being raised Christian, I was taught that the Bible was our manual for life. It was the word of God, divinely inspired. I read through the Bible literally dozens of times, and while I certainly did not memorize the whole thing, I knew what was written and heard many of the popular scriptures read in church so many times that it wasn't a matter of remembering as much as *knowing*. One of the most popular scriptures is Isaiah 11:6, which for many used to read, "... the Lion shall lie down with the Lamb", but now reads, "... the wolf also shall dwell with the lamb". (14) Needless to say, this brought a whole new level of disbelief, and I found it difficult to grasp what was really happening right before my eyes to the scripture I knew so well. I was raised with the belief that God's word does not change, yet I could see the Bible was indeed changed from the way I knew it was supposed to be. This scripture alteration was my first experience of a change with which I was one hundred percent certain.

I began looking into this more and found nearly every well-known scripture I knew by heart had been altered. And it was not just a case of a new translation coming out. This was from the same King James Version Bible with which I was raised. The very first verse of the Bible in Genesis used to read, "In the beginning, God created the Heavens and Earth"; but now it read, "... Heaven and Earth". I remember talking to my mother about this passage, and asking why there was more than one heaven when I was young.

The Ten Commandments were now written on "tables" rather than tablets, clearly a typo but still, I know it was not that way

227

before. So when was the typo added you ask? It was not added, as it exists in my old Bible, appearing like it has always been that way even though I know it was not. I noticed the word "matrix" has taken the place of "womb" in different places, such as in Exodus. In 13:12 & 15, "possessions" is now "stuff". Words like "stuff" were not in the King James Version Bible I grew up reading. Isaiah 53:5 used to say, "… by his stripes we are healed", and now it reads, "… with his stripes we are healed"; a minor change but a seemingly impossible one nonetheless.

The Lord's Prayer in Matthew chapter 6 also appears to have a few changes. In verse 10 it used to read, "Thy kingdom come, Thy will be done *on* earth, as it is in heaven". It now reads "*in* earth". I recall verse 12 originally read, "Forgive us our trespasses, as we forgive those who trespass against us", but now it reads, "… and forgive us our debts, as we forgive our debtors." For many including myself, Matthew 7:1 used to read, "Judge not, lest ye be judged", but now reads, "Judge not, that ye be not judged".

Mark 2:22 (Luke 5:37 as well) was another big change for me, because I remember sitting through a whole sermon about how you do not put new wine into old wineskins. It was the first time I ever heard of wineskins, however it appears to have always been "bottles" instead of "wineskins" now. Mark 13:10 used to read, "… and the gospel must first be preached among all nations", but now states, "… published among all nations".

There were two instances in my life when I was tasked with creating an illustration of the Bible story where the man with palsy was lowered down through the roof to Jesus to be healed. Like any artist would, I read the story several times and rendered the artwork that best represented the text from Luke chapter 5. This is where the story gets interesting: while I remember the man being lowered on a mat, the Bible now says it was a "couch". Luke 5:24 actually has Jesus now saying, "… take up thy couch and go into thine house." There is a parable in Luke chapter 19 starting at verse 12 that has had a few changes from what I remember. The nobleman who left his servants in charge of his "talents" have now been left in charge of his "pounds", and the one servant who wrapped his portion in a "handkerchief" now wraps it in a "napkin". The parable ends in verse 27 with Jesus saying, "But those mine enemies, which would not that I should reign over them, bring hither, and slay them before me." While I don't recall the exact wording of this verse, this is much more violent phrasing from my recollection of it.

John 3:16, a popular verse that I memorized, had a small change. It used to read, "For God so loved the world that he gave his only begotten Son, that whosoever believeth in him shall not perish, but have everlasting life." It now reads, "… should not perish." I remember John 8:32 read, "And ye shall know the truth, and the truth shall set you free", but it has changed to, "… make you free". 2 Corinthians 11:8 is another one I did not memorize, but I know it reads differently. Paul now says, "I robbed other churches, taking wages of them, to do you service."

There are many other changes to the Bible, so I would suggest anyone who has taken the time to memorize certain scriptures, to write them down the way you remember, and then look them up to see if they are different from the memory you have of them. Many times the new way will look familiar once you observe it, so it is important to write it down first. That is one of the strange paradoxes of this phenomenon. You can have dual memories where both versions seem familiar to you.

Other Strange Things

As if this phenomenon was not strange enough already, there is something you the reader should be aware of, if you indeed recognize any of the changes you read about in this book. You will undoubtedly feel compelled to talk to others about the changes you personally observe. You should know that the responses and reactions you receive from others can be nearly as bizarre as the phenomenon itself. I have experienced others who seem to agree with changes at first, only to switch to remembering the new way as having always been that way. Others will seem to understand what you are explaining, only to react like it is not a big deal, or have their attention pulled away to something else (changing the subject, fiddling with their phone, et cetera). Others may actually get hostile or rude. My sister kept having more important things to do, and not returning my calls to discuss it further. My brother straight out told me, "No one cares, people are just trying to pay their bills and survive." These are the people in my life who I thought I could count on if something of this magnitude were to happen, but they were not there for me, and really have not even seemed like the same people I once knew. Although I have moved on, and they would probably say the same thing about me at this point; I am okay with that. I still love them dearly. I know they never listened to most of the things I said before, so it should not have been a surprise. Just know you cannot force anyone to see this. The Mandela Effect is something that has to be experienced on a real fundamental level to get beyond the cognitive dissonance that I now realize is just a normal response to something that seems so illogical.

Another strange thing is that people who seem to be the most qualified to remember how something once was will many times have strong memories of it always having been the way it is now. Take for instance a doctor or nurse would seem to be the most likely to notice some of the human anatomy changes - like the location of the heart. I remember the heart being three finger-widths below the left nipple closer to the bottom of the rib cage, yet this is no longer the case. The heart is now much higher in the chest between the lungs and only slightly left of center. I personally had a deformed rib that was located right above where my heart was once located and wondered if it was the cause of heart problems I had many years ago. My heart, which no longer gives me problems, is now in the center and much higher, and the deformed rib is now symmetrical with the other side of my chest. I have never witnessed a change happen, only observed it after the fact. If it were not for my belly creases showing the evidence of once having an asymmetrical rib cage, I might believe I had switched into another timeline where my ribs were always symmetrical. It is mind boggling to imagine going through such drastic anatomy changes and not being aware of it.

Geographical changes to the world map are another topic you might think a pilot, ship captain, or geography teacher would be the first to recognize. However, this may not be the case. Many people recall South America being more in line beneath North America, but now they think it has moved 1000 miles or more to the east. Some people report remembering Australia as being the furthest down on the map besides Antarctica, but New Zealand is now further south. I personally had a work of art I made in 2011, in which I used a world map as a reference, and took the word love in dozens of languages and placed them over the land. When I heard people claiming the world map had changed, I found the old file on my computer and opened it. The words no longer lined up perfectly with the reference map, as they had when I last accessed the file. Dozens of new islands were now present where there had been none when I was creating the art. While this is hard evidence that a change took place that I can clearly see, and my art has been available online since 2012, there is still a natural response to think this proof was somehow fabricated years in advance of me discovering the Mandela Effect.

So, after a year of seriously looking into the Mandela Effect, I want to discuss where I am at with figuring out what is going on with these presumably supernatural changes. Why are they happening and what is causing them? I want to take an objective look at some of the main theories we hear about, using logic on why I have ruled some things out, because they seem less probable after taking everything into consideration. When one looks at this phenomenon objectively for as long as I have, you realize just how dynamic it is. The data relies heavily on individual subjective experience, and there are virtually no absolutes other than the fact that it is happening; and this is only true for those who have been able to get beyond the cognitive dissonance that pushes so many people back into disbelief and denial.

As I mentioned earlier, it took me a year from the time I first heard about it to get over that hump. Because of the dynamic nature of the M.E., (so many things change and flip-flop that the facts are only confirmed at the time of this writing, and can change by the time you read this), and lack of absolutes surrounding the effect, we are left with drawing educated, yet subjective conclusions, still well within the realm of speculation at best. No one has proven any theory concerning the cause of the M.E. yet, and perhaps never will.

Possible Causes

One popular theory is that we have slipped or merged into an alternate timeline or parallel dimension/universe, where everything is exactly the same except for minor differences. That would be why some of us are noticing these changes, while others are not - who apparently must have always been in this universe or on this particular timeline. While on the surface this sounds very scientific and seems to provide a good explanation, closer examination of the residual evidence does not seem to support this theory. Take for instance Rodin's Thinker statue, where we have people posing next to the statue and they are mimicking the old pose. If we slipped into an alternate universe where the pose was slightly different and had really always been that way, the people posing next to the statue would have changed as well to reflect the pose of that dimension. But the fact that they do not match the pose lets us know this is more than likely the same reality, timeline, dimension or universe, but the statue has been altered somehow. Add to that the fact that different changes affect people differently. It is not like if you notice one change you will notice them all.

Alternate timeline theories are often blamed on particle colliders or quantum computers since they are described as reaching into other dimensions on a quantum level to receive the computational solutions. This timeline jumping, merging, or shifting is considered by some as the side effect or byproduct of scientists toying around with quantum and atomic technology. I initially believed this as well, before seeing the micro-managed and thoughtful nature of the Mandela Effect changes.

Time travelers are another unavoidable consideration when we search for the causes of this phenomenon. While thinking of time linearly is certainly a simple way of going about viewing reality – it is not at all helpful when viewing the Mandela Effect phenomenon. Imagine a time traveler was tasked with traveling back in time and changing Earth's timeline A to B. How would he change our galactic location, geography or human anatomy? How would someone manipulate the details of the JFK assassination? How many board room meetings would have to be attended to make logo and product name changes? How many insertion points would someone have to visit in the past to change the Bible translations into what we see today? This is a complicated topic by itself, but I have looked into it enough to know someone would have needed to intervene at multiple points to give us the various Bible changes we observe today. If someone truly traveled back in time and made these changes, there would not be memories of the original timeline because it would not have happened (so there would not be any residue either). Essentially, we would all be unaware of the original timeline - because it never would have existed. Think of it this way, if you were to travel back in time to key moments in your life when you remember things the way they were, what would you see? You would see something different than what you remember, essentially rendering your memory as a false memory. No more arguing with the so-called professionals about that one, they would be right.

What do we really know about the past? Whether we think about the past from our memories, or we research the past through various resources available to us (internet, library, books, photos, audio, video, the memories of others), we always perceive history in the now. It is the only way under normal circumstances to experience the past. Our observations right now are all we can say we really know. Whomever or whatever is seemingly changing the past - is only changing our *perception* of the past in the now.

So, let us not rely only on Hollywood, media, or scientific theories as a way of figuring out what is causing this phenomenon. Remember science infers we all have false memories, so we know by their own admission, they have not seriously considered the M.E. residual data. So going with what we know to be true, all we have is our current "in the now" reality, and those affected by the M.E. know it can change or shift into something that is no longer recognizable when compared to our memories.

Some Points of Observation (I think may help lay a good foundation for understanding the phenomenon):

- All Mandela Effects (unexplained changes in matter or history) do not affect everyone, whether they consider themselves M.E. affected or not.

- Degree of familiarity with an item before it shifts or changes can affect the observer.

- M.E. shifts or changes do not happen in a single event, but seem to be ongoing. Some report it has been happening for decades, but most people just do not notice them.

- Items that have changed have been known to change back (flip-flops), or shift to an entirely new version - creating Reality C, D, and so on.

- Introducing the human mind into the history of an item can create residue of its original form (someone quoting memorized lyrics or Bible verses seem to go untouched, while items that were copied and pasted within a computer get automatically updated to the new version).

- More experimentation is needed, but it is possible that no one is exclusively bound to reality A or B, et cetera. This is certainly true of the affected, assuming every claimed M.E. is truly an M.E. change. I believe from my limited exposure to those who claim to be unaffected, if they were quizzed about enough M.E. changes - they would eventually be affected too, even if they recanted their answers once they realized their memories did not align with the current reality.   The list of proposed M.E. changes can easily number in the tens of thousands by my estimates, so there are plenty of examples to consider.

- Unaffected individuals can easily remain unaffected by denying their memories are accurate.

- By most accounts, changes are seemingly benign in terms of not causing harm. Perhaps if a change would be harmful to an individual, they would not see it, or quickly forget it (like many in the medical field not seeing reported M.E. anatomy changes, many pilots and ship captains not seeing reported M.E. geography changes).They may simply see the new change as always having been that way, so it does not affect their work.

• M.E. changes do not seem to be random or accidental - a closer look into changes can hold meaning for individuals.

• Changes can be positive or negative depending on the individual's subjective perception, and can be considered life changing.

• Observing the M.E. does not appear to be rooted in the gain of money or power for any particular person or group, although one famous atom colliding facility in a video on YouTube appeared to some to have tried to capitalize on the phenomenon, but I see no current observable gains in relationship to money or power. (15) and (16)

My Subjective Experience of the Mandela Effect (this is what I have discovered, or more specifically *felt* about the phenomenon):

1. I believe the Mandel Effect is a good thing - acting as a wake-up call of sorts. Understand I am not saying it has been enjoyable the entire time, but I have experienced a great deal of personal development in the short time I have been dealing with it. It has led to what I call a "quantum awakening", a term I use to describe my "spiritual awakening". I also feel like it has been a divine gathering of loving people I have had the pleasure of meeting as a result of the phenomenon.

2. I do feel I have gotten messages within some of the M.E. changes. Messages that point out how we have gone wrong as a society operating from a solely left-brained, analytical, selfish position, and neglecting the right-brained creative, loving, service to others position. Like Rodin's Thinker statue that has shifted awkwardly to the left with his right elbow resting on his left leg, no longer centered with the eyes closed thinking with his mind's eye, with his fist to his forehead. The first observed change had his eyes open with the back of his hand propped under his chin. The

latest version now has him looking as if he is sucking on his knuckles. This revelation of right brain versus left brain is seen in other changes as well: the American Gothic Painting in which the farmer's wife used to look straight ahead, and now looks to her left; the prohibition sign (the red circle with a diagonal line across it); the letter T in many logos missing the right side of the horizontal cross section ... just to name a few. For me, and for many others who have discussed this phenomenon with me, the main message is to get back to love and compassion for others.

3. I believe we have a benevolent higher source of some kind that is helping us. This source has manifested itself in the above described revelations accompanied by confirmatory information that has come from other people - mostly from people viewing and commenting on my YouTube videos and other YouTube channels. There have been an unusually high number of synchronistic events, like repeating and incremental number patterns that show up in all sorts of ways. Lyrics often seem to speak to the thoughts I am having, or steer me back on track. Whether over-hearing a few words in a conversation, or on the radio, or ads as I am flipping through the radio stations, even a few words of a billboard or bumper sticker ... there doesn't seem to be a limit to how a message can be delivered and received when you are aware of being in the moment and are paying attention. The more I look for these synchronicities, the more I see them.

Remembered (recreation from memory)

Current

So, this is where I am at (right now) with this whole Mandela Effect - taking into consideration all of my objective analysis mentioned earlier, and all of my life experience that has led me to this point. The Mandela Effect or Quantum Awakening is a gentle nudge from beyond this reality. I personally do not feel like it could have been caused from within this reality. I feel like some of the changes contain messages to be deciphered, while other changes are meant to benefit us in one way or another. I feel like everyone has the opportunity to see at least some of these changes, but the changes are subtle enough that they can easily be dismissed and not taken seriously. If you see the changes, but do not want to accept the gentle wake-up nudge, you can choose to accept a logical, unsubstantiated left-brain cop-out like, "I must have misremembered it", or "it must be particle colliders or quantum computers causing this."

I think it was done this way to maintain free will. No one is going to force anyone to change. The signposts are here, but we are ultimately in the driver's seat choosing which way we want to go. I personally feel I have been shown enough through my diligent seeking to know this information is real (well beyond a reasonable doubt), but so much of this personal growth has been on the inside. I do not feel like I am special in any way that would allow me to see these changes as they occur, and not everyone else. In fact, I feel like anyone hearing this should also go within for answers through prayer and meditation. Let anything you believed because someone told you that was what you *should* believe - fall away. Let it go because it can only hold you back. Be honest with yourself and trust your intuition. Realize you really do not have firsthand knowledge about much of how this reality is created and maintained. Consider the information you believe, and how much of it was passed on to you from others who blindly follow it without asking questions. It is time to consider what you actually know, and what you have actually experienced. Make a conscious decision to go within for answers. Realize that not everything may fit into how you currently view the world. The Mandela Effect certainly did not fit in with how I thought reality worked. I was hanging on to the beliefs of others that denied the Mandela Effect was even happening. I know one thousand percent it is happening, and would wager my life on that fact without hesitation. So if they were wrong about this, how do you know they are not also wrong about other things they have taught you about our reality, our world, and our place in it? This is precisely why I think this is a wake-up call, an apocalypse (disclosure of knowledge or revelation), and not the end of the world ... but maybe the end of the world as we know and understand it.

So, in considering the question of whether or not the Mandela Effect is friend or foe ... it has been a friend to me, but only because I have considered it as an opportunity and not a curse. I could have easily let pessimism and fear move me in the opposite direction, as I have seen so many others do. For me, the Mandela Effect is easily one of the best phenomena to cross my path. I feel as though I woke up in an awesome sci-fi movie where anything is possible.

Some Reported Celebrity Name Changes (by channels that cover the Mandela Effect on YouTube):

1. Christopher Reeves, now Reeve

2. George Reeve, now Reeves

3. Sally Fields, now Field

4. Steven Segal, now Seagal

5. Joel Olsteen, now Osteen

6. Joyce Meyers, now Meyer

7. Lionel Ritchie, now Richie

8. Gilbert Godfrey, now Gottfried

9. Will Farrell, now Ferrell

10. Julia Childs, now Child

11. Jim and Tammy Baker, now Bakker

12. Reba McIntyre, now McEntire

13. Charles Schultz, now Schulz

14. Dan Akroyd, now Aykroyd

15. Gordon Ramsey, now Ramsay

16. Andrew Zimmerman, now Andrew Zimmern

17. Shannon Doherty, now Shannen

18. Jim Carey, now Carrey

19. Axel Rose, now Axl

20. Barbara Streisand, now Barbra

21. Barbra Walters, now Barbara

22. Freddie Prince Jr, now Prinze

23. Courtney Cox, now Courteney

24. Desi Arnez, now Arnaz

25. Bob Segar, now Seger

26. Nicholas Cage, now Nicolas

27. Sarah McLaughlin, now McLachlan

28. Snuffleuffagus, now Snuffleupagus

29. Spike, now Stripe (from the movie *Gremlins*)

30. Leann Rhimes, now Rimes

31. Sylvia Brown, now Browne

32. Brendan Frasier, now Fraser

33. Sean Austin, now Astin

34. Selma Hayek, now Salma

35. Paula Dean, now Deen

36. Alec Trebek, now Alex

37. Mother Theresa, now Teresa

38. Kevin Cosner, now Costner

Part Three Endnotes:

1. Nelson Mandela Released from Prison, History.com,https://www.history.com/this-day-in-history/nelson-mandela-released-from-prison, accessed on 3/11/2019.

2. The Mandela effect isn't new! - 2001 callers to Art Bell talk about Mandela's death in prison, Septravarius channel, https://youtu.be/BKWTu-WNgtM, accessed on 3/11/2019.

3. The Mandela Effect, mandelaeffect.com, https://mandelaeffect.com/about/, accessed on 3/11/2019.

4. English, Jason, Mental Floss, http://mentalfloss.com/article/30153/date-1975-geraldo-aired-zapruder-film-first-time, 3.6.2012, accessed on 3.11.2019.

5. Historical Auto Attractions, Kennedy, John F. Kennedy Secret Service Car, copyright 2014, http://www.historicautoattractions.com/m/exhibit_dayindallas_cars.asp, accessed on 3/11/2019.

6. Ace Ventura Pet Detective, Warner Bros., 1994.

7. ME Conclusion using Logic and Abductive Reasoning, Unbiased & On the Fence channel, https://youtu.be/P4EMYDRljDA?t=85, accessed on 3.11.2019.

8. Berenstain, Jan, and Mike Berenstain. The Berenstain Bears. Harperfestival, 2012.

9. The Mamas & the Papas - California Dreamin', PeaceFrogMan1 channel, https://www.youtube.com/watch?v=qhZULM69Dlw, accessed 3.11.2019.

10. Carpenters "California Dreamin' ", Love Howard Banister channel, https://youtu.be/pxpMkMmGkTE, accessed on 3.11.2019.

11. Forrest Gump - "Life is like a box of chocolate", Mylife Myfilms channel, https://youtu.be/CJh59vZ8ccc, accessed on 3.11.2019.

12. 100% PROOF MANDELA EFFECT IS TRUE-FORREST GUMP DOES SAY LIFE IS..., K. Smallz channel, https://youtu.be/D2NpCcpTl0Q, accessed on 3.11.2019.

13. Apollo 13, Universal Studios, 1995.

14. Top 10 Mandela Effect examples, Unbiased & On the Fence channel, https://youtu.be/cFAl0a8AG-4?t=362, accessed on 3.11.2019.

15. Bond 1 CERN Happy Breakdown - QUANTUM SHIFT MANDELA EFFECT, R zONE channel, https://youtu.be/oMwacCZUAy4?t=84, accessed on 3.11.2019.

16. CERN Mandela Effect Explained & The Best Mandela Effect Example Yet? - Theory #1, Hidden Knowledge channel, https://youtu.be/khtqojp-ldQ?t=151, accessed on 3.11.2019.

PART FOUR

VANNESSA VA

YOUTUBE CONTENT CREATOR:

VANNESSA VA CHANNEL

www.youtube.com/VannessaVA

What Is The Mandela Effect?

The Mandela Effect is a phenomenon in which individuals have a clear memory of something that occurred in the past that has been erased from the consensus of current reality. It has been erased in a way that makes it appear as though it never occurred. It is not false memories or confabulation. Many of us, mostly total strangers, recall several of the exact same nonexistent memories with the exact same details. However, these memories are different from what is in history books, newspaper archives, et cetera. So why is the definition of the Mandela Effect provided by Wikipedia and other mainstream news sources flawed?

Mainstream news outlets, online encyclopedias and debunking websites have dismissed the Mandela Effect as merely confabulation or false memories. Labeling the Mandela Effect as confabulation or false memories is inaccurate, because the mass misremembering of thousands of specific changes to logos, book and movie titles, company names, iconic movie lines and song lyrics by thousands of individuals in exactly the same way - is statistically improbable. For example, countless individuals around the world experiencing the Mandela Effect remember the King James Bible Isaiah 11:6 verse the exact same way as, "… the lion shall lay down with the lamb", until recently when it seems to have changed to, "… the wolf shall dwell with the lamb", becoming a Mandela Effect.

If the phenomenon was attributed to only confabulation or false memories, then a plethora of variations in the way it was falsely remembered among people would be in evidence. For instance, some people could remember, "… the leopard shall lay down with the lamb"; while still others could remember, "the bear shall lay down with the lamb"; and so on with innumerable variations of the verse. Also, countless individuals experiencing the Mandela Effect remember the words "lay down" in the verse instead of other variations, such as kneel down, walk, sit down, et cetera. Not only does the vast majority of those affected by the Mandela Effect cite the lion, but so far, I have not found anyone mentioning any other verb except "lay down". The sheer number of individuals around the world remembering the exact same details changing in the exact same way - points to more than just confabulation or false memories. Despite the statistical improbability of thousands of strangers misremembering the same detail wrong in the exact same way, at the time of this writing, mainstream news outlets have not acknowledged that the Mandela Effect is a real phenomenon. Currently, the greatest amount of unbiased information about the Mandela Effect can be found on YouTube through first-hand accounts of individuals within the newly formed and growing Mandela Effect community.

The Science Behind the Mandela Effect: Schumann Resonance, Solar System Changes, and Brain Waves

The specific cause of the Mandela Effect is challenging to discern. I suspect the cause is multifaceted and relates to the Schumann Resonance, consciousness, and planetary changes. Earth as well as the entire solar system are going through some dramatic changes. On January 31, 2017, for the first time in recorded history, the Schumann Resonance climbed from its regular 7.83 hertz to 36+ hertz. The Schumann Resonance, named after physicist Winfried Otto Schumann, is the sound frequency of the Earth's electromagnetic field, which extends to the edge of Earth's ionosphere, and is made up of electromagnetic waves that are composed of electrons and ionized atoms. The Schumann Resonance fluctuates as the ionosphere becomes more or less dense, depending mainly on the amount of solar radiation striking it. Electricity from lightning affects the Schumann Resonance as well. (1)

According to Russian professor Leonidovich Tchijevsky, the Schumann Resonance has a direct impact on human beings in many ways. His research indicates that the Schumann Resonance can affect blood pressure, cardiac and neurological disease, reaction time, and neuroendocrine sensitivity. Tchijevsky's findings suggest that it even plays a role in violence and war. His research indicates that the frequency of the Schumann Resonance correlates with sunspot activity, mass human excitability, sociality, and climate change. The impact the Schumann Resonance has on the nervous systems is greatest when the Earth is exposed to heightened levels of solar radiation energy. The Schumann Resonance may also have an effect on our perception and ability to retain long-term memories by influencing our brainwaves and consciousness. (2)

At the root of all thoughts and perceptions are the communication between neurons within the brain. Brainwaves are produced by synchronized electrical pulses from groups of neurons communicating with one another. Brainwaves are best thought of as a continuous spectrum of consciousness that ranges from slow, loud, and functional - to fast, subtle, and complex. Like the Schumann Resonance of Earth, brainwave speed is measured in hertz. Each kind of brainwave relates directly to our state of awareness. Delta brainwaves are about 0.1 to 3.9 hertz, theta brainwaves measure about 4 to 7.9 hertz, alpha brainwaves are about 8 to 13.9 hertz, and beta brainwaves measure about 14 to 30 hertz. Delta brainwaves correlate with detached awareness and theta brainwaves correlate with meditation, intuition, and memory. Alpha waves are associated with relaxation, creativity, visualization, and super learning, while beta brainwaves correlate with alertness and concentration. Gamma is the highest kind of brainwave, measuring about 30 to 100 hertz, and is associated with insight, peak focus levels, and expanded consciousness. To access the gamma brainwave state the mind has to be quiet. The gamma brainwave frequency modulates perception and relates to rapid, simultaneous information processing in multiple areas of the brain at one time. (3) The higher the brainwave hertz, the more aware or spiritually evolved someone may become; and with The Schumann Resonance hertz reportedly topping 100 now, the Mandela Effect could very well be a result of our thinking in Gamma Wave hertz more often and for longer periods.

Our brainwaves are analogous to a tuned system. Research conducted by Iona Miller, Board member of The Asklepia Foundation and Dean of Faculty of The Institute for Consciousness Science & Technology confirms, "The resonant cavity formed between the ionosphere and the Earth produces rhythmic waves capable of entraining and phase-locking with brainwaves."(4) Essentially, the frequency of our brainwaves correspond with the frequency of the Schumann Resonance. Lewis Hainsworth, an electrical engineer who imparted his findings to Dr. Robert O. Becker and Harvard University neurologists, said it best in his peer-reviewed study when he stated, "A tuned system consists of at least two oscillators of identical resonant frequencies. If one oscillator starts emitting, then the other will be activated by the signal very shortly, in the process of resonance, entrainment or kindling (igniting the resonance phenomenon among the neurons) ... When waves of alpha and theta rhythms cascade across the entire brain, a resonance is possible between the human being and the planet. Energy and information which are embedded in a field are transferred. Perhaps the planet communicates with us in this primal language of frequencies." Hainsworth goes on to state, "The influence of naturally occurring Schumann's resonance signals on brainwave pattern evolution is formally stated to show that electrical fields could produce evolutionary change." (5)

This is fascinating when one considers that the hertz of the Earth's Schumann Resonance is peaking more frequently. Could it be that as the Schumann Resonance rises, the likelihood of our brainwave frequency rising also increases? Will peaks in the Schumann Resonance allow more people to become aware of the Mandela Effect? Are the individuals experiencing the Mandela Effect able to lock into a specific Schumann frequency wave that enhances their awareness and ability to remember a former reality? Or is matter in a constant state of change and spiking Schumann resonances are allowing us to see this for the first time?

Research studies, such as the work of Iona Miller, acknowledge that the electromagnetic frequency of the Earth and our brainwaves are intrinsically linked and that electromagnetic frequency can have an effect on memory. Miller affirms, "We are bathed in a sea of natural low-frequency electromagnetic (EM) fields from conception to death. The brain is an electromagnetic system synchronized by the Schumann Resonance signal that continuously stabilizes the brainwave activity. The frequencies of EEG brainwaves coincide with the range of Schumann Resonance activity." Miller maintains that electromagnetic ELF radiation waves induce altered neuron calcium ion effluxes in brain tissue. According to Miller, "Stable synchronizing of the brain's electromagnetic systems underpins thinking, emotion, memory, and intelligence. Significantly, the hippocampal wave, which exerts a decisive influence on brain function and long-term memory, shares the same frequency as the Earth's primary Schumann Resonance of 7.8Hz." (6)

Since the Schumann Resonance is erratically changing (perhaps because of the Earth's more scattered magnetic shield), some individuals are becoming aware of a different overlapping Earth reality that possesses a higher Schumann Resonance frequency than the former Earth reality's Schumann Resonance of a fairly steady 7.83 hertz. The Mandela Effect may signify a dimensional and perceptual shift that is reflected by the Schumann Resonance connection to our brainwaves. This makes sense when one considers that all dimensions may actually exist simultaneously in the same space. What separates one dimensional reality from another dimensional reality are differences in their frequency. The only factor that separates dimensional realities may be our ability to tune into a specific dimension's frequency in order to perceive it.

This would explain why some are seeing the Mandela Effect while others are oblivious to it. Individuals who do not perceive the Mandela Effect may not have shifted their brainwave frequency enough to become conscious of memories of a previous perception of reality. Some people appear to be more sensitive to changes in the Schumann Resonance than others. Unfortunately, there may always be a number of individuals who will choose to remain in a state of denial about the Mandela Effect, whether they are able to perceive it or not. However, as the Schumann Resonance continues to rise in amplitude and/or hertz, it is likely that more individuals will enter a new phase of evolution in consciousness, where changes to the material world are seen by those who are ready to wake up to the Mandela Effect.

Research conducted by Lewis Hainsworth outlines how the Schumann Resonance relates to evolutionary changes in human brainwave patterns by identifying naturally occurring factors that determine the frequency spectrum of brainwave rhythms. His work indicates, "The frequencies of naturally occurring electromagnetic signals, circulating in the electrically resonant cavity bounded by the Earth and the ionosphere, have governed or determined the evolution or development of the frequencies of operation of the principal human brainwave signals." (7)

The Mandela Effect may be a symptom of evolutionary change within both the individual and collective consciousness. Since our species began, we have evolved within a Schumann Resonance of about 7.83 hertz. Now that the Schumann Resonance is dramatically fluctuating, it makes sense that changes in the Schumann Resonance would affect human beings on a deep level. The relationship between the Schumann Resonance and our brainwaves is summarized beautifully by Iona Miller who says. "All biological processes are a function of electromagnetic field interactions. Electromagnetic fields are the connecting link between the world of form and resonant patterns. They store gestalts or patterns of information. The bridge connecting solar system resonances and brain frequencies resides in our human DNA helix, which coevolved in the Earth's environment … The Schumann Resonance modulates the set points of our consciousness and biology. Living tissues detect, absorb and utilized electromagnetic signals within some frequency ranges and completely ignore other frequencies naturally encountered in the frequency spectrum. We are in tune with Schumann resonances, which drive brainwave ELF patterns in a set range of grouped frequencies. Some describe antenna-like qualities in the brainwave." (8)

Why is the Schumann Resonance Increasingly Erratic?

It is important to note that both the hertz and amplitude of the Schumann Resonance appear to be spiking higher now. (9) and (10) The hertz or frequency is defined as how many wave cycles happen in a second. For example, 1 hertz means 1 wave cycle per second while 40 hertz means 40 wave cycles per second. Amplitude is the size of the vibration or how big the wave is. The amplitude of Schumann resonances increases when ionospheric plasma gets excited due to external factors, such as solar activity and thunderstorms. (10) A number of changes going on in the solar system may be responsible for the Schumann Resonance becoming increasingly erratic. The Schumann Resonance fluctuates as the ionosphere density changes, which depends mainly on solar activity and lightning discharge. (9)

In terms of solar activity, mainstream science has yet to delve deeply into why the Sun now seems hotter and appears to be white instead of yellow. Mainstream science is willing to acknowledge that the Sun is transitioning into a solar minimum cycle, or Grand Solar Minimum. During a solar minimum the Sun develops longer lasting coronal holes. Coronal holes are vast regions in the Sun's atmosphere where the solar magnetic field opens up and allows streams of solar particles to discharge from the Sun and permeate space in the form of solar winds. Although coronal holes are observed throughout the solar cycle, during a solar minimum, they can last for six months or more. Additionally, the number of galactic cosmic rays that penetrate Earth's upper atmosphere and affect the Schumann Resonance increases during a solar minimum. In addition to changes in the Sun, there are other remarkable changes occurring within the solar system. Pluto is experiencing global warming and a 300% increase in atmospheric pressure - even as it moves further away from the Sun. (11)

Russian physicist Habibullo Abdussamatov found that the icecaps of Mars have declined significantly, citing global warming as the primary cause. (12) Global warming is also occurring on Neptune's largest moon, Triton. (13) In terms of luminosity, the auroral brightness of Venus has increased by 2,500% over the past 40 years. Additionally, Jupiter is experiencing a 200% increase in the brightness of its plasma clouds, and Uranus is experiencing a significant increase in brightness and cloud activity. Changes occurring within the solar system are not limited to Mars, Venus, Uranus, Jupiter, Pluto, and Neptune. Saturn's equator is experiencing a significant increase in X-rays, and over the past 30 years, equatorial jet stream velocities of Saturn have significantly decreased. (14)

Oddly enough, Earth's moon has started growing an atmosphere with a 6,000 kilometer deep layer of Natrium that was not there before. Also, the Lunar Reconnaissance Orbiter recently detected oxygen, helium, carbon dioxide, argon-40, methane, nitrogen, carbon monoxide, sodium, and potassium on the moon. (15) The Earth itself is experiencing dramatic changes in the magnetic field, erratic weather patterns, and the intensification of volcano and earthquake activity.

These significant changes occurring within the solar system may be explained by what retired astrophysics professor Daniel Whitemire of the University of Arkansas and other researchers refer to as Planet X. (16) In 2016, Caltech researchers estimated Planet X's mass to be 10 times greater than the mass of the Earth, but they call this "Planet 9" now. (17) The mass index estimated by Caltech researchers corresponds with the estimations of professor Whitemire, who has been researching Planet X since the 1980s. In 1985 Whitemire and his colleague, John Matese, published their findings on Planet X in Time magazine. Although many decades have passed since their article was published, Planet X continues to make headlines in the scientific community.

In late 2017, NASA came forward and confirmed during a press conference that there is a planet with an elliptical orbit with 10 times the mass of Earth that is responsible for tilting the entire solar system due to its strong gravitational pull. [See page 52] (18) NASA's announcement has provided clarification for understanding many of the anomalies that are occurring, such as the migration of the magnetic North Pole, the increased scattering of the Earth's magnetic field over the past 40 years, the erratic spiking of the Schumann Resonance, and numerous other changes to Earth and the other planets in the solar system. NASA's announcement is also shedding light on the idea that the Sun is part of a binary star system - like the vast majority of other stars in galaxies. Up to 85% of stars belong to a binary star system. (19) A binary star system is a system in which two stars share the same gravitational link and simultaneously orbit around a common center of mass. In our case, our Sun would be considered the focal point for the common center of mass.

It is important to note that there is some confusion about Planet X's official name as it has been referred to as Nibiru from followers of the Sumerian clay tablet religious myth translations; and the 10th Planet when Pluto was still the 9th planet in our solar system. (Pluto lost its status as a planet and was recategorized as a "dwarf planet" in 2006). Biblically it has been referred to as the "great destroyer" and is believed to be related to Wormwood. In the New Testament Wormwood is mentioned once in Revelation 8:10. "The third angel sounded his trumpet, and a great star, blazing like a torch, fell from the sky on a third of the rivers and on the springs of water— the name of the star is Wormwood." The Hopi, a Native American tribe, have a similar mythical prediction, but they call the incoming stellar bodies the Blue Star Kachina and the Red Kachina that some interpret as Nemesis (our binary twin sun), and Nibiru (Planet X).

Even though Planet X has several names and is often referred to as a single planet, it could actually be one of multiple planetary bodies that make up Planet X's own mini solar system. Within its mini solar system, Planet X, as well as several smaller planetary bodies would orbit a dark brown dwarf star known as Nemesis. Nemesis and Planet X would not emit their own light, making them difficult to find, because its sun Nemesis (a binary twin to our own) would be a brown dwarf which is not bright, making it and the surrounding planets hard to see, detect and find. However, when they get close enough to the Sun they should reflect some of our Sun's light. Planet X is reported to be difficult to see in space because it is covered in a dense dust cloud of red iron oxide. The easiest way to view the Planet X system is through an infrared telescope, because it is able to see past the red iron oxide dust. Beginning in 2007, the South Pole Telescope, an infrared telescope located at the Amundsen-Scott American South Pole Station in Antarctica, gave researchers an opportunity to document photographic evidence of the Planet X system. (20)

For many decades, NASA and mainstream media outlets downplayed evidence of the existence of Planet X, and it was often called a conspiracy theory to keep it that way, but at the 2017 press conference, NASA announced the highly probably existence of Planet X aka the 9th Planet, which has yet to be located precisely, but the gravitational pull tugging on and tilting our solar system places it somewhere 20 times past the distance of Neptune. This has been seen by many as having vindicated the findings of countless independent researchers over decades who have dedicated their careers to proving the existence of Planet X, (aka Planet 10, Nibiru, now officially called Planet 9 by NASA). (21)

To many, NASA's 2017 press conference announcement signifies a major victory in the ongoing battle for truth. I believe Planet X is a catalyst for many changes within the solar system, and it is gradually influencing the Schumann Resonance which, in turn, may be affecting our brainwaves and causing people to wake up to the Mandela Effect. The following diagram outlines the chain of events that I believe have led up to the Mandela Effect awakening.

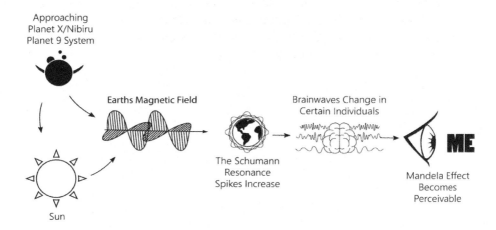

Those who hunger for the truth are more likely to be curious about their ability to perceive the Mandela Effect. On the other end of the spectrum, there are those individuals who experience the Mandela Effect, but choose not to acknowledge it and do not appear to care that matter and their reality are changing constantly. I believe it is the latter group of individuals who will find it more difficult to hang onto their original memories over time. I would encourage those who are skeptical about the correlation between changes in brainwave frequency and the Mandela Effect to think outside of the box, and consider the possibility that changes in brainwaves can alter one's ability to see a different reality. After all, when we dream our brainwaves switch from an alpha frequency to theta frequency, which causes us to enter what we perceive as a new reality within our dreams.

Often that new reality seems so real while we are dreaming, that we never pause during the dream to contemplate how our consciousness was transported to a new reality that seems just as real as the former reality we were in - before our brainwaves shifted to dream mode. Unless we become lucid during our dreams by comparing the dreamscape reality to our waking life, it is virtually impossible to realize that we are dreaming while immersed in the theta brainwave frequency. The reality constructed by the theta brainwave frequency may be only one of countless realities. Many different realities may exist within the spectrum of different brainwave frequencies. Just as many learn lucid dreaming techniques, the Mandela Effect is offering humanity an opportunity to become lucid while awake and recognize to the true nature of reality.

Is the Mandela Effect a Friend or Foe?

I consider the Mandela Effect to be a friend because of the impact the Mandela Effect has on helping individuals recognize the fluid nature of reality. Essentially, the Mandela Effect serves as an alarm clock to awaken people and invite them to embark on a journey of self-discovery about the true nature of reality. More than a paradigm shift, the Mandela Effect signifies a crossing point in the spiritual evolution of humanity within those who are curious enough to seek the truth.

Particle Accelerators

There is speculation that particle accelerators are the sole cause of the Mandela Effect, instead of multiple causes occurring simultaneously. No one knows for certain if the LHC and other particle accelerators play a role in the Mandela Effect. The Large Hadron Collider in Switzerland is the world's largest particle accelerator, with a circumference of 27 kilometers (16.7 miles) and a depth ranging from 50 to 175 meters (164 to 574 feet). It is important to remember that even though the LHC is considered the biggest and highest-energy accelerator, the Schumann Resonance encapsulates the entire Earth with a circumference of 40,075 kilometers (24,901 miles). (22) The influence, if any, that the LHC and the estimated thirty-thousand other particle accelerators (considered as an M.E. by many) have on creating Mandela Effect changes in existing global matter - is most likely minimal compared to the size of the Earth and strength of its Schumann Resonance.

How do Flip-Flops work?

A "flip-flop" occurs when a Mandela Effect change occurs, then it flips back to the way it was before it changed. The number of flip-flops that happen to a specific Mandela Effect example varies, and it is not uncommon for a flip-flop to be witnessed at different times by different individuals. A flip-flop can occur on both an individual and collective level. For example, some individuals say they witnessed the spelling of Hillary Clinton's name change from Hillary to Hilary, then flip back to Hillary at different times (23). Another example is the famous movie line, "Houston we have a problem", in the movie *Apollo 13*. A large number of people noticed the line change from, "Houston we have a problem", to, "Houston we've had a problem" … and then flip back to, "Houston we have a problem" in a relatively short span of time. (24) Based on the link between our brainwave frequencies and the Schumann Resonance, flip-flops may occasionally occur because we are still in the process of entraining our brainwaves to sync-up with the fluctuating frequency of the Schumann Resonance. This may explain how some people report having dual memories of something being both ways, before the change and after the change at the same time. This may also explain how an individual can witness a change years before another individual notices that same change. The individual who noticed the change years before the other individual may have unconsciously tuned into an amplified Schumann Resonance frequency sooner, allowing them to see the change years before. I think waking up to the true nature of reality, not a single event, is an evolutionary, transitional process that may take quite some time. Until we fully tune into a stable higher Schumann Resonance, we may continue to occasionally experience flip-flops, as we teeter between higher frequency Earth realities and the lower frequency Earth realities.

The Odd Behaviors of Those Who Won't See
or Acknowledge the Mandela Effect

The odd behaviors of some confronted with the M. E. have been disconcerting to others experiencing the Mandela Effect. Responses to the introduction of the Mandela Effect range from fearful, shocked, and interested, to apathetic and unresponsive. Many dismiss the phenomenon and laugh it off, while others become angry upon hearing about the Mandela Effect. Cognitive dissonance may be the major cause for negative responses to the Mandela Effect. Cognitive dissonance is the mental discomfort that an individual experiences when he or she is faced with information that contradicts ingrained belief systems (25). I suggest trying to remain patient with friends and family who are unresponsive when the Mandela Effect is brought up, and do not waste your time and energy on people who become belligerent. Those with eyes to see will see, and those with ears to hear will hear - when the time is right for them.

Coping with the Mandela Effect

It is normal to experience a variety of emotions when the Mandela Effect is discovered. Many describe their Mandela Effect journey as a process in which the Elizabeth Kubler Ross five stages of grief are also experienced. The five stages of grief are denial, anger, bargaining, depression and acceptance. If you are having difficulty dealing with your feelings the following Cognitive Behavioral Therapy (CBT) exercise may help.

1. First become aware of the negative thoughts that are creating negative feelings, such as fear. Negative thought examples: "Reality has become a joke." "The world is ending."

2. Stop your negative thoughts in their tracks. Take your brain off of autopilot and make a conscious effort to recognize the negative thought loops.

3. Replace the negative thoughts with positive thoughts. Positive replacement thought examples: "Reality may be changing, but at least it is no longer mundane or boring." "I am lucky that I'm alive to witness the beginning of an exciting shift in human consciousness."

Get into the habit of performing these three steps and you will be able to overcome any negative thoughts you may be experiencing.

Many are choosing to look beyond fear and see the implications of the Mandela Effect in a positive light. The Mandela Effect represents an awakening to a new way of thinking in terms of how human beings construct their reality on both an individual and collective level. Although there is speculation that technology, such as the LHC and quantum computers, is the primary source of the Mandela Effect, it is important to remember that most likely there are multiple causes involved. Many believe that the Mandela Effect is occurring naturally as mankind's spiritual evolution accelerates. Certain technology may be trying to manipulate a natural phenomenon that is more powerful than any technology. An essential part of awakening to the Mandela Effect is realizing that reality is malleable, and we each have the power to create our own reality. Remaining positive about the changes is key.

Part Four Endnotes:

1. Dr. Dispenza, Joe. "What Does the Spike in the Schumann Resonance Mean?." Dr. Joe's Dispenza Blog, 2014, www.drjoedispenza.com/blog/consciousness/what-does-the-spike-in-the-schumann-resonance-mean/.

2. Dr. Dispenza, Joe. "What Does the Spike in the Schumann Resonance Mean?." Dr. Joe's Dispenza Blog, 2014, www.drjoedispenza.com/blog/consciousness/what-does-the-spike-in-the-schumann-resonance-mean/.

3. Tchijevsky, Alexander. "Physical Factors of the Historical Process." Cycles Research Institute, Jan. 1971, www.cyclesresearchinstitute.org/cycles-history/chizhevsky1.pdf.

4. Miller, Iona. "Schumann Resonance, Psychological Regulation & Psi." Journal of Consciousness Exploration & Research, vol. 4, no. 6, 2013, pp. 599-612.

5. Hainsworth, Lewis. "The Effect of Geophysical Phenomena on Human Health." Speculations in Science and Technology, vol. 6, no. 5, 1983, pp. 439-444.

6. Miller, Iona. "Schumann Resonance, Psychological Regulation & Psi." Journal of Consciousness Exploration & Research, vol. 4, no. 6, 2013, pp. 599-612.

7. Hainsworth, Lewis. "The Effect of Geophysical Phenomena on Human Health." Speculations in Science and Technology, vol. 6, no. 5, 1983, pp. 439-444.

8. Miller, Iona. "Schumann Resonance, Psychological Regulation & Psi." Journal of Consciousness Exploration & Research, vol. 4, no. 6, 2013, pp. 599-612.

9. Dr. Dispenza, Joe. "What Does the Spike in the Schumann Resonance Mean?." Dr Joe's Dispenza Blog, 2014, www.drjoedispenza.com/blog/consciousness/what-does-the-

spike-in-the-schumann-resonance-mean/.

10. "Schumann Resonance Today Update." Disclosure News, 14 Oct. 2018, www.disclosurenews.it/en/schumann-resonance-today-update/.

11. "Solar Minimum is Coming." NASA Science: Beta, 27 June 2017, science.nasa.gov/science-news/news-articles/solar-minimum-is-coming.

12. Richardson, Valerie. "Scientist Find Evidence of Global Warming on Mars." The Washington Times, 31 May 2016, washingtontimes.com/news/2016/may/31/mars-also-undergoing-climate-change-ice-age-retrea/.

13. "Neptune." NASA Science: Solar System Exploration. 1 Feb. 2018, solarsystem.nasa.gov/planets/neptune/in-depth/.
14. Zart, Nicolas. "Weather Man Made or Natural, Climate Change Happens." LinkedIn, 11 Aug. 2015, www.linkedin.com/pulse/weather-man-made-natural-climate-change-happens-nicolas-zart. Accessed 5 Jan. 2018.

15. Sharp, Tim. "Atmosphere of the Moon." Space.com. 30 Oct. 2017, www.space.com/18067-moon-atmosphere.html.

16. Whitby, Bob. "U of A Researcher Links Mass Extinctions to 'Planet X." University of Arkansas News, 30 Mar. 2016, news.uark.edu/articles/34087/u-of-a-researcher-links-mass-extinctions-to-planet-x-.

17. Perkins, Robert. "Curious Tilt of the Sun Traced to Undiscovered Planet." Caltech, 19 Oct. 2016, www.caltech.edu/news/curious-tilt-sun-traced-undiscovered-planet-52710.

18. Brennan, Pat, and Elizabeth Landau. "The Super-Earth that Came Home for Dinner." NASA Jet Propulsion Laboratory: California Institute of Technology. 4 Oct. 2017, www.jpl.nasa.gov/news/news.php?release=2017-259.

19. "Binary Stars." Australia Telescope National Facility, 16 Jan. 2017, www.atnf.csiro.au/outreach/education/senior/astrophysics/binary_intro.html.

20. Meade, David. "The discovery of Planet X / Nibiru." Planet X news, 29 Feb. 2016, planetxnews.com/2016/02/29/the-discovery-of-planet-x-nibiru/.

21. Brennan, Pat, and Elizabeth Landau. "The Super-Earth that Came Home for Dinner." NASA Jet Propulsion Laboratory: California Institute of Technology. 4 Oct. 2017, www.jpl.nasa.gov/news/news.php?release=2017-259.

22. Cain, Fraser. "Circumference of Earth." Universe Today, 24 Dec. 2009, www.universetoday.com/26461/circumference-of-the-earth/.

23. Always thinking. "Mandela - Quantum Effect (Hillary, then Hilary, now Hillary!!)." YouTube. 11 Sep. 2016, www.youtube.com/watch?v=YQSWlSaEl5w. Accessed 14 Oct. 2018.

24. Mandela Dilemma. "Mandela Effect Flip-Flop - Houston (We Have) (We've Had) a Problem??." 10 Feb. 20(7, www.youtube.com/watch?v=5nX-z3lgWr8. Accessed 14 Oct. 2018.

25. Cherry, Kendra. "What Is Cognitive Dissonance?." Verywell Mind, 27 Aug. 2018, www.verywellmind.com/what-is-cognitive-dissonance-2795012.

Fearful & Angry Mandela Effect Testimonies
(Video Series on my YouTube Channel)

Reactions to the Mandela Effect vary and include both negative and positive responses. The following personal experiences are adapted from comments and videos posted on YouTube from 2016 to 2018. These testimonies embody the personal experiences of people who are trying to navigate through life after waking up to the Mandela Effect, and they have given us permission to include their personal Mandela Effect stories here. Only their first names are used in order to protect their identities.

Testimony 1

It is real and there's so much more to it than probably what you know. There are so many different facets of this – it's just totally crazy. I mean it blows me away. Some days I'm up all night. It's really perplexing and it's hard to wrap your head around it. Ever since I found out about this, I've been trying to wake people up and let them know what's going on. What I found is that out of the maybe 20 people, only two or three of them have any true belief that the Mandela Effect is happening. It has profoundly touched the ones that have been affected. Some have problems sleeping, and are always looking around and saying, "What is this place? It's weird now". The ones that the Mandela Effect hasn't touched - they just don't seem to want to hear about it. Sometimes they get hostile, or they just totally ignore it and act like you're a freaking nut or crazy person.

I'm one of those people that can normally get anybody to at least hear me out, but on this subject it is very strange because I just can't get them to even comprehend it, or talk about it. Nothing. It's weird man. I don't know why. It's really freaking me out. This is something that has taken over my life, since I realized what was going on. I mean it is just kind of one of those "A-Ha" moments when you really start to think about your life, how you could have done things differently, and what you should be doing from here on out. Of course, if you look at the mainstream definition of the Mandela Effect, it says it is a group of people misremembering things. Alright, well let me give you a little info about me. I love movies. I love music (I'm actually a musician). Those two things are probably the top things in my whole life. There are so many movies that are different from how I remember them now. Big, epic movie quotes like Darth Vader in the movie Star Wars saying, "Luke, I am your father"; and Forrest Gump saying, "… life is like a box of chocolates". They never ever said that now. What?! Now those movie lines say, "No, I am your father." And "… life was like a box of chocolates". I know better. It is much, much more than that. I mean the way bands names are spelled differently now. All this stuff is what brought me into the Mandela Effect at first, but then the more I started really looking into this thing, the more I started noticing important changes like the Lord's Prayer had changed in the Bible. How is that possible? What is going on? Then I noticed Isaiah 11:6 had changed. Then I started thinking that about how there will be a famine in the land for the Word of God, and to me, if the Bible has changed - then it is no longer the Bible. It is just an object used to blaspheme God.

I'm not a religious zealot of any kind, but when these things come to pass that are happening right now, then you better get right with God. That's what really hooked me in, and I've spent six weeks on this thing every single day. I knew something was different in the world. I'll give you an example. Last year when I was constantly working outside, I just couldn't understand why I couldn't handle the heat anymore that whole summer. It was like the heat was taking me out and knocking me down. It felt different outside. At first, I thought maybe I'm getting a little older and I just don't have the stamina I had last year - that wasn't it though. The Sun is different now – it is bright white. There used to always be a yellow Sun before, but for some reason it has changed and I do not react well to it anymore. I don't know what that is all about.

Another big change I like to talk about is geography changes. South America has moved to the east of North America - look it up. Also, your kidneys have moved. The heart has moved. Your liver is larger and has a left and right lobe. Everything is really strange right now. I haven't figured out if I have come from somewhere else, which sounds totally freaking crazy. I mean it all sounds crazy, but when you know it is real, you feel like you have to speak up about it, to let other people know that this thing is real and tell them that they just need to wake up too.

I've done two videos on YouTube now. I'm going to learn how to edit videos. I want to know how to put this stuff together so I can try to start reaching people. I want them to know what is going on. I feel that it is that important. I mean it is very, very important when the Bible starts changing. I can deal with pop culture changes. I can deal with "Sweet dreams are made of this" (instead

of these), but when my Bible, my holy book, starts changing you better get right with God at that point.
Ben

Testimony 2

The strangest thing for me wasn't the changes themselves, but the reactions of those around me when I would tell them about it. I have since learned that the majority of people we interact with here on a daily basis are shells/dolls/clay. They are connected to an A.I. hive-mind that keeps the true soul beings trapped in this pernicious construct, under the illusion that they are real. The being who has hacked into our false 'reality' is making the changes to free us, to show us that these people are not like us - they are empty soulless vessels. This was the only way we would wake up and desire to exit the matrix. This entire construct is a fowler's snare. There was no other way to extract us except by altering the very substance of our 'reality', so we would 1. question it, and 2. detach from our family and friends who are illusions, not actually sentient beings, no more than virtual reality characters. These changes have been going on for a very long time, but we've only recently started noticing them in large numbers - which shows that we are disconnecting from the technology here and beginning to free ourselves. Our cosmic prison break is at hand.
Jamie

Testimony 3

I just wanted to share some thoughts with you guys this morning. Have you guys ever given any thought to how much programming we are subjected to from the time we are children all the way into adulthood? When you think about it it's a tremendous amount of programming. We experience literal television programming and societal programming, as well as religious programming and racial programing. I mean its craziness when you think about it. A few years ago, prior to the realization that I had experienced a quantum effect shift, I was on this quest to deconstruct the programming in my head. I have been on this journey for a while. An exercise or mantra that I do literally every morning is getting up for the day and asking myself, "What else is in your head". I do it because I was a victim of a tremendous amount of programming that included religious, societal, and military programming. I'm always on a quest of trying to clear out these constructs that are in my head. I have been thinking about that - in light of the quantum effect or Mandela Effect.

The Mandela Effect challenges our notions and mental constructs. When you really think about reality changing, and what that does to the psyche – it is pretty profound. When we first discovered the Mandela effect we all went through that period where we lost it, because we had been relying so much on the construct of solidity/realness, that we had been taught about what reality was. When we first woke up to the Mandela Effect we found out the construction of reality is not the way we thought it was. Now, a lot of people affected by the Mandela Effect seemed to have reached the point where we have accepted that the concept of shifting to multiple realities is not something that is scary to us anymore. It is something that we are starting to accept as a possibility. We change and evolve. I think when I look at the Mandela Effect it is an opportunity to recognize what we can do to change our lives, and it can be a new lease on life - an opportunity to make life what you want it to be.

One of the questions that I've been thinking about this week is what would we do if we knew it was possible that we couldn't die. Do you ever think about that? I'm pretty sure if we knew we couldn't die, then we would all be a lot more brazen and a lot more carefree. We would probably take more risks in life and pursue things that we are afraid to do. We are afraid to pursue certain things because we don't want to risk losing our life over that pursuit. In a sense, I think we have to apply that with the Mandela Effect. I wonder if reality has changed and we have shifted into a different reality, because we have possibly already died and passed that threshold. I say that because the new reality that we find ourselves in is obviously something completely different and completely alien to our recollection of how reality used to be. I think a lot of us are going through our Mandela effect experiences with clarity.

What if we realize that quantum immortality is a fact, and that you don't really die, but instead you transfer to this place or construct? What if what we call reality is actually us projecting reality from our own consciousness? That seems to be a quite a possibility. I think we have to get out of the victim mentality. When I first came to realization that the Mandela Effect was real, I really went into a victim mentality mode. Back then I felt like something, or someone had done something against me. I questioned what or who took my consciousness to this reality against my will. Honestly, there was a lot of fear and a lot of anger. Anger generally is used to mask fear. I was afraid, but then once I kind of came back to center and found my balance and wasn't afraid anymore - then I could start appreciating the opportunities within the Mandela or quantum effect.

It seems there is this conscious effort to feed off of our fear. It kind of it reminds me of the kiddie movie called Monsters Inc. where the plot was centered around a whole society or parallel dimension on the other side of the movie characters' closet doors that would create and collect fear energy by scaring the children. I think that a lot of these movies are telling the truth. Maybe it is the subconscious mind that is revealing the truth. Maybe it is someone on the outside of this matrix that is sending us messages within the movies and through other means to allow our subconscious minds to pick them up. It is very probable that there is some sort of energy exchange in which entities feed off of our energy because our emotions and our thoughts are quantifiable and powerful. The energy has got to be going somewhere, right? What if they are beings that feed off of that energy and benefit off of that energy? It is a possibility, especially when you consider that we are more powerful than we know, and we are co-creators of this reality.

Our individual reality and this amalgamation of collective reality plays a role in constructing this reality. We are co-creators of our individual reality and the collective reality. I call it a construct because this place is kind of like the matrix. It is a world where we load programs. It seems to be a very strange place, but it's not so bad you know. I think we have to be able to challenge our notions, and challenge these constructs in our heads about what we think we know - things we are battling with, and things that we need to let go of.

For me, I think one of the big ones I had to analyze was religion. I came up in a very fanatically religious home, and I was always pushed to be a part of that through excelling within a particular religious construct. I didn't want a part of it. It was not my path. One thing about being raised in that type of environment is that I learned fear. I was taught that I should fear God. They would always talk about having a healthy fear of God. There are all these concepts that are constructs of man that seek to entrap our souls, damage us, and divert us from our path of who we really are as beings (creator beings and eternal beings).

Children naturally come into this life with this light/innocence and then it gets corrupted overtime. I think that religion is one of those things we have to look at because it generates fear. The goal is to stay out of the fear matrix, especially at this time. It is becoming very clear that there are these entities that benefit from negative energy. There are positive and negative entities in this playing field. There and those people that work with the negative entities and serve as their hosts. I think that is a reality. If you look at this reality on a spiritual level and energetic level you can see it within people. I think that is why a lot of us are experiencing jarring changes in our relationships with people. We are starting to recognize that it may be that our family is not really our family, and our friends are not really our friends. They are shadows of their former selves. These beings are lining up on one side and they may not be on the same side that we are on. That seems to be a revelation and a realization that I had to deal with. I had to grasp that in dealing with some of my former friends. I used to be close to these individuals, but not anymore because we are lined up on opposite sides of the playing field so to speak.

So I think it is about acceptance of that. It is okay because in that energetic exchange you find that whatever you lose, you end up gaining on the other side of the playing field with the family over here on this side. I just wanted to share that with you. Also, when it comes to this world and creating your own reality you have to ask yourself what your happy ending is to your story. Do you visualize that? You should. What is your happy ending to this story right now? Visualize it and work toward that. For me, my happy ending is leaving this plane and passing as an old man surrounded by my wife, children, grandchildren, and maybe some great grandchildren. My happy ending is knowing that I lived my life as a good man, a good father, a good husband, and a good member of my community who helped others. That is my happy ending. I mean what more can you ask for in life? That is my dream. I think this is the kind of world that we want to create for ourselves. It is about acceptance. I accept that and so I'm going to create that reality. Just food for thought.
Blake

Testimony 4

When you tell somebody about the Mandela Effect, they do almost a uniform thing where they shun you, or they have a fake explanation for everything. They say, "It's you and it's just your memory." And with people like that I really want to tell them "fxxk you". I really get pissed off about that because it's like they're telling you that you're crazy and you're not right in the head.

Back in 2009, I watched videos taking about how polar bears were in danger of extinction because the North Pole was melting so much. Where I'm from, people would talk about how if the ice caps melted at the North Pole, then we would have flooding, and the water all around the world would rise several feet. I remember that. These people that debunk the Mandela Effect have programed explanations. It is ridiculously crazy and dumb. I use to have a Jehovah's Witness come over here all the time wanting to come in my house to preach the word of God. The last time he knocked on my door, I asked him if he remembered Isaiah 11:6 saying: "The lion shall lay with the lamb," and he agreed that was what the verse said. I then said open up your bible. He opened up the book and read: "The wolf shall dwell with lamb," from the same Isaiah 11:6 verse. Then he did this blank stare thing and said, "oh yeah, yeah. I remember now. It's the wolf". After that, those Jehovah Witnesses never came to my house again. I guess their asses got scared. They witnessed that Bible change themselves. They kept asking me if my Bible was the exact same Bible, and I assured them it was the same one. Those people are gone now and I haven't heard from them since.

I don't understand how anyone could walk around and be normal about this. I know those Jehovah's Witnesses know those famous Bible lines, and they weren't misquoting it before I showed them the verse. Elvis even wrote a song about the lion laying down with the lamb. I don't think he misquoted the Bible. I don't believe that there's no such thing as the lion laying down with the lamb. Also, it reads suspicious now because of the negative connation that the wolf has. This shit is getting ridiculous and every morning I wake up and I think to myself, "What's going to happen next?" And I almost don't even want to look to see what has changed. I've constantly been seeing the double digits 33 everywhere, but that's a whole other subject.

My message to people who are experiencing this Mandela Effect is that you need to get your sanity, and you need to make sure that you are solid on something that changed in terms of being totally certain that it was changed by the Mandela Effect. That's why I go back to this Bible, because I'm rock solid on this being changed by the Mandela Effect. I saw this change with my own eyes. In the beginning of the Bible, it now says, "In the beginning, God created the heaven and the earth". There is no "s" there at the end of the word "heaven". I showed that to the Jehovah's Witness and compared it to their Bibles, and they agreed that my Bible was a bad translation, which was evidence that they also saw the change and they remembered that the verse use to say, "In the beginning, God created the heavens and the earth" with an "s" at the end of the word "heaven". Two weeks later, my Bible flip-flopped and switched from saying, "In the beginning, God created the heaven and the earth," to saying, "In the beginning, God created the heavens and the earth" with an "s" at the end of the word "heaven" again. So, I just always remember that my Bible changing is my rock solid evidence that I hold on to and use to remind me that the Mandela Effect is real.

People will try to come at you and challenge your mind and memories and try to shatter your mind and memories, but I use my rock solid evidence of the Bible changing to help me hold on to my original memories, and not forget the Mandela Effect changes. All it takes is one solid piece of evidence of a change to know that the Mandela Effect is real. If your instincts are telling you that something has changed and the way it is now is wrong, hold firm and know that it is wrong and that what you remember is the truth. Your God-given instincts are telling you something is not right. You have to be strong-minded enough to disagree with people who aren't able to remember the way things used to be, before the Mandela Effect changes happened.

People will debate you and try to break you. For example, a lady I saw on YouTube believed the Mandela Effect was real because she was seeing the changes, then a couple months later something happened to her, and now she is in denial about the Mandela Effect being real. Now she makes videos attacking others for being able to see the Mandela effect. I'm like what are you talking about? She flipped her entire script and her original memories shattered and changed for some reason. I refuse to let my original memories be erased, because I hold on to my rock solid memory of the Bible changing as my anchor memory and proof that the Mandela effect is real. I saw my Bible physically change and that is my solid evidence, so if people want to try to convince me that the map changes and other Mandela Effect changes aren't real and I'm just misremembering everything - then I remind myself of my rock solid anchor memory of the Bible changing.

They are in denial. I mean, look at my girlfriend. My girlfriend is more interested in playing video games than hearing about the Mandela effect. This is really taking a toll on me. The strain of this is making me feel alone. I'm separated and nobody knows what I'm trying to explain to them. They are void and empty. There's very few of us that are able to maintain and keep those original memories and collection of thoughts. So, my message to you is to keep a solid piece of evidence as your rock, so you know where you came from. And so that way later on when changes grow - you will be able to still hold on to your original memories. The changes are just going to keep getting crazier and crazier, and everyone around me seems to be going along with the changes and accepting them. Apparently, for some reason they can't remember the truth of how things really were. They can't remember the way it was before, and so they're not going to be of any help to you. You're just going to be alone, so you need to keep a solid piece of evidence of an original memory of something you knew for sure.
Tony

Testimony 5

It is important that we don't lose sight of what can transpire. I wish that none of this had ever occurred in my lifetime or anyone's lifetime, but it seems to be occurring, so if we're going to be brave then we need to look at what we're being told, what we're being shown, and what has been foretold in this process. I watched a video the other day from a great guy. He is trying to deal with this as well, and I can see the pain on his face in his videos because he's a very wise young man (I call him young because he's younger than me). He's pained and I'm pained because I can tell that we come from similar understandings of Biblical readings. Even though we may have different backgrounds the lord has led many to the same place. In his video, he says that he hopes that this is a process that is going to take a long time and we'll be able to live with these changes well into old age ... but if we are going to be truthful with ourselves and to these signs that we are given, then we have to accept the reality of the unpleasant parts of the prophecies if they are true. If you haven't read them, I would suggest that you read the next chapter in the Book of Revelations, chapter 13. It is an unpleasant read, but we're going to have to deal with it if it's truly where we're heading. And I think that if we are heading that way, then these things will culminate quickly.

The lord said the days will be shortened for the sake of the elect. Who are the elect? Anyone who the lord decides so, even if I'm not the elect and even if you are not the elect, the days are going to be shortened. I suggest you read them. I'm going to prepare something for myself that I can present and it is going to be soon, because things are going to change rapidly within the next 12 months. I don't want to be some prophet of doom. No one does. Only crazy people and people full of resentment who want to feel important want to run around yelling: "it's the end of the world". I don't want to be that guy, but I have to be responsible to this calling as we all do. If you have the eyes to see and the ears to hear then you must have the voice to cry out. It is part of the process. Prayer is a big part of the process so, let's pray for peace, for love, and for a peaceful transition.
Terry

Testimony 6

I stopped trying to inform people about the changes taking place. I got tired of being called crazy. Too many blank stares, name calling, and anger towards me. Even when they realized I was right, they just wanted to ignore me. They are not ready for it. Let them remain oblivious of other changes. The Mandela Effect will never be recognized universally. Prepare to be shunned after people become aware that you accept the Mandela Effect as fact. We are modern day lepers. We will continue to be ostracized.
Ufoguyspaceman YouTube Channel

Testimony 7

Everything is not so great with me this afternoon. I left work early. I'm a church secretary. At this church we have two bulletins. You have your morning service and your earlier morning service. In the bulletins, in the first service we have the full Lord's Prayer. Of course, the Lord's Prayer used to say "trespasses" back in May. Shortly after that, I started to realize that things were going to keep changing, and that it wasn't corporations just changing stuff and denying it just to drive people nuts. I don't know at what point it was, but the Lord's Prayer changed. I made a template so that we did not have to type the prayer every time during church service. The template was kept in box form and it was never changed by anyone including the pastor. A of couple months after I made the template, it changed from saying "sin" to "sins".

The second bulletin also had a template and it was just a little passage. It used to say, "forgive us of our trespasses", and no one changed it either. I had been watching that second template closely to track any changes, because when the first template changed I really didn't notice when it changed since I didn't really look at it much. So last week the second bulletin still had the word "trespasses" in it. I had been watching it. When I did the bulletin today it had changed. So yeah, my heart's pounding. The only way it could have been changed is if I changed it and I didn't. It's disturbing.

I know we're all struggling and I just want to say hi to everyone and show myself. It is so hard to discern who you're talking to online, so I think it is really good to show ourselves. I have a lot of things to say, but because of my business I don't know if I'll be able to keep a lot of my videos up that show my face.

My family are not the same people. I mean I love them, but they are not the same people. They are very status-driven. They are going to do whatever some authority tells them to do. They are the type of people who would go right to a doctor or a psychiatrist and ask them what they should do. So, who needs that? I do not need that. I'm just trying to be as good to them as I can, and try to get to know them the way they are now. Yeah, I just feel for you guys out there and I just want to say God bless you, and don't feel guilty about things like leaving work early if you have to. Just take care of yourself. Your soul is not dependent upon where you work. Breanna

Testimony 8

I spend a lot of my day thinking about the stuff that is happened to me in my past that just doesn't make sense as a rational adult in the world that I was born and raised in. I know that some stuff is wrong. It is just blatantly obvious. In the passage in Isaiah 11:6 it used to say, "The lion shall lay with the lamb." Now the same verse says, "The wolf shall also dwell with the lamb." The thing is, a lot of us remember it differently because you can't change what the heart remembers. Whatever this Mandela Effect thing is, it can't change what has been written on our hearts.

Nobody has encyclopedias anymore because we live in a world where everything is digital. Maybe there was a reason for that. If anyone has a book with old maps in it you should go check them out and see what you find.

So, I don't know why this is happening. Some people say it's CERN. Some people say it is the d-wave quantum computer. I do find it quite odd that in Stephen King's book, *The Dark Tower* ,there are all kinds of different worlds that people can go into. People just say that all of the sci-fi is made-up, and sci-fi isn't real. I find it very strange that there are some things that are mirrored in the world we live in. I don't know why it is happening. Some people will say they believe that the worlds are colliding, or being pushed together because things are changing that we don't remember. I honestly believe that there is something trying to separate us, because of the power that comes when "two people are gathered in my name", like the Bible says. I don't know exactly how it works - I just know that something is changing.

There are a lot of people recognizing the Mandela Effect, and for this reason I think it is causing the elect to be deceived. Obviously, the strange thing is that when I go to people of faith in my community and speak to them about the Mandela Effect, they really don't have an interest in it. They don't seem to care. They are like, "What's the big deal when it comes to the wolf dwelling with the lamb?" The big deal is that it is written on my heart differently, and that it has been changed. The changes with Sally Fields to Sally Field, and "Luke, I am you father" are changes too, but the Bible is a bigger deal. These smaller changes are evidence of the much bigger picture. It is evidence of a little piece of matter that has changed. There is something to it, and I think we should all be aware of it. I find it very strange that some of the people I talk to about this - I believed to be men of faith - and they just don't care at all. They say, "Well it's got no bearing on your salvation." That's true because I think you get saved through Jesus, but it is as if these people who got saved years ago don't even care anymore about what the enemy is doing to us.

There's something to it. The Mandela Effect is not just there for no reason. I highly suggest if you don't know anything about the Mandela Effect that you research it. Please research CERN and how much things have changed since they actually started using it. Research the d-wave computer and that guy who is running it - he's just blatantly talking about speaking to gods and other dimensions, but he tries to pass that off as normal terminology. Check them out. It is something I can't get my mind off of, and there's got to be a reason for it. I'm just trying to share whatever

God puts on my heart.

Something's going on here and I don't know what it is, but there's hundreds of thousands, if not millions of people seeing it, and it at least needs to be discussed. It is something important. If this world really belongs to Lucifer then he's trying to do everything he possibly can through these experiments to figure out how to break down the elect. He's going to do whatever he can to separate them from each other, and then just work on that one individual person. I do what God places on my heart. I feel the need. I really can't explain the stuff about the Mandela Effect and how it affects us spiritually other than the fact that we see it and we know it is real, and now it is trying to change the Bible. I really do believe that they are trying to take the knowledge of Jesus out of the bible, but they can't remove him from our hearts. I see an agenda there. We may be far from the agenda being completed, but right now it is like the boiling frog analogy is happening now. They're not going to just change all of history in one day. It may be a gradual process in which bits and pieces are changed over time slowly. Then one day when you're 70 years old, the kids that are in school during that time will be learning a history completely different from what you knew.

Alex

Testimony 9

I am a loan processor and underwriter. I deal with mortgages. That's been my job. I'm in a professional field. If I get caught making Mandela Effect videos, then I won't have a job because my reputation is on the line for talking about something that sounds absolutely insane – crazy. But I don't mind anymore because it doesn't matter. We're in a form of tribulation where we are seeing something that is on a mass scale, and at the end of the day it doesn't fxxking matter how much money we make. The nice cars, all my things, and the job that I have doesn't matter. Right now, I could work at McDonald's and just have enough money to pay my rent because I have to focus on this.

We're waking up to new changes to our history that include new records, landmasses, human anatomy, etc. and we're being told by these people who act like demons to stop worrying about the Mandela Effect, stop looking at it, don't pay attention to it, and continue to work and don't be a burden on society. There is something about those people that is odd. They seem empty and void. They are scared of truth. They can't listen to anything and they have no logic. Some close loved ones that you have known forever don't have some of the memories that you made with them while you were together in the past. When you try to tell them about the Mandela Effect they don't want to hear it and they get very aggressive. People didn't use to act that way. That is not normal. They aren't normal people. I don't know what the fxxk is going on, but I know that it is not normal. We're dealing with something on a whole other level and we're surrounded by these people.

The number one thing that I think most of us who see the Mandela Effect have in common - is that we have a ton of people around us that we know personally who don't share our memories. These people don't have the same personalities anymore and don't want to listen. They have a low attention span, they change the subject, and they are evasive. A lot of thc time I think to myself that these are not my friends and my family. Where did these people come from? These people act totally different and don't want to hear the truth.

We are surrounded by these people and they could quite possibly be demons or possessed in some kind of way. When you try to explain the Mandela Effect changes to them they don't have any real argument and they'll just go straight into attacking you. It's funny to me in some sense. Right now, it is pretty obvious for us to see, but I don't know if these people get smarter later on and hide it better. We're obviously going to be infiltrated and there's going to be fake people pretending like they know what is going on with the Mandela Effect, but really they just want to listen in and see how much we in the Mandela Effect community know. A week or two later after pretending to be affected by the Mandela Effect, a switch will get flipped and they'll be on the total opposite end disregarding the Mandela Effect like the rest of the world.

So, what I say to you people out there who are experiencing this is that you just have to know that these are not the people that you once knew. I don't know how this is being done. I don't know if we're in a simulation or something, but I think our consciousness are in a place where some people's normal consciousness has left their body and has been replaced by a different consciousness. Maybe their bodies were empty, void and something else has entered these people's bodies.

The spirit of some of these people seems to be gone. It just seems to be an empty set of eyes that I'm looking at when I talk to some of these people and I don't know how I'm picking up on this. I'm able to just see it. I'm not some sort of a spiritual freak or anything. I just have the ability to look at these people and see that. I approached four different people who are strangers and asked them some questions and I got the exact same uniform responses back from different people that don't know each other. Their words as well as their facial muscles and mannerisms looked totally the same.

It was like they had the same script and it freaked me out at first. I just keep seeing it happen and I keep asking the questions. The other day I talked to my sister on the phone and asked her about the Statue of Liberty. She lives in New York. She has been to Ellis Island where the Statue of Liberty was at, and she's been in the torch so she was shocked to know that they are claiming that nobody has been in the torch since the early 1900s. I almost got her to wake up which is great, because I have not gotten anybody really to wake up. It is impossible to wake some people up, and I don't even think that we're supposed to be trying to wake certain people up.

I know we're seeing the Mandela Effect for a reason, but I don't know if we are supposed to be waking people up. I've tried over and over again and it is almost impossible. It is hard to tell if the people who won't wake up are lost, or if something else is going on. I would expect to hear about the Mandela Effect on more media platforms than YouTube. I don't hear about it that much. I thought we would be hearing about the Mandela Effect on major news networks and in the churches, but we haven't. The churches just aren't saying anything. I get that same aggressive feeling from a pastor that I get from people when I tell them about logo changes. When I try to talk to the pastor about the change in Isaiah 11:6 in the KJV Bible about the lion changing to the wolf – it is the same feeling. You guys out there need to go off your gut feeling and your memory. That is what we have left. So I'm just talking about the Mandela Effect and I'm going to talk about it even if it means that I may not ever get another professional job again. At this point, what kind of job I have really doesn't matter to me.

Jacob

Testimony 10

My video is for those who don't believe that the Bible has

changed and get absolutely defensive whenever someone brings it up. There's a large community of us that are now here on YouTube because that is the only place that we haven't been ostracized from (though many attempts have been made). We all see the changes. There are thousands of us that recognize this. I don't know how this Mandela Effect works, and why some of us remember it differently than others do. There are all kinds of theories out there as to why this is happening, and why it is affecting a lot of us. I pray that people will find truth and will find the real answers they are looking for.

There are many people that are telling us that we're horrible and what we're doing is actually absolutely blasphemous. I want to give a bit of a history lesson. I was raised Catholic. Since I was a little boy, I went to a private school from kindergarten all the way to seventh grade, which means we went to mass every week in school and then on the weekend on Sunday. We would do about 30 or 40 different repeated prayers over and over. You will no longer find in the KJV where it says the word "trespasses" in the Lord's Prayer. That is completely changed and it has changed in bibles that I've had for years. Now am I and thousands of other people remembering that wrong? I bring that up because I recited that prayer over and over for years throughout my youth, because I was told that was what we were supposed to do. That is what our religion did and it always started with, "Our Father who art in heaven, hallowed be thy name, thy kingdom come, thy will be done, on earth as it is in heaven." Well now you can't find "forgive us our trespasses" at all. It's not there.

I know these changes aren't happening all at once. The Bible says that there will be a famine for the word of God. I'm not here to convince anybody. I'm only asking those that say that the Mandela Effect is impossible to please search your heart and test the spirit of where those thoughts are coming from. The Bible also says the elect would be deceived - it talks about how there is going to be a famine for the word and it has started. There are hundreds of changes. I don't care how crazy it sounds.

As crazy as this claim sounds, I watched Billy Graham's funeral for the second time today. I don't mean I watched it twice today. I mean last November 2017, the day before Thanksgiving I didn't see any family or do anything for Thanksgiving. I was home alone and I watched his funeral and I was watching other people online talk about how Billy Graham had just passed away. I remember specific things about his funeral, but the key here is that it was not

the same funeral that I saw today. There was a completely different background and setup. Could I convince anyone? No, because if you need convincing you are never going to believe me anyway. I know that I'm not mentally ill.
Chris

Testimony 11

Tens of thousands of people have experienced the Mandela Effect so far in little ways, and speaking as one of those people who's having this happen to them, I'd appreciate it if they would turn off that damn quantum computer because I really feel that I'm losing my mind here. I certainly don't want to come off to you as crazy, but you know that thing they call the Mandela Effect? I'm pretty sure you know about it. Just about everybody knows about the Mandela Effect now.

I was one of the first people to notice the Mandela Effect back in 2009. It really irks me. It is important that you realize this was back in 2009. I have an incredible memory and I have an incredible eye for detail, and little things really irked me, so I went searching the internet. Everybody thought I was crazy. Well in 2008, they developed the first working quantum computer. Now if you don't know anything about quantum computing let me try to explain it to you in the simplest way possible. Quantum computers take advantage of alternate realities to solve mathematical equations that would be impossible to solve with regular computers. It is really complicated but there are plenty of YouTube videos out there that will explain quantum computing to you. Watch them all and you'll get it. I have watched them all. That is kind of what it took for me to get a clear grasp of quantum computers.

One of the things that has changed with the Mandela Effect is of course Nelson Mandela. Some of you may remember Nelson Mandela dying in the 80's like I do. I remember clearly hearing about it on the news because at the time I didn't have cable. I remember hearing about it at school and we flew the flag at half mast. I remember watching the funeral on television. I remember I saw footage of the back of his wife and daughter walking away from the funeral. It was a pretty big event in my life.

The Bernstein Bears (children's books and TV show) apparently is now spelled Berenstain. A lot of the news media and online encyclopedias will say that we are just remembering it wrong, but I'm not an idiot. I have an eye for details and I remember Berenstain being spelled Berenstein. This is one of the pivotal books in my life. It is one of the first books I learned to read by myself. I had the entire collection of the Berenstein Bears. I had six read-along books on tape, and I even had a Berenstein Bears record with the book that I played on my little record player so, when they say you're just remembering this wrong it really kind of irks me. I'm not remembering it wrong. My point being that these Mandela Effects or quantum computing effects are growing. They're continuing to happen. I'm trying really hard to stay calm. What is happening is that they are inputting these problems into the quantum computers and the quantum computers are changing things. They are not changing everybody's lives. They are just changing certain people's lives. Maybe it was done accidentally. Not everybody, but just certain people have experienced the Mandela Effect. Please, if you know anything about the quantum computing, or if you have anyone that is involved in quantum computing - tell them to shut this thing off. It is very, very irritating. Dylan

Testimony Excerpts

Testimony 12

I've been thinking that it is possible that the Mandela effect itself is not actually created by man or by atom smashers, but is instead a fulfillment of Bible prophecy. Just like you and I do, the powers that be have the ability to read the Bible and see what is predicted to happen. This may be hard for some people to believe, but the great minds of our time, the elite, the globalists, and those in charge know that God is real. They know he exists and they'll do anything to cover him up, hide him, and to keep you from believing, so the Mandela Effect could be their attempt to do that because they knew that certain things were going to occur based on Bible prophecy. Now that these prophetic things are starting to occur they may be rolling out this technology that allows them to literally manipulate matter to create some of the Mandela Effect examples by using quantum mechanics, quantum physics, and quantum computing ... the agenda was to hide the real cause behind the Mandela Effect changes, trying to take credit for it so that instead of us believing this is Bible prophecy, God is real, and it is the end of days so to speak, we're running around like chickens with their heads cut off trying to figure out how science is doing all of the Mandela Effects.

They also are trying to show that man has more power than God. This is where I think the discrepancy exists, because you'll see the control system simultaneously exposing Mandela Effect examples, while at the same time debunking other Mandela Effects and making fun of people who believe in the Mandela Effect. While that's happening, simultaneously they will have scientists out talking about parallel universes and the power of quantum computers. How confusing is that? The Bible says that God is not the author of confusion. The confusion comes in when you start to wondering how they are doing this, and why they are simultaneously covering it up and ridiculing people for believing in it - while at the same time telling us they have computers that can literally access thousands of other parallel universes.
Kim

Testimony 13

Your precious ego gets torn to shreds when people close to you (whose opinions you hold in high regard) start to write things off and think that what you are saying is crazy talk. It really does terrible things to you inside. Your ego gets trampled upon and gets torn to ribbons. At your core, you always want understanding and affection from your closest family members. You want them to have a basic amount of respect for you and not write off things you're saying because they think you're crazy. I never thought I would ever find myself in that kind of situation. Personally, I was always a black sheep kind of person but it's never like anybody thought I was crazy. I would always have little tidbits and facts for people that would be enlightening. I like to help people learn. I always want to learn.
Tammy

Testimony 14

I've been called crazy, psychotic. I've been told that I am suffering from a lack of sleep. I've been told that I'm a victim of a psychological operation by the military aka a psyop (psychological operation), and it is all because I have seen the Mandela Effect. I'm just going to get to the source of some things and show you just how affective this Mandela Effect is. It is not a psychological operation. What's happening is that our third dimensional world is merging with a fourth dimensional one and we're losing some stuff that can't cross over. Eventually we will understand what the fourth dimension is. That is what's happening at CERN right now. CERN is finding that they're learning more and more about the fourth dimension. They have already talked about it. They don't bring it up much, because it is dangerous, but when they turned on the hadron collider they opened up a portal and they said they saw something. You can look it up for yourself. It happened.

Additional proof of the Mandela Effect is Neil deGrasse Tyson. He's one of the most renowned minds in the world. He's an astrophysicist who breaks down everything for people in a way that we can understand. Neil deGrasse Tyson has been heard on videos mentioning that we are on the Sagittarius Arm of the Milky Way galaxy. But now we were on the Sagittarius arm of the Milky Way, because we are not on it any more - we are on the Orion Spur now. So, what happened? People still want proof of the Mandela effect. Neil deGrasse Tyson is the most known astrophysicist in the world. This dude is the voice of Cosmos. We've always been on the Sagittarius Arm and now we're suddenly on the Orion Spur? It's not a psychological operation. That happened. Just like Nelson Mandela dying before 2013 happened.

The Mandela effect is actually two dimensions merging. We're getting ready to hit the cusp of something beautiful. We're getting ready to discover the fourth dimension. When the third dimension witnesses something that happens in the fourth dimension there is no way for our brains to explain it.

Jerome

Testimony 15

With the Mandela effect, one of the things that I've realized since waking up to this five weeks ago is the level of shock that comes with the realization and the need to find acceptance. I'm sure this is true for everybody. There's that level of shock, surprise, wonder, and disbelief and that human impulse to push it aside and say, "This isn't really happening, and even if it is - what's the big deal. It hasn't changed my life." Still, the Mandela effect demands a level of acceptance. The ability to come to the acceptance of the changes is going to be very important, because

the changes as far as I can see are not going to stop. At some point, there's going to be drastic changes that are undeniable-- irrefutable changes in our reality. I think that is going to come in the fourth and final dimension of this shift. In the fourth and final chapter of what I think is the harvest we'll be completely cut off from our understanding of our past and we'll be living in a present reality. During that time, we'll be in a purely present reality and that's the process of acceptance that we have to come to in order to survive this psychologically and emotionally.
Toby

Testimony 16

They're messing with particle collisions, so they're continuously trying to create this big bang thing. They know exactly what they are doing with devilish precision, so basically they are trying to create dark matter. They're trying to bring the underworld to this realm. I guess that most likely explains the Mandela Effect. When particles collide, they create quantum entanglement which causes the Mandela Effect to happen. We now have new species that we've never heard of, new fruits, new plants … our anatomy is changing. The reality of what is happening is going to trip me out to the point that I'm going to be stunned with my mouth open processing too much information at once. I'm not sure how to feel about it. It's too much. There's actual proof. Either it's time-travel fxxkery or it is CERN.
Yolanda

Testimony 17

So, it's been a year for me now since waking up to the Mandela effect. When I first woke up I was ranting and raving about the Sun changing and the plethora of changes that had occurred. I was scared that I had died and that the this was all a death DMT release in my brain before going to the afterlife, or a maybe a trick to get my mind to accept my death. I was afraid, but that didn't last. I was extremely interested in the Mandela Effect changes and what each change meant. I expounded on a lot of theories. It has been an interesting year with logo and movie changes here and there. There have been anatomy changes, continent changes,

and all these things are fantastic. They make us wonder about the reality that we live in, but at the same time if you want to impress me - then change the hearts of men. That will impress me. Make a change to the world to where children don't have to suffer. I was born to a psychopath. My father was a sadistic psychopath and my mother was a religious zealot and a narcissist. So, that was my reality that I was born into. I had a sister that died of malnutrition. I had a daughter that died on the operating table. I've lost friends at war and I've been homeless. I've been shot at. My life here in this world has not been an easy one and that's the truth. It has made me a misanthrope which is a person who hates people. I don't care for people at all and I avoid people. The most positive interactions I've had is with the Mandela Effect community and I love you guys. To me that's the most positive and beneficial thing that has come out of the Mandela effect.
Louis

Testimony 18

I'm a Twilight Zone addict - I have the entire Twilight Zone collection. I think there are a hundred episodes. I'm a writer. I like to write and so with every Twilight Zone episode I wanted to know which episodes were written by Rod Sterling, because I wanted to see his flavor. I'd watch each show and I'd wait for the credits and see that it was written by Rod Sterling, so I'd have a really good idea of his writing style. I already went through and watched all one hundred episodes. Then I heard about the Mandela Effect, and I go back to look at the spelling of Rod Sterling's name and they all say "Serling" without the 't'. I was dumbfounded! I was literally dumbfounded and now I have to listen to people say, "oh you're just mistaken". I have to listen to these people telling me that I have a faulty memory. I don't know. It was really, really bizarre. And no, I don't take medication and I was not taking drugs. All you stubborn donkeys out there just need to accept that weird things happen and there's things that happen in life that you can't explain. It's a fact that you're going to have to live with. You're going to have to deal with that.
Clarence

Testimony 19

For those of us who understand, see, and are affected by the

Mandela Effect or reality shifting, I've been seeing a lot of people on the Mandela Effect Facebook groups really losing their minds and feeling really sad, upset, and disturbed (not only over experiencing these changes, but also over the havoc it wreaks in their life). Oh my goodness guys! It is by far the worst kind of mental anguish and trauma I could ever possibly imagine. Knowing the whole Earth is changing, your whole reality is changing, and having to keep that quiet from the people around you and the people that you love like friends and family is hard. Having the Mandela Effect takeover your entire life, but having to pretend in your day-to-day life that it doesn't exist is so mentally taxing that I could cry for a whole week straight about it. I have to be in my work mode form half the time, and that is so extremely taxing to have to edit myself and pretend there is absolutely nothing wrong. Because all I want to do is just let them know that the world is quantumly changing, and we don't have time to watch every single episode of their favorite Netflix series. I want to be able to tell them that the north pole is still missing. Sometimes it just feels good to vent and see other people on YouTube talking about how upsetting it is to exist in this new reality. It's a new reality where you feel like you've stumbled upon this hidden information that you know most other people in the world have no clue about.
Victoria

Testimony 20

We call it the Mandela Effect because things are starting to change. Our reality is starting to change. We're having memories of things that are no longer there. The monopoly man does not have the monocle anymore, and there are many other changes that you can look up on different YouTube videos. Well, what a lot of people aren't talking about is how we are changing. Our memories are changing. It is scary enough to know that things are changing, but when you start to realize that you are also changing and people around you are also changing it is very scary. If you can see the Mandela Effect, then consider yourself lucky because you still have your memory. A lot of people don't. A lot of people are still asleep to the Mandela Effect. So I'm trying to make videos to wake people up because this is not a game, this is not a joke. This is real. This is really happening and not enough people are talking about.

Chelsey

Testimony 21

I want to discuss the whole Mandala Effect in terms of getting people to see it. Do you find that even the people who do acknowledge the Mandela effect is real just are as concerned or involved with the whole effect as you are? Before you were affected by the Mandela effect, we're you always the type of person that people would consider to be a conspiracy theorist? Someone who was always looking at the things that no one else seemed to be concerned about? The Mandela effect is much grander than any conspiracy theory. This is no longer a conspiracy when you realize that it's really happening and it is not just a theory. It is an actual thing that is happening. You have to try to understand that with these other people who don't see the Mandela Effect there's really no difference between the Mandela Effect and any other conspiracy theory you bring up to them. So do you feel like a different person? People say you seem like a different person. I feel like I'm a different person. Other people seem like different people and they don't seem to realize that this is a pretty big deal. It is a life-changing event, so just take it to heart and understand that from their point of view you probably do seem like a different person because you are a different person. Don't get too freaked out by it. Understand that these changes are a good thing, and it is a good thing that you are seeing them. It is a bad thing that other people aren't seeing them, but you can't make people see. You can show them and you can present it to them, but you can't make people see. Anyways, I just feel like you guys should not be fearful no matter what happens. I've heard conspiracies about alien invasions and all sorts of stuff, but no matter what happens, just understand that it is all part of the plan and the good guys are the victors in this whole situation.
Devon

Testimony 22

In the interest of truth seeking and honesty and questioning my own conclusions, I'm coming to realize that no one knows for certain what the cause of the Mandela Effect is. I'm willing to challenge my own theories, put them aside, and just wipe them away in order to have a different perspective because this is what

the process is. I don't believe in dogma. I'm not here to tell you what the Mandela Effect is. I don't want anybody telling me what it is. We're all working from different bases of experience. I can only work from my experience, so from a purely Christian esoteric perspective, I think Christians have waited for a promise to be fulfilled in the Gospels. We've been told that Christ would return and we have lived with the Bible which has, in my opinion, been consistent in its text and its teaching. We've been given the gospel. We've been given the teachings, so that we can live a Christ-like existence and have a relationship with our God through Christ. We've been waiting and waiting, and now things have finally begun happening in our reality.
Kelly

ABOUT THE AUTHORS

Eileen Colts

Eileen grew up in the suburbs of Chicago, Cairo and the coconut jungles of Trinidad & Tobago. She opened the first expatriate nursery school in Maadi, Egypt in 1979, and then completed her B.A. magna cum laude from Loyola University, Chicago with a major in journalism and minor in (child) psychology, 1985.

Fortunate to land her first post-university job at the Chicago NPR affiliate radio station, she started as a producer/reporter in children's programming, but left for a European network five years later as the morning news anchor and City Hall reporter. Eileen initially joined the German national broadcasting network Radio Deutsche Welle as a news editor, reporter, director and host for their international English Service, but eventually left to freelance report Eastern European news, based in Cologne, Prague and Bucharest, for National Public Radio (NPR), Associated Press (AP), Pacifica Radio, Canadian Broadcasting Corporation (CBC), Radio France, and Vatican Radio.

In London, Eileen worked as a media consultant for

international corporations and energy companies, before starting a family at 39 and settling down to open one of the country's first organic nursery schools. She became a healthy childcare writer, speaker and advocate (published under her maiden name Eileen McIntyre).

Though her professional life primarily involved children and media, her private passion focused on world religious myth and quantum physics. Looking for God and the *meaning of life*, she was certain it would cross the boundaries of the mystical and the scientific, so her studies involved science, philosophy and world religions. She credits her NDE in Egypt in 1977 for leading her into the mystic's private life, after remaining fully conscious and watching a medical team resuscitate her lifeless body following anaphylactic shock to an immunization.

Eileen returned to the United States in 2012, where the Mandela Effect soon caught her attention. She found likeminded people on YouTube putting a name to something she has experienced since 1995, and recalls her mother experiencing Mandela Effects since the 1970s. She began her YouTube channel *One (Eileen Colts)* in 2016 on the advice of Shane to share Mandela Effect experiences and observations, but soon moved into the spiritual metaphysical realms of quantum science and contact disclosure.

She considers the Mandela Effect a Quantum Awakening of consciousness in humanity. "The New Human will easily understand this phenomenon and so much more. This is the beginning of a major evolutionary change. Consider it a marker or a signpost for generations to come. When did people first start to see how their collective thoughts affect matter collectively? When they started seeing the Mandela Effect."

Eileen is a contributing recipient of a Corporation for Public Broadcast (CPB) Award 1989 for Live Concert Production (Director); and a National Education Association (NEA) Award 1986 for Excellence in Children's Programming (Producer/Host).

Paulo M. Pinto

Paulo is a metaphysical researcher, author, reiki practitioner, father of two and professional economist. Born in Recife, Brazil, he graduated as an Electrical Engineer in 1995, before marrying and moving to Australia three years later. In Sydney, he completed a Master of Economics (1st Class Hons), and started a career in economic analysis, modelling and policy advice for a number of Australian government agencies, universities and private institutions.

His first fiction book, *Imersão (Immersion),* was written in Portuguese in the mid-1990s and self-published in 2001. It contains many utopian and dystopian predictions about aspects of society and technology that materialized twenty years later.

Paulo successively delved into many spiritual traditions including Catholicism, Seventh Day Adventism, Rosicrucianism, and Franco-Brazilian Spiritism. He studied the teachings of the Buddha, the works of French spiritual pioneer Allan Kardec, the messages of Brazilian medium Chico Xavier, the metaphysics of Erwin Laszlo, the American *RA: Law of One* books and philosophies developed by the L/L Research Group and critiqued by scholar Dr. Scott Mandelker.

Paulo's undergraduate studies facilitated the familiarization with the concepts of Einsteinian physics, mathematical multi-dimensionality, and quantum mechanics - especially the de Broglie-Bohm pilot wave interpretation of quantum phenomena espoused by Nassim Haramein. All these scientific pillars are the foundation of Paulo's internet video channel *Spiritwalker*, available freely on many platforms including YouTube, where aspects of the physics-metaphysics interplay are workshopped. They also provide the basis upon which the *Spiritwalker* section of this anthology *Mandela Effect: Friend or Foe?* was written.

In 2018, after three years of training, Paulo became a reiki practitioner in the Usui-Tibetan tradition, having been tuned by Brazilian Reiki Master Herzil Jr. Unexpectedly, reiki helped bring about a torrent of professional turmoil, ostracism, friendship break-ups, loneliness, anxiety, financial tension, introspection and eventually the end of a marriage. These adjustments began the clearing of negative behaviors and unhelpful thought patterns that are needed for the emancipation of consciousness.

Today, Paulo focuses on researching how we can develop a peaceful, prosperous and inclusive society in which human potential can thrive. In parallel, he continues to investigate the universal language of metaphysics; and to pursue – through study, meditation, reiki, kindness and coherent faith – that which can hardly be put into words.

Shane Cornell Robinson

Shane was born on March 30th, 1974, in St. Louis, Missouri. He was the youngest of three in a multi-racial Christian home. Shane questioned everything about life like, "How and why are we here?" and, "If God made everything - where did God come from?"

Shane would usually get the typical mainstream Christian response, and if the question was too deep, his mother would tell him, "I don't know, when you get to heaven you can ask God." That would shut him up for a while, but he never stopped wondering and searching for answers to life's biggest questions.

Christianity is the only religion Shane has ever associated with, even though he moved through a few denominations before realizing religion was only a steppingstone to a deeper relationship with the divine. Shane began to unravel what he felt was man-made religious doctrine from the core values he was raised to live by. The Golden Rule: treating and loving others as you want others to treat and love you. This is what Shane believes is the foundation of what many great spiritual teachers taught, including his role model and hero, Jesus.

After a life-long journey of searching for deeper truths to the meaning of life, Shane felt as if this journey had finally come to a dead end, and that there were no answers that could satisfy the basic, yet fundamental questions he had about our existence here on Earth. This would ultimately lead to what Shane considers his 'dark night of the soul' in late 2016. Life had become utterly meaningless - like King Solomon talks about in the book of Ecclesiastes. By February 2017, in a desperate attempt to alleviate the meaningless feelings he was experiencing, Shane decided to start a YouTube channel to explore different world views and ideas held by others. The initial goal was to help others realize we are more the same than we are different, and to help unite people in love, rather than divide us over differences in beliefs. Not long after starting the channel, Shane realized the Mandela Effect was a very real phenomenon.

After extensive research into the possible causes of the Mandela Effect, Shane felt no explanations fit as well as the consideration that this was a supernatural event caused by some benevolent force or agency trying to awaken humanity without violating free will. This idea was confirmed when he read the book, *The Three Waves of Volunteers and the New Earth,* by Dolores Cannon. In chapter twenty-three, "The Best Agenda for Earth", the book seems to describe the Mandela Effect when higher-level beings discuss whether or not to make observable material changes to our dimensional reality. That realization put Shane back onto a more spiritual path of trying to get the word out, wake up others, and bring together loving people in the endeavor to raise human con-sciousness to a more unified, loving, Christ Consciousness.

Vannessa VA

Vannessa is a Qualified Mental Health Professional (QMHP) and currently works as a counselor at a crisis stabilization facility in the northern Virginia area. Vannessa specializes in a variety of treatment modalities, including cognitive behavioral therapy, dialectical behavioral therapy, and music therapy. She graduated with a Master of Science in Clinical Mental Health Counseling from an accredited university in 2015. Before devoting her work fulltime to adults in crisis, Vannessa worked to meet the mental health needs of children and adolescents. Person-centered therapy, that focuses on building each client's strengths, has always been Vannessa goal.

In July 2016, Vannessa became aware of the Mandela Effect and experienced a dramatic change to her paradigm of reality. After processing the initial shock, she started to notice a pattern within the Mandela Effect community, in terms of the lack of support from the loved ones of individuals impacted by the Mandela Effect. The lack of support from the friends and family of many individuals experiencing the Mandela Effect, including herself, inspired Vannessa to launch her YouTube channel, *Vannessa VA*. One of the main objectives of her channel is to combat isolation by giving Mandela Effect affected individuals a voice to express themselves, and an opportunity to relate to others who are having similar experiences. Vannessa has compiled hundreds of personal testimonies of people sharing their Mandela Effect experiences. She also provides support by encouraging members of the Mandela Effect community to participate in her "Mandela Effect Helpline" via YouTube livestreams.

In addition to doing livestreams and compiling personal testimonies, Vannessa has proposed a number of theories outlining potential causes of the Mandela Effect. Many of her theories integrate elements related to consciousness, philosophy, and spirituality. The conceptual framework behind Vannessa's theories are rooted in the work of independent thinkers, such as Rupert Spira, Dr. Robert Lanza, Dr. Bernardo Kastrup, and Paul Levy.

In July 2018, Vannessa hosted the first Mandela Effect Conference, which marked a cornerstone within the Mandela Effect community, and helped solidify many friendships. Individuals from across the country gathered to meet with like-minded people, many of whom had been completely physically isolated from others experiencing the Mandela Effect. The conference provided an opportunity for participants to discuss the Mandela Effect, and express themselves openly without any fear of ridicule. A sense of unity and acceptance was felt by everyone who attended, as participants took turns sharing their M.E. experiences.

Vannessa is passionate about issues related to mental health, spirituality, and philosophy. She is also passionate about exploring the nature of consciousness and the dreamlike nature of reality. Vannessa believes the Mandela Effect signifies an awakening that will forever change the evolutionary path of humanity.